Letters from Hollywood

Inside the Private World of
Classic American Moviemaking

COMPILED AND EDITED BY

Rocky Lang & Barbara Hall

ABRAMS, NEW YORK

For cousin Joan—the rudder of my life

Rocky Lang

For Val—my leading man

Barbara Hall

Contents

Foreword by Peter Bogdanovich

What a great idea! Who wouldn't want to peek into some of the business or personal letters from Old Hollywood, or as the book's subtitle puts it, "Inside the Private World of Classic American Moviemaking"? Who wouldn't want to read what John Barrymore wrote in praise to Edward G. Robinson in 1932? Or what Mary Pickford wrote to Gloria Swanson in 1937? Or Garbo, for Pete's sake, to Marion Davies a year later? The letters are not only reproduced in their original form, but they are also commented on succinctly, brightly, and informatively by the two compilers-editors, Rocky Lang and Barbara Hall.

There are riches here. Reading Ingrid Bergman's poorly typed, scribbled-on letter to Cary Grant, thanking him for his loving words when he accepted the Oscar for her in 1957, gives you a better understanding of Bergman, a closer look at what she was like. Cary and Ingrid had just worked together on *Indiscreet*, having first appeared in one of Hitchcock's best pictures, *Notorious*. She calls Cary her "wonderful friend." And this brief letter exemplifies their friendship beautifully.

Just some of the gold in this book: Audrey Hepburn to director George Cukor, bubbling over with excitement at having just recently signed on to play Eliza in *My Fair Lady*; her lovely suggestions for wardrobe and, particularly, shoes, since she has long had trouble with her feet from having danced ballet—you can hear Audrey in the letter, and it's beautifully written.

Groucho Marx to Jerry Lewis—mainly one-liners, but you can hear Groucho doing it, so it's funny.

Marlene Dietrich to Ernest Hemingway begins: "Well, you, my eternal love, have been silent for so long that my batteries are running dangerously low..." and continues like that for a fairly well-typed two pages on London's Hotel Dorchester stationery. To stress the intimacy of this marvelous, excited, open, and personal letter, she signs it: "your Kraut."

There is a marvelously insolent and amusing letter from Humphrey Bogart to John Huston, as they prepared to make their sixth movie together. Bogie begins: "Dear fly in the ointment" and continues "because I always open my wife's mail, I read your insidious and immoral proposals to my wife. It is perfectly safe to promise Miss Bacall a leading part in your picture, as soon as you are perfectly sure that she is knocked up—by me, that is." He then turns fairly serious trying to convince Huston that the picture (*Beat the Devil*) would be more successful in color than in black and white.

And then there's Bette Davis's handwritten letter, arguing for a new contract from her boss, Jack L. Warner: "For the first time in my life, I don't care whether I ever make another picture or not. I am that overworked." She goes on with specifics: "My contract is ridiculous. I have no protection whatsoever. I must have limited pictures—I must have time off between." She concludes: "Would appreciate your not communicating with me—it upsets me very much... Also, arguing with me is no use—nor do I want to come back until it is settled..."

There are a total of 137 letters here—including a number from more contemporary figures like Francis Ford Coppola, Paul Newman, Charlton Heston, Tom Hanks... This is a delightfully intimate and illuminating way to learn about Hollywood history.

Introduction by Rocky Lang

In the fall of 2016, I received a letter from the Academy of Motion Pictures Arts and Sciences. The letter was from Howard Prouty, the acquisitions archivist at the Academy's Margaret Herrick Library, the home to millions of items from the history of Hollywood.

Howard remembered me from when I was a directing fellow at the American Film Institute in 1980. Back then, he was just starting out in his career as an archivist and I as a film and television director. Howard had enclosed a copy of a letter he had discovered at the library that my father, Jennings Lang, wrote in 1939 to the famed Hollywood literary agent H. N. Swanson, who represented the likes of F. Scott Fitzgerald, William Faulkner, and James M. Cain. The letter revealed that my father had just arrived in Los Angeles and was without a job. Though my father was only twenty-four years old at the time he wrote it, the letter showed many of the personality traits that he had later in life. Looking at this letter was like looking back through a window in time to see who my father was at the start of his incredible life. Within the letter was a glimpse into my father's young voice, his soul, and his hopes and dreams. It was powerful, and it brought his voice back and forced me to reflect on his life and on mine. My father never got the job with H. N. Swanson, but he went on to become a powerful agent in Hollywood and later a successful producer and studio executive for MCA/Universal. He produced more than thirty movies, including *Earthquake*, the *Airport* sequels, and *Play Misty for Me*, and he jump-started the directing careers of

Clint Eastwood and Steven Spielberg. It was quite a world I grew up in as my mother, Monica Lewis, was also in show business. She was a successful singer who appeared on the very first *Ed Sullivan Show*, was under contract to MGM in the 1950s, and was the voice of Chiquita Banana.

As I have become older, I have been consumed with preserving my family's history and also the history of others and events in their lives that have faded away with time. This passion has permeated my writing and my film production and various projects that involve documenting a person's life. I was so moved by the letter Howard found, I asked him to lunch and then he showed me the archival storage areas of the Margaret Herrick Library that contains millions of photos, letters and poster art, and other documents dating back to the beginning of Hollywood. On the way home from my visit with Howard, fighting Los Angeles traffic, I conceived this book. I wanted to document the history of Hollywood through letter writing and, hopefully, move others as I was moved. In some small way, I wanted to preserve the voice of the letter writer and the time they lived as seen through their writing.

As much as I knew about the history of Hollywood, I knew the research for this project would be daunting. Writing a book like this can be like quicksand, and once I put my toe in, I might never get out. I knew I was in trouble and I needed help. It was then that I was introduced to film historian and archivist Barbara Hall, who has forgotten more about film history than I will ever know. I asked Barbara to join me on this journey and to be my writing partner. Happily, she agreed.

Letters from Hollywood required thousands of hours of research. Once we'd found the letters we wanted, we needed to find the authors or the estates to obtain permission to reprint the letters. It was demanding, frustrating, and fun. Some of it felt like six degrees of separation, as it took multiple connections to finally find the estate holder who controlled the rights and could grant us permission to publish the letter. Sometimes we did our due diligence only to find that the family line and the estate had ceased to exist decades ago. Many times, descendants had changed their names or taken the name of their spouse. Sometimes

Rocky Lang with Monica Lewis Lang and Jennings Lang, 1977.

people simply didn't want to be found. We used investigative tools, a research assistant, and even a private eye. When we finally found the estate holder—usually a family member—they were often delighted to discover a letter that opened a window into their loved one's past. This made all the hard work worth it. With those who are still alive and still working, seeing a letter that they wrote decades ago, often before they had achieved success, brought back memories of a time gone by, and with it, tremendous joy in seeing the letter. Just like movies bring us back to another time, so do these letters.

Sometimes in life we take a journey with an anticipated destination, and with this book, the destination was this publication. However, along the way, we saw many forks in the road, and yes, sometimes we did take the road less traveled. This journey took me to places I never dreamed of going, and I met the most interesting people, many of them the sons and daughters of the movie icons who often gave context to the letters we had found.

The history of Hollywood through letter writing is not just important to the families but to those who love Hollywood. Preserving history is crucial in this digital age. So much is recorded, but so much is forgotten. The art of letter writing is pretty much gone, and with it, so is the romantic and intimate way people shared their feelings, their fears, their hopes, and their dreams.

Introduction by Barbara Hall

When Rocky Lang first approached me about collaborating on a book of vintage Hollywood letters, I was immediately intrigued. I didn't grow up in Hollywood the way Rocky did, but I did grow up watching old movies on TV with my parents and sisters, going to the vintage 1920s Fox Theatre in my hometown of Redondo Beach, California, and hearing about the time my grandparents got dressed up in their finest and went to see *Gone with the Wind* at the beautiful Carthay Circle Theatre in Los Angeles. Eventually, I became a film historian and archivist and spent a lot of time working with cinema-related archival collections, so when this book opportunity arose I loved the idea of sharing some of my favorite letters with a wider audience. But I also knew that putting together a cohesive collection would be quite a challenge. Luckily, Rocky and I agreed on an approach. We decided that the book would take readers back in time to get a glimpse of what it was like to work and live in Hollywood in the decades before the advent of the fax machine, email, and social media. Each letter included in the collection would represent the unique voice of its writer at a specific moment in his or her career, but taken together the correspondence would form a loose historical timeline that we hoped would offer some new insights into how the film industry operated in Hollywood from the 1920s to the 1970s. Naturally, many of the letters would be written right here in Los Angeles and provide a look at life in what was sometimes known as the "movie colony," but we knew that our book would also include a number of letters written from across the country and even

a few from around the globe. With those goals in mind, we set out to collect potential material from libraries and archives, as well as through collectors, estates, and friends and acquaintances.

The selection of correspondence that emerged from our research and is now reproduced on these pages is an eclectic assortment of letters, telegrams, and memos written by more than 130 members of Hollywood's expansive filmmaking community, from Harry Houdini in 1921 to Jane Fonda in 1976. These first-person accounts shed light on the making of many of Hollywood's most iconic movies and offer perspectives on important facets of Hollywood studio history, such as censorship, the star system, World War II, and the blacklist. But alongside these pieces that focus on film production and the industry, we also made a point of including a number of letters—to friends, family members, and colleagues—that either have nothing to do with work or touch on both personal and professional matters. These pieces of correspondence are especially interesting, not only because of details they provide about the letter writers' private lives—including their social circle—but also because of what they reveal about overlapping spheres and unexpected connections within the Hollywood community. Though the letters span over fifty years of film history, it's remarkable how consistently insightful they are about living and working in Hollywood, the challenges of the creative process, the foibles and flaws of the movie industry, and the many exceptional people who worked both in front of and behind the camera.

LA-118—Fox Carthay Circle Theatre, Los Angeles, California

1B-H1019

The talented cast of characters that populates these pages runs the gamut from the famous to the obscure, and includes movie stars, directors, screenwriters, and producers, as well as agents, executives, artists, and craftspeople. In order to keep the focus on the film community, we decided early on to limit ourselves to letters between people in Hollywood's orbit (broadly defined as anyone involved in the movie business, or their close family members) and chose not to include correspondence to or from fans or people in other walks of life, such as politicians, academics, scientists, or novelists—unless they also tried their hand at writing movies. We also decided, with a couple of exceptions, to include just one letter per person, even though this meant making some difficult choices. This allowed us to get more voices into the mix, and to bring in a wider range of stories and experiences. Knowing that some of the letter writers are less well known and might need to be introduced to readers, we also determined that each letter would be accompanied by an extended caption that would provide some background on the writer, information about people and films mentioned in the letter, and historical context.

While we did obtain some letters from private collectors and estates, most of the research for the book was undertaken in film libraries and archives where we worked our way through dozens of collections and hundreds of files. Some of this work was done remotely via computer—using online finding aids and searching digital repositories—but the majority of the letters included in the book were found as a result of conducting in-person research in archives and having conversations with archivists and curators who generously shared their knowledge and expertise with us. It was a somewhat overwhelming process, and one that was limited by time and resources, but I do think the selections included here amount to an excellent introduction to the kinds of personal and studio correspondence that can be found in cinema-related archival collections, both here in Los Angeles and at selected archives across the country. The sources for all of the items, as well as the permissions, are listed at the end of the book. We hope that readers interested in finding out more about any of the correspondence we have selected will use that information as a jumping-off point for further research.

It was always important to us that *Letters from Hollywood* be made up of reproductions of original documents, so we are very grateful to all of the archives and our private donors for furnishing us with high-resolution scans of all of the letters, memos, and telegrams included in the book. This format not only affords our readers the chance to read the unedited contents of the correspondence but also the opportunity to study the handwritten and typed documents as pre-digital artifacts, complete with interesting letterheads, embellishments, coffee stains, postscripts, colorful ink, cross-outs, additions, typos, and drawings. We hope that in each case, traces of the personality of the letter writer and a feel for the time when the letter was composed come through on the page. We also hope that having a chance to engage with these original materials encourages readers to support and maybe even visit the archives and libraries in their communities that preserve letters, telegrams, and memos like those found in our book—and to save their own family correspondence for future generations to discover. There's nothing like reading a letter written seventy or ninety years ago to make you realize how much, and how little, the world has changed.

The Letters

HOUDINI PICTURE CORPORATION

CANDLER BLDG.

220 WEST 42ND STREET

NEW YORK CITY

Phone Bryant 5519

July 16, 1921.

Mr. Adolph Zukor,
Famous Players-Lasky Corp.,
469 Fifth Avenue,
New York City.

My dear Mr. Zukor:-

Tried to get you on the 'phone a number of times
this week but unfortunately failed to do so.   Am
starting on my second super special.   My first production "The Man from Beyond" is finished and is a
competitive picture to "Way Down East," referring to
the thrill finish wherein we have our episode on the
brink of Niagara Falls.   Would like to make arrangements to show you this picture any time to suit your
convenience and any place you designate.

May I suggest the possibility of bringing
it to your home and running it as you did "The Grim
Game."   As I stated above, I am working in the day
time on my next picture but I could come out any evening
or Sunday.   "The Man From Beyond" is a full seven-reeler
and really believe I have a great, big financial success.

Regards,

Sincerely yours,   *Houdini*

We took six months to make The man from Beyond.

Harry Houdini (right) during production of *The Grim Game*, 1919

Harry Houdini to Adolph Zukor

JULY 16, 1921

Harry Houdini was the most famous illusionist and escape artist in the world when he wrote this letter to Adolph Zukor, the powerful head of the Famous Players-Lasky Corporation, and his former employer. Houdini had been exhibiting films of his daring outdoor escapes at his live performances since as early as 1906, but he first made the leap into narrative films in 1918 with the serial *The Master Mystery*. The following year Houdini signed with Famous Players-Lasky and went to Hollywood to make two films, *The Grim Game* and *Terror Island*, both featuring a series of real escapes and stunts that gave movie audiences a chance to see Houdini in action on the big screen. The films were not as popular as expected, however, and following their release Houdini decided to return to New York and form his own company, the Houdini Picture Corporation. In *The Man from Beyond*, his first independent production, Houdini plays a man who is mysteriously revived after being frozen in the Arctic ice for a hundred years. Houdini not only produced and starred in the supernatural film

but also cowrote it, and he was probably hoping that if he arranged a screening for Zukor he might convince him to distribute *The Man from Beyond* through his company. This is also probably why Houdini tries to impress the studio head by comparing the film and its Niagara Falls climax to *Way Down East*, the acclaimed melodrama directed by D. W. Griffith that concludes with a suspenseful rescue of Lillian Gish from a fast-moving ice floe. In a handwritten postscript, Houdini also notes, "We took six months to make *The Man from Beyond*," another detail clearly intended to convey to Zukor how impressive Houdini's film was. Houdini followed *The Man from Beyond* with *Haldane of the Secret Service*, released in 1923, but that film proved to be his last foray into feature moviemaking. For the next few years, until his untimely death in 1926, Houdini focused on astounding audiences with live performances of his escapes and illusions, further cementing his legacy as one of the world's greatest magicians.

Roscoe Arbuckle and Mabel Normand in the 1916 short *He Did and He Didn't*.

Roscoe Arbuckle to Joseph M. Schenck

OCTOBER 1, 1921

Roscoe "Fatty" Arbuckle was one of Hollywood's most famous and successful screen comics, but his life took a tragic turn when the fun-loving star went to San Francisco over Labor Day weekend in 1921. By the time he wrote this letter to his close friend and business partner Joseph M. Schenck a month later, Arbuckle had been accused of raping and killing the actress Virginia Rappe during a drunken party at the St. Francis Hotel and had just been released on bail after spending eighteen days in jail. Even before Arbuckle's arrest, newspapers across the nation were attacking him and printing outrageous stories about Rappe's death, and before long Arbuckle was denounced by women's groups and others who used the scandal as evidence of the rampant immorality of Hollywood. In his letter, Arbuckle pleads his innocence and insists that he is being targeted only because he is a celebrity. He also makes a point of assuring Adolph Zukor and Jesse Lasky, his bosses at Paramount, that he would weather the storm and return to work. Unfortunately, he was mistaken. Arbuckle endured three sensational manslaughter trials before finally being acquitted in April 1922, only to be banned from the screen a week later by Will Hays, the industry's recently appointed morality czar. Hays lifted his ban at the end of 1922, but fear of a backlash kept the studios from bringing Arbuckle back to the screen. He later found work as a writer and director, using a pseudonym, and also went back to performing on stage. He returned to acting for the screen in 1932, but his comeback came to an end when he died in 1933 at the age of 46.

Oct. 1st, 1921

My Dear Joe..

It seems I never write to you unless I am in trouble. But this is one time Joe I was not to blame and when something happens in a half an hour that will change a man's whole life it's pretty tough especially when a person is absolutely innocent in deed word or thought of any wrong.

I can't get into details about this affair as it would take me a week to tell you about it and explain it to you in detail so you would understand it. However Joe I want to tell you now, and I have always come clean with you. I have never lied to you or crossed you in one single act or statement since I have known you and I am telling you now that I am absolutely innocent of all the accusations you have heard against me. I simply tried to help someone in distress, the same as you or anyone else with human instincts would have done in the circumstance.

I want you to have explicit faith and confidence in me and tell Mr. Zukor to have the same. I have done no wrong, my heart is clean and my conscience is clear and when it is over I have got the guts to come back and I will come back and make good.

I realize the position of Mr. Zukor and Mr. Lasky and I know what it means to them in more ways than one and their attitude during this affair has been wonderful and I want you to tell them that I appreciate it. I know what they have tied up in me at present and irrespective of whether we ever do business together again I will come out of this affair clean and vindicated so that they can realize on their tremendous investment.

I am not asking for sympathy or forgiveness, I have done no wrong, but I do want you and the ones financially as well as personally interested [to know] that I am innocent, a victim of circumstance, the only one of prominence in the party and therefore I had to be the goat.

Tell Mr. Zukor before passing judgment to remember the Boston party. He knows what a shakedown is.

Joe perhaps I needed a bump to wake me up, but I think I got considerable more than was coming to me, needless to say the kind of life I will lead from now on.

Best regards Roscoe

ROSCOE C. ARBUCKLE
649 WEST ADAMS STREET
LOS ANGELES, CALIFORNIA

Oct 1st 1921

My Dear Joe..

I seems I never write to you
unless I am in trouble. But this
is one time Joe I was not to
blame and when something happens in a half an hour that ~~it~~
will change a mans whole ~~life~~ life its
pretty ~~tought~~ tough especially when
a person is absolutely innocent in
deed words or thought of any wrong.

I cant go into detail about this
affair as it would take me a week
to tell you about it and explain

it to me in detail so you would understand it. However Joe I want to tell you now, and I have always come clean with you. I have never lied to you or crossed you in one single act or statement since I have known you and I am telling you now that I am absolutely innocent of any all the accusations you have heard against me. I simply tried to help someone in distress, the same as you or anyone else with human instincts who would have done in the circumstance.

I want you to have explicit faith and confidence in me and tell Mr. Ouker to have the same.

I have done no wrong, my heart
is clean and my concurne is
clear and when it is over I have
got the guts to come back and
I will ~~come to~~ come back and make
good,

I realize the position of Mr.
Zukor and Mr. Lasky and I know
what it means to them in more
ways than one and their attitude
during this affair has been wonderful
and I want you to tell them that
I appreciate it. I know what they have
tied up in me at present and
irrespective of whether we ever due business
together again I will come out of this
affair clean and vindicated so that

they can realize on their tremendous investment.

I am not asking for sympathy or forgiveness, I have done no wrong, but I do want you and the ones financially as well as personally interested that I am innocent, a victim of circumstance, the only one of prominence in the party and therefore I had to be the goat.

Tell Mr. Zukor before passing judgement to remember the Boston party. He knows what a shakedown is.

Joe perhaps I needed a bump to wake me up, but I think I got considerable more than was coming the me, needless to say the kind of a life I will lead from now on Best Regards Roscoe

3089 W. Seventh St.,
Los Angeles, Calif.

Mr. Adolph Zukor,
c/o Famous Players Lasky Corp.,
New York City.

My dear Mr. Zukor:-

I know it's wrong to take up the valuable time of
a man in your elegant position but I do need your
advice, so I take my pen in hand, and if you throw
this letter away before reading it through, I will
never go to see your pictures again.

I had a fine business - a hairpin factory, but since
that Mrs. Castle became famous a couple of years ago
and everyone has bobbed their hair, all that's left
of my fine business is the machinery and myself.
Everyone tells me I look like Mary Pickford - in
fact, they tell me I have her beat a mile. I am 7' 9"
in heighth, have the palest blue eyes you ever saw,
a very large nose, and they do say, a most extraordinary chin. It's a bit receding, but it would be
a novelty for your cinematographers to practice on.
(That word sounded so French and intricate that I
looked it up in the dictionary - I hope you will like
it). I have very good ears. In fact your corporation
would save a lot of money in not buying megaphones
for your temperamental directors.

The reason I am such a demon for detail is because
after I told the manager of the theatre in our town,
who runs your pictures, how I was going to describe
myself to you, he told me not to change a line. Do
you think he is spoofing me?

Lest I forget to tell you about my hair - it is
exactly like Sid Grauman's.

I am enclosing a photograph and I hope you will consider me.

The reason I wrote all the above was because I hope you get it right after you have had a conference with Sydney Cohen.

I know my delay in acknowledging your lovely flowers which you sent me when I was ill seems unpardonable, but better late than never, so please forgive me, and my sincere thanks for your kindness and thoughtfullness.

Mabel Normand

May Thirtieth,
Nineteen Twenty two.

Mabel Normand to Adolph Zukor

MAY 30, 1922

Mabel Normand, one of the most talented comediennes of the silent era, shows off her wit in this charming thank-you note that pokes fun at the alarming number of "movie-struck girls" who flocked to Hollywood in the 1920s to become stars on the silver screen. In addition to referencing Hollywood's reigning queen, Mary Pickford, Normand mentions the dancer and actress Irene Castle, who had popularized the bob, a short haircut then trending among young, modern women. Theater owner Sid Grauman and Paramount studio executive Sydney Cohen also get gently teased in Normand's humorous letter. Despite her lighthearted tone, this was a difficult time for Normand. Only a few months earlier, on February 1, 1922, the director William Desmond Taylor had been murdered under mysterious circumstances, and Normand was caught up in the scandal that swirled around the unsolved crime. Normand continued to make films, but the controversy took a toll on her career and her health. She died of tuberculosis in 1930 at the age of thirty-seven.

Irving Thalberg to Erich von Stroheim

OCTOBER 6, 1922

Universal executive Irving Thalberg was only twenty-three when he wrote this termination letter to the brilliant but difficult actor-writer-director Erich von Stroheim during the production of *Merry-Go-Round*, the filmmaker's fourth movie for the studio. Thalberg's decision to fire the autocratic von Stroheim resonated throughout the film industry, which was in the process of moving from a system where powerful directors called the shots to one where producers had the final authority. For Thalberg, the issues that he raises in his letter were all central to efficient studio management, and the unpredictable and uncontrollable von Stroheim was a clear liability. Ironically, the two adversaries were brought together again two years later when *Greed*, von Stroheim's hyperrealistic adaptation of Frank Norris's novel *McTeague*, landed at Thalberg's new studio, Metro-Goldwyn-Mayer, due to a company merger. Over von Stroheim's adamant objections, Thalberg supervised a drastic reediting of *Greed* that cut more than three hours of material from the director's five-and-a-quarter-hour version, which is now considered a lost masterpiece. Von Stroheim's volatile career as a director burned itself out by the early 1930s, but he continued to work regularly as an actor. In 1950, he delivered a memorable performance as a silent movie director turned butler in *Sunset Boulevard*.

UNIVERSAL FILM MANUFACTURING COMPANY

PACIFIC COAST STUDIOS

UNIVERSAL CITY, CALIFORNIA

October 6th, 1922.

Office of General Manager
  Irving G. Thalberg

Mr. Eric Von Stroheim,
Universal City, California.

Dear Sir:-

Ever since the execution of your contract of employment with us dated May 19th, 1920, we have labored patiently
and conscientiously with you for the purpose of endeavoring
to secure your cooperation in the production of the pictures
which you were making for us.   We have been particularly
anxious since the completion of "FOOLISH WIVES" to do our
utmost to produce "MERRY GO ROUND" on an efficient and
commercially profitable, but at the same time, artistic
basis, and to avoid the costly blunders made by you in
connection with the earlier production.   Your contract of
employment with us provides for the completion of two
feature motion picture productions a year.   You have completed exactly one production under your contract, namely,
"FOOLISH WIVES", and are,at present, engaged in the production
of your second, "MERRY GO ROUND".   The fact that more productions have not been completed is due largely to your
totally inexcusable and repeated acts of insubordination, your
extravagant ideas which you have been unwilling to sacrifice
in the slightest particular, repeated and unnecessary delays
occasioned by your attitude in arguing against practically
every instruction that has been given to you in good faith,
and by your apparent idea that you are greater and more
powerful than the organization that employs you.

After the completion of "FOOLISH WIVES", the situation
was discussed with you in detail at a time when it was our intention to permit you to direct no further pictures.   After repeated assurances and promises on your part that you would be
more responsive to our demands in the future, and after you
gave what appeared to be evidence of your ability to produce
"MERRY GO ROUND" on a satisfactory basis, we agreed to let you
direct this picture, making no attempt to exercise the right
which we believed we possessed to terminate your employment
with us because of your many and repeated acts of insubordination in connection with the production of "FOOLISH WIVES"."
We naturally expected, however, that you would perform conscientiously and in good faith, all services reasonably and
properly required of you under the terms of your employment
contract.   We regret to state that we have been bitterly

disappointed in your failure so to do, and particularly in your
general attitude toward the company, its officials and employees.

Shortly after the commencement of the actual photo-
graphing of "MERRY GO ROUND" we realized that your promises
were not to be relied upon, and that unless drastic action was
taken by us, this picture would be as unnecessarily expensive
as "FOOLISH WIVES". Hoping to remedy this situation without
having to take drastic action, we engaged Mr. J. W. Hum as manager
of your production, and placed him in charge thereof. You were
notified that he was the representative of the company and were
instructed to follow his instructions at all times. This you
have failed to do, and moreover, you have repeatedly been guilty
of flagrant disrespect and insubordination toward Mr. Hum and
have employed profane language not only in talking to and about
him, but in speaking of various other officials of the company,
and time after time have exhibited such an attitude of contempt
to us, that other employees working for you have been tempted
to display the same spirit. In spite of the fact that you
have occupied a position of trust, dignity and confidence on
the lot, you have time and time again demonstrated your dis-
loyalty to our company, encouraged and fostered discontent,
distrust and disrespect for us in the minds of your fellow
employees, and have attempted to create an organization loyal
to yourself, rather than the company you were employed to serve.

Among other difficulties with which we have had to
contend, has been your flagrant disregard of the principles
of censorship and your repeated and insistent attempts to
include in the scenes photographed by you, situations and in-
cidents so reprehensible that they could not by any reasonable
possibility be expected to meet with the approval of the
Boards of Censorship.

For the foregoing reasons, and each of them, as well
as for other reasons which it is unnecessary to cite at this
time, you are notified that you are discharged from our employ,
your discharge to take effect as of this date. You will be
paid your salary in full up to and including October 7th, 1922.
Your closing check will be mailed or delivered to you tomorrow.

This action on the part of the company is without
prejudice to any other rights to which it may be entitled.

Very truly yours,

UNIVERSAL FILM MANUFACTURING COMPANY
By _____
General Manager.

WESTERN UNION TELEGRAM

Form 1206A

CLASS OF SERVICE DESIRED

Telegram
Day Letter
Night Message
Night Letter XXXXXXXX

Patrons should mark an X opposite the class of service desired; OTHERWISE THE MESSAGE WILL BE TRANSMITTED AS A FULL-RATE TELEGRAM

Receiver's No.

Check

Time Filed

NEWCOMB CARLTON, PRESIDENT   GEORGE W. E. ATKINS, FIRST VICE-PRESIDENT

Send the following message, subject to the terms on back hereof, which are hereby agreed to

Copy
(Original filed under Zukor)

May 10, 1923.

Adolph Zukor,
Famous Players-Lasky Corp., 485 – 5th Ave.,
New York, N. Y.

I am deeply appreciative of your attitude toward Ten Commandments and of your faith in me, as I fully realize the responsibility of the enormous sum of money that I am spending stop. I can assure you that to the best of my belief the picture will have those qualities of love, romance and beauty which you so rightly suggest are necessary to any picture, and as an evidence of my appreciation and of my faith in this picture, I hereby waive the guarantee under my contract on this picture, other than the regular weekly payments stop. I am delighted that you and Mr. Kent are going to be here while I am on the big location and can see some of the vast machinery in operation. I believe it will be the biggest picture ever made, not only from the standpoint of spectacle but from the standpoint of humaness, dramatic power and the great good it will do. I am confident that nothing equalling it has ever been filmed. Kind personal regards,

Cecil B. DeMille.

(CHG. LASKY ACCT.)

Cecil B. DeMille to Adolph Zukor

MAY 10, 1923

In 1923, Cecil B. DeMille was one of the movie industry's most successful commercial directors, known for stylish, racy melodramas like *Male and Female* and *Why Change Your Wife?* However, he outdid himself with his production of *The Ten Commandments*, which combined a stunning biblical prologue depicting Moses and the Exodus with a modern story about the relevance of the commandments to contemporary life. Clearly, it resonated with audiences, becoming the second-highest-grossing film of the year. In this telegram to studio head Adolph Zukor, DeMille displays some of his characteristic bravado, while at the same time reassuring Zukor that the studio's financial investment will pay off. The "big location" that DeMille refers to was located on the Guadalupe-Nipomo Dunes near Santa Barbara, where studio craftsmen built one of the largest and most extravagant sets in movie history for the film's Egyptian scenes. Though DeMille worked in many genres during his career, he became especially identified with biblical epics such as *The King of Kings*, *The Sign of the Cross*, *Samson and Delilah*, and the 1956 remake of *The Ten Commandments*, which all featured DeMille's signature combination of sex, spectacle, and Christianity. In an interesting footnote, some of the remains of the *Ten Commandments* set, which was dismantled and buried when shooting was completed, were discovered in the sand dunes in 1983, and volunteers continue to search for remnants of the set in the dunes, which are now treated as an archeological site.

Lou Marangella to Irving Thalberg

OCTOBER 2, 1924

Only a publicity man could have written this upbeat description of the filming of *Ben-Hur*, the massive production then being undertaken in Italy by Metro-Goldwyn-Mayer studio. MGM had inherited the project when the studio was formed in early 1924 but scrapped most of the work that had been done before and started over with a new director and crew on the ground in Italy. In this letter to MGM executive Irving Thalberg, publicist Lou Marangella chooses not to mention any of the myriad problems on location, instead focusing on the extravagant scale of the production and the accomplishments of its new director, Fred Niblo. In reality, the galley-slave sequence Marangella describes was disastrous and

may have resulted in the death of several extras; many animals were injured or killed during the shooting; and the chariot-race footage that was filmed in Italy was deemed unusable. The entire company eventually moved back to Culver City, where much of the film was reshot, including the chariot-race sequence. Despite its chaotic production history, *Ben-Hur* created a sensation when it was released in December 1925, becoming one of the highest-grossing films up to that time, and putting MGM on the map as one of the top studios in Hollywood.

Fred Niblo directing *Ben-Hur* in Italy, 1924.

Marcus Loew
President

METRO-GOLDWYN-MAYER PICTURES CORPORATION
1540 Broadway, New York, N. Y.

Louis B. Mayer
Vice-President
In charge of production

BEN HUR

Fred Niblo
Director General

Now in course of production
JERUSALEM - BETHLAHEM - EGYPT - TUNIS - ROME

H. E. Edington
General Manager

CINES STUDIO
51, Via Veio (S. G.)
Roma, Italia

October 2, 1924.

Mr. Irving Thalberg,
Goldwyn Studios,
<u>Culver City</u>, Cal.

My dear Mr. Thalberg:

The "Ben Hur" production is being produced in great style.
Unquestionably it will be the greatest feature attraction that has ever
been shown to the public.   Of course, it is needless for me to try to
exaggerate anything to you, but my enthusiasm is so great that I cannot
help but express my sentiments in the highest and most flattering phrase-
ology.

At the outset let me state that no tribute can ever be great
enough to compensate Director Fred Niblo for the way in which he has won
the complete respect, admiration, and whole-hearted cooperation of
thousands of Italian men, women, and children, including a band of swarthy
black men and women imported from Tripoli, and a group of Arabs. Within
three days after the first scene was shot the people here were literally
eating out of Niblo's hands; and I do not believe that there is any other
American director who could have achieved Niblo's results within this
remarkably short period.

Marcus Loew
President

METRO-GOLDWYN-MAYER PICTURES CORPORATION
1540 Broadway, New York, N. Y.

Louis B. Mayer
Vice-President
In charge of production

BEN HUR

Fred Niblo
Director General

Now in course of production
JERUSALEM - BETHLAHEM - EGYPT - TUNIS - ROME

H. E. Edington
General Manager

2.

CINES STUDIO
51, Via Veio (S. G.)
Roma, Italia

The entire working staff of the production, I may say, is working in harmony.   I have never seen so courageous a crew of American workmen and artists banded together for one big purpose.

Here are some facts that will unquestionably interest you:

From Germany we have secured 10,000 costumes; from Hungary several hundred beautiful stallions which are being used in the mob scenes, and which will also be used in the chariot race sequence, have been imported; from Tripoli a large group of swarthy black men and women were brought on; from Tunis, North Africa, a veritable caravan of camels were secured after an Italian army officer penetrated the heart of the desert for 1000 miles in order to get the type of camel prevalent during the Caesar Augustus period.

The exterior scene of action is about seven miles from the studio. On this territory, which comprises some 400 acres of ground, there have been constructed the massive Joppa Gate of Jerusalem, the tribunal, the Jerusalem city, Jerusalem streets, palaces, homes, stores, etc; a huge wardrobe department some 800 feet square in which the costumes are housed, and to which are attached several large dressing rooms capable of accommodating from 3000 to 8000 extras at one time; the stupendous Circus Maximus, wherein the chariot race scenes will be filmed covers fully about half a mile of territory.   This structure is still in the making, and should be completed by the time you receive this letter.

Marcus Loew
President

METRO-GOLDWYN-MAYER PICTURES CORPORATION
1540 Broadway, New York, N. Y.

Louis B. Mayer
Vice-President
In charge of production

BEN HUR

Fred Niblo
Director General

Now in course of production
JERUSALEM - BETHLAHEM - EGYPT - TUNIS - ROME

H. E. Edington
General Manager

3.

CINES STUDIO
51, Via Veio (S. G.)
Roma, Italia

    At Leghorn, Italy, (a seacoast town some six hours' ride from Rome)
the galley fleet was constructed.   Here at this writing Niblo is filming
the galley slave sequence. The weather is ideal, and there is every
indication that it will remain so until he gets through with the entire
~~scenes.~~   The galley ships are veritable transports, beautifully constructed by Italian craftsmen. A view of these ships manned by thousands
of Roman soldiers, sailors and galley slaves, out on the Mediterranean Sea
is an awe-inspiring spectacle.   Mr. Niblo is getting some wonderful
results with them, and I am sure that when the production is finally shown
to the public they will cause a sensation.

    There are many more weeks of hard work ahead of us, but we are all
determined to carry on even if it is necessary to remain here until we grow
beards that will wind around a pilot's wheel.

    I have sent Mr. Condon a batch of photographs which I am sure he
will be able to use judiciously in the Coast newspapers.   This batch is
merely the first of a number of others which I will send to him from time
to time.   In order to avoid any confliction the Home Office is notified
as to just how many photos have been sent to the Coast.

    With kind personal regards and best wishes, I am,

        Sincerely yours,

        Lou Marangella

Mr. Carl Laemmle, President   July 3d, 1925
Universal Pictures Corp.
New York City, N.Y.

My dear uncle Carl,-

            Please let me extend to you my heartfelt thanks for
the wonderful opportunity you have just given me. Although I
expected to become a director within the next few months, the
joyful effect caused upon me by your favorable answer to my
wire is beyond words. As it happened it was on my birthday
anniversary, and you gave me the most wonderful gift that I was
ever given, namely the opportunity to direct. Now, the rest is
up to me, I know, and I feel fully confident that I will make good;
in fact I feel surer of mys elf this time than in anything I have
ever attempted. This for two good reasons: first beacause I frankly
believe that I have the material within me to develop some day
into one of your best commercial directors; and then because
you, Carl Laemmle, have enough faith in me to give me the
opportunity to prove the first reason, which makes me all the
more confident as to the success of my latest attempt and the
results thereof. Once more you have proven that you are only
58 years young, for you believe in giving young people the chance
which shows that you yourself are still young and progressive
in ideas and action. Anyway, this is one promotion you will never
regret, for I am positive the result of it spells success. I shall
be forever grateful towards you and no matter what happens I will
stick by you as long as you will have me.

I am glad that you have finally decided to make
your annual trip to Europe, knowing that it is your only chance
of getting a little rest which you certainly deserve more than
anybody I know. My folks will probably look you up in Paris;
please give them both Robert's and my love. As you know they
expect to start on their journey to California this coming
fall and we are extremely happy at the thought of living here
with our parents and kid brother. Although my mother has
the real american spirit of optimism, my father, I believe,
needs a little more encouragement; but once they have arrived
in Los Angeles my brother and myself will lookout and provide
if necessary for their happiness and general welfare.

Hoping that this letter will find you, also dear
Rosabelle and Junior to whom please give my best love, in
a perfect state of health, I wish you all a most happy and
enjoyable trip.

Once again let me express my sincere gratitude
towards you, dear uncle Carl, with my best love,

always your nephew

William Wyler to Carl Laemmle

JULY 3, 1925

This letter from a young William Wyler thanking Universal studio head (and Wyler's second cousin) "Uncle Carl" Laemmle for the opportunity to direct shows a remarkable maturity and sense of purpose. Born in Mulhouse, Germany, Wyler came to America in 1920 thanks to a job offer from Laemmle. After starting as a shipping clerk at Universal's New York studio, Wyler moved to Hollywood in 1922 and worked his way up to being an assistant director before getting his chance to direct his first film, the western short *The Crook Buster*, in 1925. Wyler was just one of many relatives to benefit from "Uncle Carl" Laemmle's generosity; in fact, the studio head was frequently mocked in the industry for hiring so many members of his family, including his son Junior, who became Universal's head of production in 1928. Family was also important to Wyler. He was extremely close to his older brother Robert, who worked with him on many of his films, as well as to his parents and younger brother, who all eventually moved to Los Angeles from Europe. Wyler, who went on to become one of Hollywood's most respected filmmakers, directed more than forty features during his long career, including *Mrs. Miniver*, *The Best Years of Our Lives*, *Roman Holiday*, *Ben-Hur*, and *Funny Girl*.

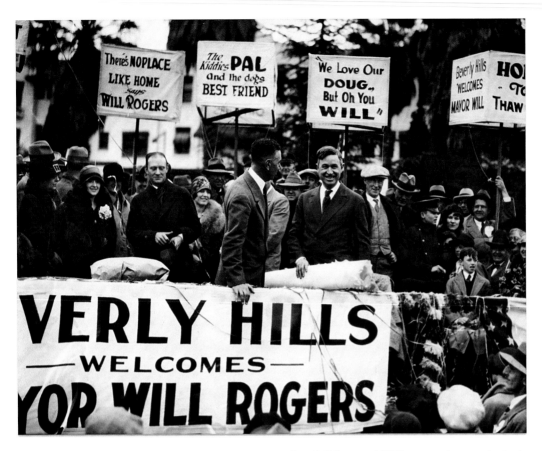

The signs read:

"There's NOPLACE LIKE HOME says WILL ROGERS"

"The Kiddies PAL and the dogs BEST FRIEND"

"We Love Our DOUG., But Oh You WILL"

"Beverly Hills WELCOMES MAYOR WILL"

"Beverly Hills HO[...] -- TO[...] THAW[...]"

VERLY HILLS —WELCOMES— [MA]YOR WILL ROGERS

Beverly Hills mayor Will Rogers getting an enthusiastic
welcome from his constituents, 1926.

Will Rogers to Cecil B. DeMille

CIRCA 1926

In this letter to the director Cecil B. DeMille, the humorist Will Rogers uses his abundant charm to dodge DeMille's request that he speak to a group of bankers at a private soiree. A storyteller and cowboy who had become a movie star after hitting it big in vaudeville, Rogers was known for his folksy wisdom and populism, which he shared not only on stage and screen but also on the radio and in a syndicated newspaper column. He was often referred to as "the most trusted man in America." Rogers also regularly delivered after-dinner speeches to all kinds of groups, including businessmen and bankers, so his lack of interest in DeMille's offer is intriguing. The mention of a bathtub thief is a sly reference to DeMille's reputation for including provocative bathing scenes in his movies. Rogers and his family settled in Beverly Hills in the 1920s. He was the honorary mayor of the city from 1926 to 1928, which may explain the Beverly Hills Hotel letterhead. In 1952, a park across from the hotel was renamed in his honor.

Beverly Hills Hotel and Bungalows
Beverly Hills, California

Dear C. B.

 Last semester you arote me something about amusing
some Bankers somewhere while they eat, Now I would
have answered you sonner but I only answer mail once
a month and this is my replying time,
 Now I have reformed from all that foolishness of
gabbing around, Its one of the lowest forms of art
there is, is after dinner speaking, and besides I am
an Actor now, they are on the verge of putting me in
sex parts, (thats not six, thats SEX)
 But all seriousness aside I would like to go up
there and be with the old Sylocks, and watch em play
Golf and raise the interest on everybody, But I
just havent got time, I am borrowed up to my
capacity so whats the good of standing in with em,
 Say did you see in the papers tonight where x
a Burglar in Hollywood stold a Bathtub, I thought of
you and figure that that old Boy was one of your fans,
 I will see what I am doing when dinner time
comes, If I am not doing anything, I willfind
something to do for an Alabi to keep from going,
 You tell it to em up there, You know em
better than I do,
 How they coming anyhow?.
 Regards to you and your troop,

Will Rogers.

WILL H. HAYS
PRESIDENT
CARL E. MILLIKEN
SECRETARY

OFFICE OF THE PRESIDENT

Return to Mr. Doane —

Hollywood, California.
July 10, 1926

Mr. Warren Doane,
Hal E. Roach Studios,
Culver City, California.

My dear Mr. Doane:

Referring further to the discussions at the Association
meeting.

Again I particularly call your attention to the imperative
necessity of:

(1) Making certain that into no picture there be allowed
to enter any shot of drinking scenes, manufacture or sale of
liquor, or undue effects of liquor which are not a necessary part
of the story or an essential element in the building up of the
plot. That is, there should be no picturization of liquor, its
manufacture, use or effect which can be construed as being
brought in unnecessarily as a type of propaganda. It is one
thing, of course if the use of liquor in a picture is a natural
and necessary element, but quite another thing if the manufacture,
use or effects of liquor are brought in unnecessarily in any
way which can be construed as being for any ulterior purpose or
which in any way promotes any disrespect for law.

(2) Making certain that into no title there be allowed to
enter any word, phrase, clause or sentence that directly or in-
directly encourages the slightest disregard for law. There might
be a tendency to make light of prohibition on the theory that
it is a type of humor and might bring the laugh that sometimes
follows, but any such treatment of the subject is, of course, a
belittling of the statute itself, and it is the earnest purpose
of the Association to make certain that the screen shall never
be used in a manner which promotes the slightest disrespect for
any law, whatever that law may be.

As suggested in the meeting, I am sure it is unnecessary to emphasize either the wisdom of this course, its propriety, or our duty in the premises. There is much talk today of personal liberty. Very well. But let us not confuse liberty with license. Liberty to make our laws does not give us a license to break them. Liberty to make our laws commands a duty to obey them ourlseves and enforce obedience by all others in their jurisdiction. "Liberty is fire on the hearth -- license is fire on the floor."

The motion picture has a definite duty, still more emphasized at the present, of not allowing itself to be misused in any situation such as exists at the present. Further, it has the continued duty of a positive support of law, order and authority, and the great opportunity which is in pictures measures exactly their great responsibility.

I again call your attention also to the discussion relative to the importance of avoiding scenes of undue nudity in the pictures. The tendency in certain of the stage plays is well known. It is very important that this tendency be avoided in pictures. This should be watched carefully.

I am leaving it to you to make certain that the directors of the pictures made by your company are appraised of the importance of these suggestions.

With kindest personal regards and best wishes always, I am

Sincerely yours,

Will Hays to Warren Doane

JULY 10, 1926

In 1922, besieged by scandal and threats of censorship and boycotts, the movie business formed a trade group called the Motion Picture Producers and Distributors of America and hired a Republican Party official and former postmaster general named Will Hays to run it. As the chief spokesman for the movie industry, Hays tried to dissuade producers from making films that would rile up the moral crusaders who had turned their sights on Hollywood. In this formal letter to Warren Doane, general manager at the Roach Studios, Hays expresses concern that movies showing illegal drinking and general lawlessness would make the industry vulnerable to government censorship efforts. Despite his tough talk, however, Hays had very little leverage with the studios, which mostly disregarded his edicts in favor of making movies that were popular at the box office. Though officially against censorship, Hays continued to demand that the industry regulate itself, and eventually he engineered the adoption of the Production Code, a set of moral guidelines that shaped filmmaking in Hollywood for more than thirty years.

The National Guide to Motion Pictures

PHOTOPLAY

JANUARY
25 CENTS

Madge
Bellamy

Diet, *the*
Menace
of
Hollywood

Winners of
$5,000⁰⁰ Contest

Sol Wurtzel to Madge Bellamy

FEBRUARY 20, 1928

Sol Wurtzel, the head of production at Fox, gives some not-so-subtle advice to Madge Bellamy, one of the leading actresses under contract to the studio. At the time, Bellamy was considered one of the great screen beauties, but she also had an independent streak that led to a reputation for being difficult. In her autobiography, published in 1989, Bellamy wrote that Wurtzel once told her she could have an upcoming role if she lost twelve pounds.

To get the part, Bellamy recalled that she "got down to one hundred pounds in two weeks by eating nothing but canned spinach and canned tomatoes." Wurtzel, who remained friends with Bellamy long after she left the studio, also mentions in his letter that she should "keep on looking younger with each picture." Bellamy was twenty-eight when she received this helpful suggestion from her boss.

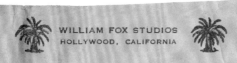

WILLIAM FOX STUDIOS
HOLLYWOOD, CALIFORNIA

February 20, 1928.

OFFICE OF
GENERAL SUPERINTENDENT

MISS MADGE BELLAMY:

I am sending you herewith article
which I know you will be pleased to
read.

I call your attention to the last
paragraph which I have marked
with an X and circle.

I noticed in the last few days'
work that either something is wrong
with the photography or you have
been adding a little weight.   I am
inclined to think you haven't been
careful in checking your diet lately,
and I thought you have taken on
a few pounds.

I would suggest you give this
matter your thought and if I am
correct and you have taken on some
weight, that you start on a diet.

Keep faith with the man who wrote
the article and keep on looking
younger with each picture.

GENERAL SUPERINTENDENT.

RONALD COLMAN

5th August, 1928.

My dear Abe:

Sorry I did not see you yesterday and that tomorrow I shall be away from the studio on location.

With reference to the additional clause to the contract, - I would rather not sign this, at any rate just at present. Except as a scientific achievement, I am not sympathetic to this "sound" business. I feel, as so many do, that it is a mechanical resource, that it is a retrogressive and temporary digression in so far as it affects the art of motion picture acting, - in short that it does not properly belong to my particular work (of which naturally I must be the best judge).

That the public are for the time being demanding this novelty is obvious, and that the producer is anxious to supply it is natural, and for the actor to dispute this situation or contend against it would be foolish. After four years' experience with myself, the firm should have no doubt as to my reasonable co-operation in this matter - as in others.

For me to function conscientiously before the microphone is one thing, but to sign a legally phrased document authorising this is a very different matter and would logically presuppose my approval of this mechanical accessory to my work.

Furthermore, if the original contract embraces such developments in motion picture making, then the amendment is superfluous. If it does not, I would not care to have it added.

I hope I have made this clear, Abe. May I request that the company will respect these convictions and leave the matter where it is.

Kind regards always,

Ronald Colman

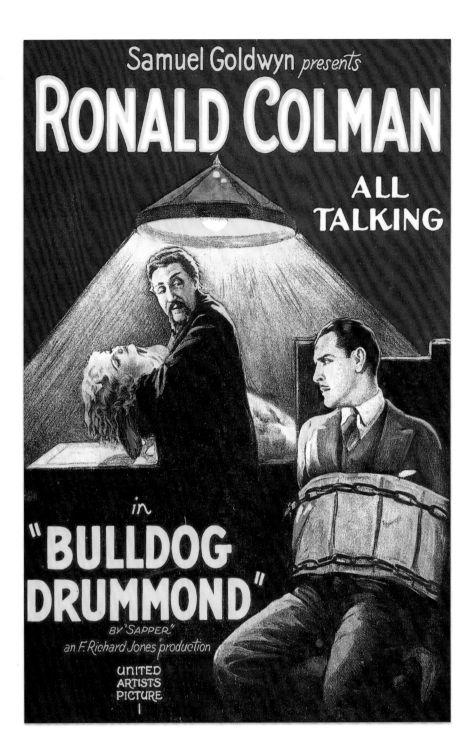

Ronald Colman
to Abe Lehr

AUGUST 5, 1928

While it may seem today that the development of sound technology was an inevitable advancement for motion pictures, there were many artists, in front of and behind the camera, who thought that talking pictures might be a passing fad. That certainly seems to be the case for British actor Ronald Colman, a Goldwyn star with very definite opinions who shared his thoughts in this painfully shortsighted letter to studio executive Abe Lehr. Of course,

Colman, who had acted on the stage for many years before becoming a movie star, turned out to have a beautiful voice that was ideally suited to recording and greatly admired by fans. Unlike many silent stars whose careers ended when they had to face the microphone, Colman made a triumphant transition to sound and was a reliably dashing leading man throughout the 1930s and 1940s. In 1947, he won an Oscar for playing a murderous actor in *A Double Life*.

Jack L. Warner to Hunt Stromberg

Gambling was a popular and expensive pastime in Hollywood, as this letter from studio head Jack Warner to MGM producer Hunt Stromberg illustrates. This note refers to a poker game that Stromberg had organized in May at the Roosevelt Hotel, but this group of friends also bet on horseracing and college football, and played high-stakes games of poker, bridge, and craps at private homes, at the Hillcrest Country Club, and at venues like the Clover Club on Sunset Boulevard. Stromberg, who in another letter called himself the "timekeeper, stakeholder, and payoff man" for these games, attempted to make sure everyone got paid, but it seems to have been very complicated to keep track of the bank. In one letter, Stromberg mentioned that the director Harold Franklin, one of the regular players in their group, had raked up losses of $33,000.

Warner Bros. Pictures, Inc.
WEST COAST STUDIOS
LOS ANGELES, CALIF.

OFFICE OF VICE-PRESIDENT

July 29th, 1929

Dear Hunter:

Many a moons, have come and gone since the indulgence in a game of chance at your big party at the Roosevelt Hotel.

So far, all I received was a breath of spring, and a bad breath too -- not even the breath of halitosis. If you have not, as yet, mailed the $1055.00 you will find me located at the above address.

All kidding aside, as a friend - everybody who has played in the games recently where you are in charge of the monies, are continually squaking. As a good friend of yours Hunt, something should be done as it is hurting your reputation and harm is being done every minute, on account of the monies not coming from the gambling games.

I am only writing this because I like you personally, and if I were you, I would get the thing straightened out and would not have anything to do with the settling up of gaming monies again. Take this advice for what it is worth -- and I repeat - it is just because you and I have been such good and close friends that I am taking the liberty of telling you, and certainly not because of the 1055 I have coming.

With kindest regards,

Sincerely,

Jack Warner

Mr. Hunt Stromberg,
Metro-Goldwyn-Mayer Studio
Culver City, Cal.

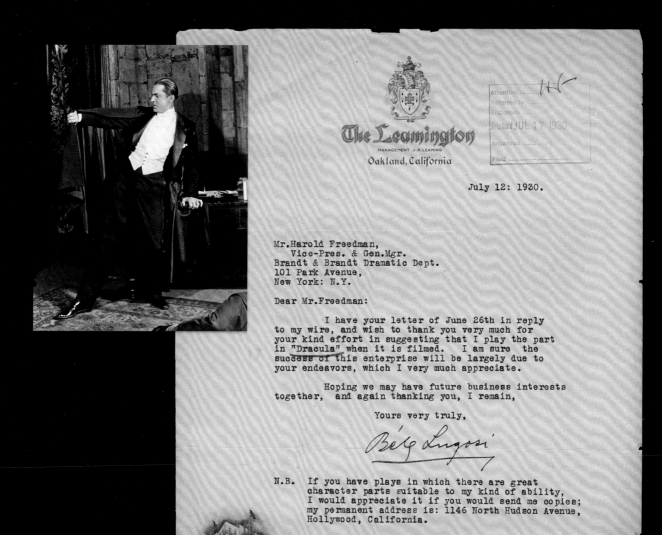

The Leamington
MANAGEMENT J.K.LEAMING
Oakland, California

July 12: 1930.

Mr.Harold Freedman,
      Vice-Pres. & Gen.Mgr.
Brandt & Brandt Dramatic Dept.
101 Park Avenue,
New York: N.Y.

Dear Mr.Freedman:

          I have your letter of June 26th in reply
to my wire, and wish to thank you very much for
your kind effort in suggesting that I play the part
in "Dracula" when it is filmed.   I am sure the
success of this enterprise will be largely due to
your endeavors, which I very much appreciate.

          Hoping we may have future business interests
together, and again thanking you, I remain,

                    Yours very truly,

                    Béla Lugosi

N.B. If you have plays in which there are great
      character parts suitable to my kind of ability,
      I would appreciate it if you would send me copies;
      my permanent address is: 1146 North Hudson Avenue,
      Hollywood, California.

Bela Lugosi to Harold Freedman

JULY 12, 1930

In this letter to theatrical play agent Harold Freedman, actor Bela Lugosi goes all out to land the leading role in the upcoming film version of *Dracula*. Lugosi was in his mid-forties and had been a working actor for years when he was cast as Count Dracula in the 1927 Broadway adaptation of Bram Stoker's gothic novel. After the New York run, Lugosi signed on for the West Coast tour, reprising his performance in San Francisco, Oakland, and Los Angeles, and campaigning for the lead role in the film adaptation being planned by Universal. Audiences who had seen Lugosi play the role on stage were excited at the prospect of his bringing the character to the screen, but Universal's executives were not convinced, and made plans to cast a known movie star like Lon Chaney (who died just six weeks after this letter was written), Conrad Veidt or Paul Muni. Finally, Universal and director Tod Browning agreed that Lugosi was the logical choice, and he was signed in September 1930.

Mrs. Alonzo Richardson (center) surrounded by members of her church group, 1942.

Mrs. Alonzo Richardson to Jason Joy

JUNE 22, 1932

Mrs. Alonzo (Zella) Richardson of Atlanta, Georgia, was a prominent clubwoman and member of the Better Films Committee who took over the position of Atlanta's film censor in 1925. Though the movie industry adopted the Production Code in 1930 in order to head off local censorship efforts, officials like Mrs. Richardson and other reformers continued to give Hollywood grief by editing release prints to suit their own local standards or, in some cases, banning films outright. In this letter to Colonel Jason Joy, the head of the Studio Relations Committee in Hollywood, Mrs. Richardson weighs in on the Jean Harlow comedy *Red-Headed Woman*, condemning it not only for its humorous depiction of a sexually rapacious female but also because it has personally shaken her faith in humanity. Mrs. Richardson was not alone. Many local censor officials, religious groups, and social scientists were calling for movies to clean house, and eventually the industry, faced with boycotts, gave in. In 1934, outspoken Catholic Joseph Breen was installed as head of the Production Code Administration and started enforcing the Code. For her part, the colorful Mrs. Richardson continued to share her thoughts with Breen and his colleagues until her retirement in 1945. In her handwritten postscript, Mrs. Richardson notes, "I haven't mailed the original. Am wondering whether I shall – whether it's worth while." She is referring to another letter about *Red-Headed Woman* that she wrote to Carl Milliken, the right-hand man to Will Hays, the head of the Motion Picture Producers and Distributors of America. Though she was wavering, she did end up sending the letter, which also condemned the film and bemoaned the effect it would have on young viewers.

BOARD OF REVIEW

406 CITY HALL

MRS. ALONZO RICHARDSON, Secretary

JUNE 2ND 1932

Dear Col Joy,-

It seems I cant stop quarreling to save my life, and I am naturally so peacefully inclined, and as my children tell me, gullible to the last degree! Maybe I am old, crabbed, ill-natured, and gullible, but as I sat this morning with my young granddaughter to whom life is so beautiful, previewing Jean Harlow in THE RED HEADED WOMAN, I felt I had made such a terrible mistake, to think I could have forgiven this hussy her behavior in HELLS ANGELS, to the extent I could believe she could do a decent enough thing, for me to risk taking a young girl to see her. BUT I DID, and with the result I have chronicled, in the letter to Governor Milliken, copy inclosed.

Now, for an old fashioned mid-Victorian lady, the word I have used regarding miss Harlow, is used for the first time, by yours truly, but to save my life after seeing her this morning, I cant think of any other which fits her performance. I just cant call her a lady, in fact only the one word suggests itself to me, and with shame I use it.. Picture your own lovely daughters seeing this nasty thing, then why do other peoples daughters have to see it?

Of course as to my own, the fault was entirely mine, I should have known from previous experience, previous pictures, that I should not have taken the girl;. but Since the world is restless, uncertain, and people looking and longing for entertainment which the family can enjoy together, and which will lift them out of the perplexities and cares of the day,- why give them such as this? Girls go home, doubting their fathers, knowing that even these are helpless against the wiles of the woman in the case, also that there is a way to reach any man, (which she probably had never dreamed of before.) Miss Harlowe's repeated "isnt he a man?" I think one of the filthiest things I have ever heard on the screen.

Perhaps I am a bit too prudish, for as one of the critics wrote me "if people wish to go 'merrily to hell' why stop them, it is no concern of ours". To neither your daughter nor to mine, will the "way" continue to to be "merry" and surely it is not ours to show them the way.

I guess I have lived too long, but deep in my heart is a hurt, that we who profess to want to pass on to the next generation so much of strength wisdom and courage to meet conditions that even we have not yet faced, it is a great sorrow to show them the things we are showing them in such pictures. Maybe you think I am all wrong. Maybe I am. Maybe I HAVE lived too long, to cling to ideals of clean living decent family life, and decent men and women. I wonder..

Love to all the Joys.

Cordially

I havent mailed the original. Am wondering whether

Mrs R

I shall - whether it worth while.

OUT OF THE THUNDERING CAVALCADE OF HISTORY COMES THE SCREEN'S MASTERPICTURE!

•

Towering head and shoulders above the screen giants of the past...Climaxing Warner Bros.' greatest production year..."SILVER DOLLAR"! Roaring, brawling record of America's most amazing empire builder, who lived to beg in the cities he had built. Men sang his glories... Women whispered of his sins ...America will shout its praise of this stupendous drama of his life and times!

Already 4-starred by Liberty Magazine. "A picture you must show," says Hollywood Reporter. "A honey"—Variety Bulletin. "Marvelous picture —it has everything!"—Hollywood Herald.

•

VAST CAST INCLUDING
BEBE DANIELS
ALINE MacMAHON
Directed by Alfred E. Green
A First National Picture

Watch Denver Premiere Dec. 1

VITAGRAPH, INC. DISTRIBUTORS

EDW. G. ROBINSON

SILVER DOLLAR

It's a Gift from WARNER BROS for Christmas!

John Barrymore to Edward G. Robinson

DECEMBER 1932

It must have been a thrill for Edward G. Robinson to receive this note of appreciation from John Barrymore, the great American stage and screen actor whose family was considered theater royalty. In 1931, the thirty-seven-year-old Robinson had rocketed to stardom after his breakthrough role as Rico in the iconic gangster movie *Little Caesar*, and for the rest of his career he was often cast in similar roles. But Robinson's studio, Warner Bros., also gave the experienced actor the opportunity to shine in other types of stories. *Silver Dollar*, the film that inspired Barrymore to write this "mash note," was a historical

drama about the rise and fall of a nineteenth-century Colorado silver tycoon, and in 1932 Robinson also played a Portuguese fisherman in *Tiger Shark* and a Chinese assassin in *The Hatchet Man*. That year, Barrymore also distinguished himself on the screen, appearing opposite newcomer Katharine Hepburn in *A Bill of Divorcement* and Greta Garbo in *Grand Hotel*. Barrymore's letter was written from Palm Springs, a popular desert getaway for movie stars in the winter months. At the time, Barrymore was married to his third wife, the actress Dolores Costello.

Desert Inn
Palm Springs

Dear Mr. Robinson –
    My wife & myself saw "The Silver Dollar" here last night and I cannot help writing you a "mash note" about it. You were really most extraordinarily moving and superb. It seemed to me to be a superlative piece of cumulative natural acting and made one proud to be in the same game! The way you got a little weaker & weaker in the "chassis" as things got tougher was great—and the scene in the opera house beautiful.
    Congratulations—and every good wish to you. My wife reiterates these sentiments with equal warmth.
    All the best to you and Mrs. Robinson.

Jack Barrymore

The way you got a little
weaker & weaker in the
"chassis" as things got
tougher was great and
the scene in the opera House
beautiful— Congratulations.
and every good wish to you.
My wife reiterates these
sentiments with equal warmth.
all the best to you and
Mrs Robinson—
Jack Barrymore.

following spread

Bert Glennon to Katharine Hepburn

FALL 1933

One of Hollywood's most respected cameramen, Bert Glennon already had more than forty credits under his belt when he photographed *Morning Glory* and *Christopher Strong*, two 1933 RKO productions starring Katharine Hepburn. As this breezy letter from Glennon shows, the two became fast friends off the set as well, and clearly enjoyed sharing news about their extracurricular activities as well as industry gossip. In the 1920s and 1930s, Glennon photographed four films for the mercurial director Josef von Sternberg, including two of his collaborations with Marlene Dietrich. This would explain why Glennon has such insights into the tempestuous relationship between the director and his star, who at this time were working on *The Scarlet Empress*. Glennon's mentions of Hepburn's upcoming adventures in New York refers to the fact that Hepburn was temporarily leaving Hollywood and heading east to star in the play *The Lake*, which opened on Broadway in December 1933. The "business manager" that Glennon mentions is Leland Hayward, with whom Hepburn was romantically involved at the time. "Laura" is Laura Harding, Hepburn's close friend and frequent companion.

Monday

Dear Madam Kate,

Sorry you got away without a "so long for awhile," but I guess you'll get along O.K. without those salutations.

We're still going nite & day and strange to say getting some interesting results. Dietrich & Von haven't fought yet—Oh! yes, it happens at least once a picture—but we're all expecting the boiling over to come as soon as they start doing scenes that require emotional stress—or is it strain?

What's this I hear about you, Darling, and your business manager—or is it just an amusing insinuation of our *Hollywood Reporter*. Of course I don't blame the young man. Pretty soon they are going to discover some of the things I know about your personality and you will not have a moment's peace of mind.

Gee! I envy the fun you are going to have in good old N.Y.—(Good if you know people)—and the work. I know everything is going to be O.K. So keep the feet on the ground "old gal" and come back to gullible California full of new ideas.

Took a blond for an air ride Sunday and I think I have found the location of your <u>new</u> bandit's lair. Any way I had the pleasure of saying—"I bet that's Madam Hep's new joint."

Hello to Laura.
Bye,
Bert

Mondays.

Madam.

Dear , Kate .

Sorry you got
away without a "So long for
awhile", but I guess you'll
get along O.K. without ~~those~~
salutations,

We're still going
nite & day. and strange to
say getting some interesting
results. Dietrich & Von haven't
fought yet — Oh! yes, it
happens at least once a
picture — but we're all expecting
the boiling over to come
as soon as they start
doing scenes that require
emotional stress . or is it
strain ?

Whats this I hear about
You; Darling, and your
business manager — or is it just
an amusing insinuation of
our Hollywood Reporter . Of.
course I don't blame the .

young man. Pretty soon they are going to discover some of the things I know about your personality and you will not have a moments peace of mind.

Yes! I envy the fun you are going to have in <u>Good</u> Old N.Y. — (Good if you know people) — and the work. — I know everything is going to be O.K. So keep the feet on the ground. 'Old gal'. and come back to gullible California full of new ideas.

Took a blond for an air ride Sunday and I think I have found the location of your <u>new</u> bandits lair. Anyway I had the pleasure of saying — "I bet thats madam Haps new joint"
Hello to Laura
Bye
Bert

Jean Bello to Arthur Landau

SEPTEMBER 1933

Jean Harlow Bello, also known as "Mother Jean," was one of the most domineering stage mothers in Hollywood. Her daughter, Harlean Carpenter (whom she always called "the Baby"), was transformed into the movie star "Jean Harlow" thanks to relentless promotion from Mother Jean, though most of the credit should go to Harlow's considerable talents as an actress and comedienne. In this letter to Harlow's agent, Arthur Landau (who the young actress affectionately nicknamed Pops), Mother Jean shows that she was not only protective but also shrewd, as she eviscerates MGM studio chief Louis B. Mayer and his lieutenant Eddie Mannix for their indifferent response to Harlow's brilliant star turn in *Bombshell*. Produced by Hunt Stromberg and written by Jules Furthman and John Lee Mahin,

the satirical behind-the-scenes Hollywood comedy stars Harlow as a likeable scandal-plagued movie star looking for true love and Lee Tracy as the studio publicity man who is always one step ahead of her. The mention of Harlow's having "finished the concrete at the Chinese" refers to the process of placing her hand and foot prints in the forecourt of Grauman's Chinese Theatre in Hollywood, where the young star was immortalized in cement in September 1933. Harlow died in 1937 at the age of twenty-six.

Jean Harlow (second from right) and her mother, Jean Bello, dining with Arthur Landau and his wife Beatrice, 1934.

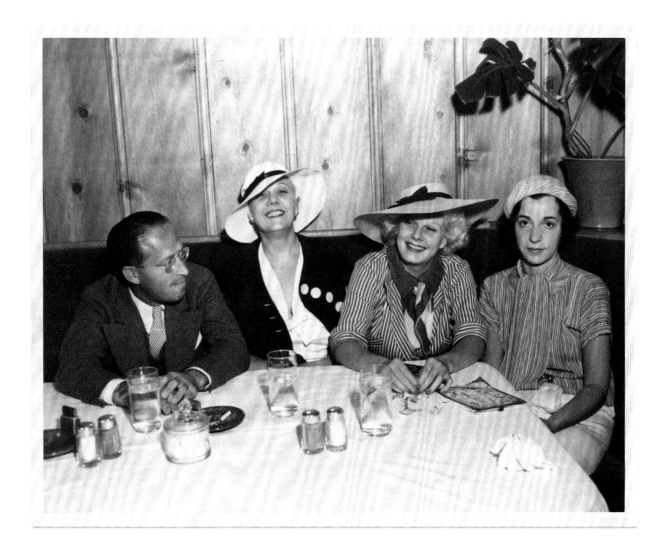

Popa darling, this will please you.

Bombshell was a SENSATION, a WOW, a SUCCESS and what an
evening.
The wires poured in here and Hunt Stromberg sent the Baby a huge box of
roses with this note " To my favorite actress, with my appreciation for
a perfect performance" Love Hunt. Which made the Baby cry with gratitude.
A huge box of cut orchids from Jules Furthman (from his own greenhouses)
with an exqyisite note of appreciation for the most perfect performance he had
ever seen and that NO one could have done what Harlow did, and how proud he
was to have his name on the sheet with hers. Wasent that lovely?
We are so grateful and happy for the Baby.

L. B. sat in front of us and when he and Mannix came in the did not EVEN speak
to t he Baby ONLY nodded. When it was over and the audience Was WILD L.B. stopped
at the Babys side and started to explode he caught himself and said ,GOD TRACY
has great lines. Now Pops if I had not heard it I could NOT have believed that.

Not even " Jean your work was nice" Not one word except JUST what I have
told you. CAN you imagine such a fool as to think he could intimidate three
people like us with such childish tactics. Really those people must think
we are of very limited intelligence and ef very lowly birth to accept such
childish tactice. BUT Pops if I had anything to do with the situation I
would make that gentleman pay in blood for tha insult.
Yeaterday the Baby finished the concrete at the CHINESE and we are so
proud to have her name among the biggest of the industry.
I have only met Miss Dressler once but Pops will you please tell her I am
a really devoted fan of Dressler the magnificent woman as well as Dressler
the great actres? I adore her.

Tell Mrs Landau when she returnes I will haveto hear about all the pretty
new styles.

Love to you both

Mother

                                        Tuesday night.

Dear Howard:- (STRICKLING)

I have just talked to Joe on the telephone after trying vainly to locate
you.   Anything I can tell you in# this letter will be stale by the time
it reaches you,   but so you'll get a complete picture I'll re-hash
the happenings of the last few days -- and, God forbid! nights.   I've
slept four hours since Saturday night and don't expect to get much sleep
tonight.   Lee is lost somewhere.   The press association gang keep me
posted every few minutes, but there's nothing new.   I told Joe I
thought he was sleeping in Chihuahua, and won't worry about him until
tomorrow.

It all started Sunday shortly after# noon. I was having luncheon down
stairs when one of the lads from the A. P. came rushing in and said Tracy
was standing on the balcony overlooking the Avenida Juarez, the main
drag here, absolutely naked. Further, he was shouting obscenities
and making bawdy gestures at the crowds who were out to see the miles-
long parade celebrating the anniversary of the revolution.   It was a
holiday comparable to our Fourth of July, only tremendously more intense
in its national spirit.   To cap the climax, Tracy was hurling ribald
and obscene remarks at the cadets from Chapultepec who happened to be
marching by; they are the West Point boys of Mexico.   The crowds in
the street were in an uproar and the cadets were on the point of coming
after Tracy en masse.

By the time I got to his room he was just throwing out the first of the
many policemen# who eventually arrived.   Lee went for the cop, and the
cop retreated to await re-inforcements.   Then all the cops in town began
to arrive, until eventually there were probably thirty there, uniformed
men and detectives.   By this time Lee had passed out cold in his room
while we were all holding the cops in the hall; it was a blessing,
because they were all for beating him to a pulp and throwing him in jail
pronto.   When he passed out we were able to convince them that he could
 not be moved. They left two men on guard, one in his room and one in the
hall, and it stayed like that all night.

First thing Monday they took him to the police station, then back to the
hotel for breakfast. Then back to the station and into a cell.   By that
time I had the A.P. and U.P. boys working for me -- they had the story,
of course, but agreed not to use it.   They took me to the Embassy and
to xxx the chief secretary to the Ambassador, who## is an American-born
Spaniard and knows all the intricacies of Mexican politics. Through
his good offices I was able to get Lee out of jail at 12:30 noon with the
blessing of the General who is Chief of Police, and the Chief of
Detectives.   It looked like it was all over.

                                                                        5697
VINA VILLA - LEE TRACY INCIDENT 1933

Don Eddy to Howard Strickling

NOVEMBER 21, 1933

One of the most notorious studio public relations disasters of the 1930s is documented in this intriguing partial letter from unit publicist Don Eddy to MGM publicity department head Howard Strickling. In Mexico shooting *Viva Villa!*, a film loosely based on the life of Pancho Villa, leader of the Mexican revolution, MGM was already on thin ice with the Mexican authorities and facing harsh criticism from community leaders when things came to a head in Mexico City on Sunday, November 19, 1933, during a parade celebrating Mexican independence. The popular actor Lee Tracy, who was playing a reporter in the movie, was accused of drunkenly shouting and making indecent gestures toward the crowd from his hotel room balcony, and to add insult to injury, according to some observers, he was naked or only partially clothed at the time. After being arrested and detained, then released, Tracy managed to make it across the border to El Paso before additional charges could be filed by the Mexican government. Studio head L. B. Mayer scrambled to control the damage by promptly firing Tracy, who was under contract to the studio. Mayer also sent a widely publicized telegram to the president of Mexico apologizing for the incident, but relations were so strained the company quickly wrapped up its work and returned to California to complete the film. Though accounts at the time varied (Tracy, for instance, claimed his room didn't even have a balcony), most of the overheated press coverage focused on the insults and gestures Tracy exchanged with the crowd, and the fact that he was in a "state of undress." Years later, however, the story began to include another previously unreported detail: that Tracy had urinated from the balcony onto the crowd below. Though none of the press coverage, or this letter from Eddy, includes that accusation, the film's first (uncredited) director, Howard Hawks, later claimed that was the case in interviews, and the story has been repeated in many sources, including the autobiography of actor Desi Arnaz and biographies of Mayer and producer David O. Selznick. In fact, in his book *David O. Selznick's Hollywood*, Ronald Haver quotes from this very letter, but includes the line, "I got there just in time to see him urinating on the cadets from Chapultepec, the West Point boys of Mexico," a statement that does not appear in the copy of the letter reproduced here. On the other hand, the cinematographer Charles G. Clarke wrote in his autobiography that he witnessed the incident from the street and that Tracy did nothing inappropriate on the balcony. Not surprisingly, the story dogged Tracy for the rest of his life. When he died in 1966, *Variety* recounted the scandal in his obituary and wrote that he was "credited with showering available greetings upon marchers from his hotel balcony."

Gregg Toland to Fred Zinnemann

APRIL 27, 1934

Cinematographer Gregg Toland captures the exciting and exhausting life of an in-demand studio cameraman in this letter to his friend Fred Zinnemann, who had worked as an assistant on the set of several of Toland's movies. One of the top cameramen with Samuel Goldwyn productions, the twenty-nine-year-old Toland was preparing to shoot *Resurrection* (released as *We Live Again*), an adaptation of the Tolstoy novel starring Anna Sten, a recent Goldwyn discovery, and directed by the "camera conscious" Rouben Mamoulian. *Barbary Coast*, which Toland was expecting to work on next, was postponed by a year and eventually photographed by Ray June, who also shot *Kid Millions*, the Eddie Cantor vehicle referred to in the letter as *Treasure Hunt*. Toland, who worked primarily for Goldwyn but also at other studios, photographed more than sixty films between 1931 and 1948, including *Dead End*, *Citizen Kane*, and *The Best Years of Our Lives*, and was responsible for many innovations that advanced the art of cinematography, including the deep-focus technique that he perfected for *Kane*. In his letter, Toland addresses Zinnemann as "amigo" because the young director, who was still finding his footing in Hollywood, was then in Mexico making an independent film called *Redes* (*The Wave*). According to a profile of Toland published in the *New Yorker* in 2006, he met his second wife, Helene Barclay, at the Chateau Marmont, where he was living when he wrote this letter. They were married in 1934.

April 27th. Nite Int.

Dear Amigo Fred;

So sorry sorry sorry not to have answered your
letter sooner but picture taking business would not permit.
After my quickie at M.G.M. which was finally titled "Lazy River"
I did seven weeks of "Tarzan" and then back to Goldwyn to get
ready for "Ressurection". Have traveled 4400 miles in last three
weeks doing projection backgrounds and have some swell ones.
They realy 'give'. Made one trip into Oregon around the Hood
River and photographed the apple blossoms add a lot of shots for
suggestion of spring in Russia. Very swell. Then found a very
excellent wheat field and some lovely (kidney shaped) plowed
fiels up north. Did a lot of really startling shots. All set to
leave for Panama on the Empress of Britan next Sunday to do
backgrounds for next Cantor picture, and fly back from Panama
but Goldwyn wouldn't hear of it. Wouldn't even discuss it. So-
arranged to get Bert a first card for three weeks and he leaves
day after tomorrow. Lucky Bastard- Hope you see the capital B.
Thats ehough about me- except that Mamoulian seems very camera
concious which is swell. Now about yoy- and please excuse my
mistakes on the keys.

Read your last letter to Bob MacIntyre and sure
hope you get back soon. Here is the dope as nearly as I can get
it. We must start "Ressurection" not later than May 14th says
Goldwyn. Thats the reason he wouldn't let me go away. Reason
for starting sooner than expected is that Swanson is out of
"Barbary Coast" and sten is in. So the director, Wellman and his
crew are standing by for "Barbary Coast" until we finish. So you
see we must start soon. Be on "Ressurection" at least eight
weeks. So you see "Barbary Coast" can't start before July 15th.
In my personal opinion Cantor will start about August first. His
picture is called "Treasure Hunt" and is laid in Africa. As far as
I know we will only do three this year. Goldwyn wants to go to
China this year and wants to leave in September. Of course he'll
never get away then, but thats an indication of how things are
lining up. I'm certain you can catch the Cantor picture. Ray will
do that one. Perhaps I'll do the numbers- who knows ?

I do hope your picture down there is a huge
success and I'm sure the photography will put us all to shame.
Saw the few print tests Bob had and they were grand. Keep on and
do your best. Remember that people up here might see it, and try to
make every scene the best in the picture.

I'm very very very very much in Love. Really divine-
or something or other. At least everything seems perfectly exposed. Good Luck Fredie- I'M certain you'll do swell.

Amigo-Gregg.

New address above- Have a cute little pent house here.

BORIS KARLOFF
Universal Studios,
Universal City, Cal.

August 22nd, 1934.

Mr. Albert Hergesheimer,
147 N. Eighth Ave.,
Mt. Vernon, N. Y.

Dear Mr. Hergesheimer:

Perhaps my most important superstition is the
continuance of the chain of events which have proved
fortunate.

For example, in making "Frankenstein" a few
years ago after all the hours spent in the make-up room,
in going to the set it happened that I always turned to
the right as I left the make-up room.   As you know, it
was a very lucky picture for me so now, whenever I leave
the make-up room I always turn to the right even if it
means a longer walk to the particular set I am going to.

This sounds rather silly but there you are!

Good-luck to your column.

Very sincerely,

Boris Karloff

Boris Karloff during production of *Bride of Frankenstein*, 1935.

Boris Karloff to Albert Hergesheimer

AUGUST 22, 1934

The veteran character actor turned horror star Boris Karloff (born William Henry Pratt) was between pictures but soon to star in *Bride of Frankenstein* when he wrote or dictated this quick note to writer Albert Hergesheimer. Fan magazines and movie gossip columns were filled with tidbits like this that were planted by Hollywood publicists in order to give movie fans a look behind the camera and a sense that they might learn what a star was really like. A consummate professional, the English-born Karloff was very genteel, in contrast to the frightening characters he usually played on screen. A founder of the Screen Actors Guild in 1933, he was also a dedicated advocate for the rights of his fellow thespians.

271 Bronwood Avenue,
West Los Angeles.
July 9, 1936.

Dear Fritz,

Anne and I saw FURY last night and we want to tell you how thoroughly we agree with the general opinion that you did a superb job with your story. (We asked Alice if she wanted to go with us, but when she heard it was a picture about lynching she said No, she had only been born a bout a month ago and that being born was more harrowing and terrifying than any lynching could possibly be.)

Some critics which I have read said the story fell away in its last half, but outside of the kiss in the courtroon which I know they put over across your dead body, I did not agree with them, nor did Anne. The psychology of Wilson's relenting from his vengeance seemed to us absolutely valid and authentic. The only regret we had was that he was so spruced up and neat when he came into the coutroom. We would have liked to have had him still dishevelled and wild-looking, still showing the effects of the night's horror and hysteria. Tracy certainly put on a splendid performance. Sylvia's was good too, but I thought her makeup a bit too sleek and tailored, something which made her a bit artificial for me.

There are many touches of yours I would like to comment on, but I'll have to see the picture a couple of more times so that I can take them in. Things like the swinging door in the barber shop, for instance.

And I don't think I have ever seen anything more effective than the use you made of your camera when it took the place of the mob advancing to the jail entrance. That shot was terrific. All I can say is that I hope to Christ, more than ever, that PATHS OF GLORY may someday come to the screen under your direction.

I don't know what contribution Cormack made to the dialogue, but obnoxious louse that I think he is, I must say that I thought the lines were excellent and uniformly in the right key.

It is really a source of great personal satisfaction to both Anne and myself that your first picture in this country is such a splendid job and all credit is due you for having produced it in the face of Hollywood and all that Hollywood stands for. Sincerest congratulations from us both.

Yours,

Humphrey

Humphrey Cobb to Fritz Lang

JULY 9, 1936

Fritz Lang was one of the most famous of the filmmakers who emigrated to the United States in the 1930s after the Nazis came to power. A giant of the German industry who had directed *Metropolis* and *M*, Lang landed in Hollywood in 1934 and signed a contract with MGM. His first American production was *Fury*, a hard-hitting expose about lynching that starred Spencer Tracy and Sylvia Sidney. In this perceptive letter about the film, the novelist and screenwriter Humphrey Cobb praises Lang's command of cinematic language, while also hinting at the challenges the independent director faced as he adjusted to the realities of working in the often restrictive Hollywood studio system. "Cormack" was Bartlett Cormack, who cowrote the script with Lang, based on a story by Norman Krasna. Cobb, who died in 1944, was the author of *Paths of Glory*, a powerful anti-war novel set in France during the First World War. Cobb's 1935 book was eventually adapted for the screen in 1957, but it was directed by Stanley Kubrick, not Fritz Lang.

Tallulah Bankhead in the 1936 Broadway play *Reflected Glory*.

following spread

Tallulah Bankhead to David O. Selznick

DECEMBER 25, 1936

In December 1936, as the publicity machine around David O. Selznick's production of *Gone with the Wind* started to heat up, the inimitable stage actress Tallulah Bankhead traveled to Hollywood and shot several silent screen tests with George Cukor, who was then slated to direct the film for Selznick. Bankhead was performing on Broadway at the time, in the play *Reflected Glory*, but had been discussing the role of Scarlett with Selznick and his team for several months, working especially closely with Katherine Brown, Selznick's New York-based story editor and trusted associate. Born in Huntsville, Alabama, to a prosperous, well-connected Southern family, Bankhead in many ways had the perfect pedigree for the role of Scarlett O'Hara, and by all accounts she was committed to winning the part. This letter from the actress to Selznick, written just a few days after

returning from Los Angeles, shows that she is confident about her ability to play Scarlett, but not willing to be put on a back burner while Selznick reviews his options. It was in response to a telegram from Selznick in which he said that he was "Still worried about the first part of the story and frankly if I had to give you an answer now it would be no but if we can leave it open I can say to you very honestly that I think there is a strong possibility." He also told her she would probably need to do more screen tests before he could reach a decision. In the end, Selznick considered hundreds of actresses for the role, and his staff shot screen tests with more than thirty of them. The "Search for Scarlett," as Selznick's overeager publicity agents called it, ended in January 1939 when Selznick signed the English actress Vivien Leigh to play the tempestuous Southern belle.

PRIVATE OFFICE
MAX A. HAERING
RESIDENT MANAGER

The Gotham

5TH AVE. AT 55TH ST.
NEW YORK CITY

December 25, 1936.

Dear David:-

Thank you very much for your wire, which I have read and thought about many times before I am writing my reactions to it.

First of all, I want to say that I sincerely appreciate your original interest and the cooperation of all concerned. I want you to believe me when I say this letter is not written in any spirit of hurt, arrogance, or bad temper, and if these elements should creep in, it is only because I haven't a sufficient gift of words to express myself clearly.

The whole situation, thru no fault of yours or mine, has been under the strain of lack of the time element involved, but I think under the circumstances everything has been done that could be. As I see it, your wire to me means one thing - that if no one better comes along, I'll do. Well, that would be all well and good if I were a beginner at my job. It would be a wonderful thing to hope and wait for, but as this is not the case, I cannot see it that way, and I feel it only fair to tell you that I will not make any more tests, either silent or dialogue, for Scarlett O'Hara, on probation.

I know and George knows that the part of Scarlett O'Hara, as an actress, would be safe in my hands, and I assumed that you were of the same opinion. As to my being able to look the part in the early sequence of the picture, that is entirely out of my jurisdiction, but I have been assured by several ace cameramen in their vernacular that " its a cinch ". I claim no credit for their genius.

I realize your feeling of responsibility and the desire for the perfection of the production of "Gone With The Wind", and I also know

DIRECTION

Stop at Recognized Hotels

The Gotham

5TH AVE. AT 55TH ST.
NEW YORK CITY

how harrassed you must be by the many conflicting opinions and
suggestions which you receive daily, but if you were to abide by
them all, poor "Gone With The Wind" would never see the light of day.
The decision ultimately must rest upon your shoulders and those few
upon whom you will place the responsibility for the success of the
production, of which I feel George is the keynote. For his sake and
yours, I hope the miracle happens and that you find your ideal Scarlett
because I am as sentimental and rabid on the subject as all the others.

In closing, I want to especially thank you for the assistance of
Kay Brown, who has been an angel about the whole thing. It goes without saying how much I appreciate what George has done and felt, and I
want you to know I am sending him a copy of this letter incase I have
unintentionally misinterpreted his sentiments on the subject.

Thank you again, and my best wishes for your continued success.

Tallulah

Dashiell Hammett
to Lillian Hellman

SEPTEMBER 9, 1937

Dashiell Hammett, the acclaimed author of *The Thin Man* and *The Maltese Falcon*, was temporarily living and working in Los Angeles as a screenwriter when he wrote this letter to his companion Lillian Hellman, the celebrated playwright and screenwriter. Hellman had recently returned from a much-publicized trip to Russia, and Hammett was taking this opportunity to bring her up to date on the goings-on in Hollywood. Though he seemed to shy away from regular socializing, Hammett was well-connected, and his letter gives a great feeling for the social scene in the movie colony at this time, particularly among friends like John Huston, William Wyler, Albert and Frances Hackett, Hunt Stromberg, and Charles Brackett. Wyler and Hellman were both under contract to Samuel Goldwyn, and Wyler had directed two films written by Hellman, including, most recently, *Dead End*. In addition to parties and events, such as the memorial concert at the Hollywood Bowl for George Gershwin, who had died in July, Hammett reports to Hellman on the progress of the struggling Screen Writers Guild, which was in the process of trying to build up its membership. He and Hellman were dedicated members and were involved in the ongoing battle to sign up new recruits and gain recognition for the Guild from the studios, which were undermining the effort by backing a rival group, the Screen Playwrights. As mentioned in the last paragraph of his letter, Hammett did obtain a divorce from his wife in 1937, but he and Hellman never married.

The Beverly-Wilshire
Beverly Hills, California

September 9, 1937

Dear Lilishka,

There's a lot of missing of
you going on around here, personally speaking, and maybe it's not only me: I seldom
see Charley Brackett that he doesn't put in
his vice-presidential two-cent's-worth.
Maybe you've got something there.

The Gershwin concert last night
seems to have been a smash. I didn't go,
afraid to take a chance on the great outdoors with the tail-end of my flu (practically gone now, thank you) but it sounded swell
on the radio.

I saw Lou Holtz night before
last. He's taking a screen test for David
Selznick, thinking about marrying a girl with
two children, and has had a successful eight
weeks in a Chicago night club. Don't say
I don't give you the news.

Willy Wyler is giving a cock-
tail party for John Huston tommorrow, and
the Arthur Sheekman's one for themselves
Saturday. No, I'm not going.

The Hacketts cabled me from
Stockholm that Hunt had wired them from
Biarritz to cable me asking about the story.
Hunt will be back on the 19th.

Eddie Knopf phoned me yester-
day with his tongue hanging out trying to

get hold of you. He had just run across the
Hollywood Reporter's little item saying you
had left Goldwyn in a huff over the Follies,
and seemed disappointed when I told him it
wasn't exactly so.

Dead End, I suppose you know,
is doing terrific business and a lot of nice
things are being said about what you did to
the play.

Life this week has pictures of
you week-ending at the Kauffmans': one bad
one of you playing tennis, one good one of
you knitting, so I guess you're more the
domestic type.

I haven't seen the Goldwyn's
since you left; I ran into Haight one night
at the Clover--where he was gambling and I
wasn't--and saw Freddy and Maxine at the
Trocadero. Freddy, very drunk, was trying to
find out if it was wrong of him to think that
Lois got on his nerves sometimes.

Speaking of Lois, believe it
or etc., she borrowed thirty dollars while
she was here and sent it back as soon as she
got home. I think she's a little peeved
because I didn't take her out, but maybe that
is just my male vanity.

Arthur's play, according to
always reliable Variety, has picked up again
and is good for a few more months.

Moss Hart's mother died a day
or two ago; the 21-Trocadero deal has fallen

The Beverly-Wilshire
Beverly Hills, California

for the twentieth and supposedly last time;
our Labor Board hearing is slated for the
27th of this month; I was divorced in Nogales,
Sonora, Mexico, on the 26th of last month;
Al Lichtman still says the chemin-de-fer's
no good since you left town; my gambling has
not been doing me any good financially; the
Guild has been signing up an average of
about twelve members a week, including a few
from the Playwrights; and the weather remains
pleasant enough, though I've been out only
twice briefly in the past two weeks.

        I hope and imagine you had a
swell time in Russia.

        Love,

        Dash

Somewhere in Kansas.

Gloria dear:

Forgive the typewritten letter, but the train
is too jiggly to write in longhand.

In the excitement of preparing the Carl Laemmle
speech, in which you so ably helped me, I forgot to
thank you for your charming Christmas thought. I
know how busy you are and it makes me appreciate all
the more your thinking of me.

You will be amused to learn that in the part of
my speech where I am supposed to say, "You, Mr.
Laemmle, are one of the structural pillars of our
industry, etc., I was punished for my naughtiness
earlier in the day, before a large and distinguished
audience, by saying, "You, Mr. Laemmle, are a structural
pill pill pill pillar" - much to my confusion and
embarrassment and to the merriment of the distinguished
representatives of the industry who were standing back
of me. As Uncle Carl is deaf, he, of course, smiled
blandly at me.

I am play scouting and should I see anything
I think would be good for you, I shall immediately
wire you.

As ever

Affectionately yours,

Mary.

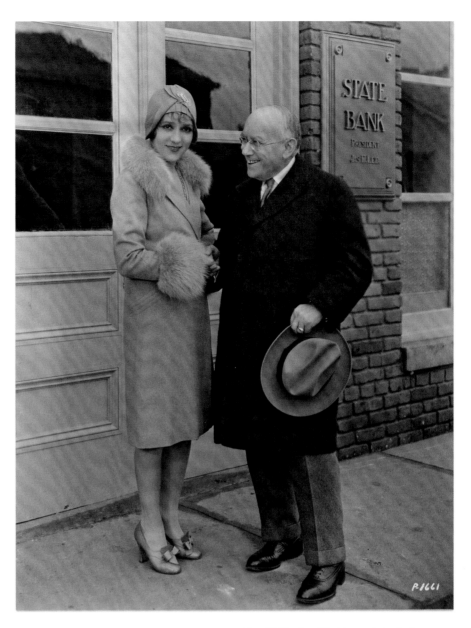

Mary Pickford and Carl Laemmle in the late 1920s.

Mary Pickford to Gloria Swanson

CIRCA 1937

This undated note from Mary Pickford, the biggest movie star of the silent era, to actress Gloria Swanson not only shows Pickford's likeable personality but also sheds light on the important role she played as a spokesperson on behalf of the motion picture industry. Carl Laemmle, the beloved film pioneer and founder of Universal Pictures whom she was honoring, was one of Pickford's first bosses in the movie business, and she clearly felt that she owed him a debt of gratitude. Pickford retired from acting in 1933, but she continued to play an important role in the industry as an executive at United Artists, the company she had cofounded in 1919. Though this note is undated, the goodwill tour celebrating Laemmle may have taken place in 1937, which would have been the twenty-fifth anniversary of the founding of Universal Pictures. In another clue as to the year of this letter, Pickford's third husband, Charles "Buddy" Rogers, whom she married in 1937, was born in Olathe, Kansas, and this train trip may have coincided with a visit to his home state around the time of their wedding.

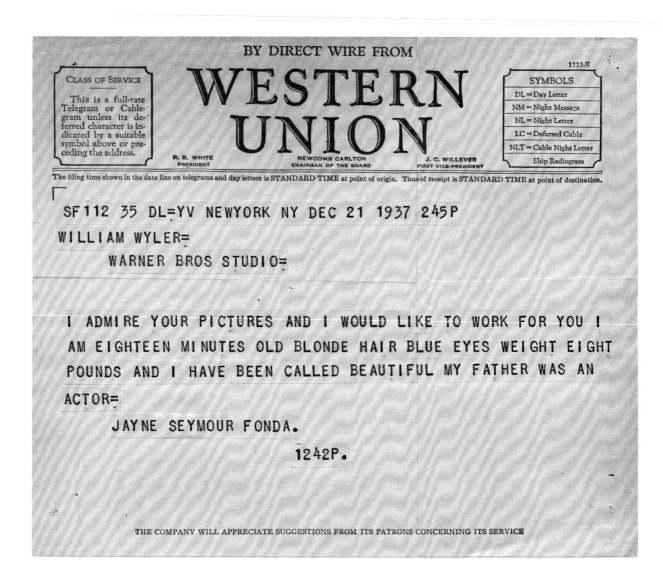

SF112 35 DL=YV NEWYORK NY DEC 21 1937 245P

WILLIAM WYLER=

WARNER BROS STUDIO=

I ADMIRE YOUR PICTURES AND I WOULD LIKE TO WORK FOR YOU I AM EIGHTEEN MINUTES OLD BLONDE HAIR BLUE EYES WEIGHT EIGHT POUNDS AND I HAVE BEEN CALLED BEAUTIFUL MY FATHER WAS AN ACTOR=

JAYNE SEYMOUR FONDA.

1242P.

Henry Fonda to William Wyler & Wyler's Reply

DECEMBER 21, 1937

Henry Fonda was in the middle of shooting *Jezebel* with Bette Davis when his daughter Jayne Seymour Fonda (aka Jane Fonda) was born in New York on December 21, 1937. In this witty exchange of telegrams, Fonda is remarkably prescient about his daughter's future career, while director William Wyler and his other comrades back in Hollywood,

dubbing themselves "The Jezzies," take the opportunity to rib Fonda about his acting abilities. Jane's mother was Fonda's second wife, Frances Ford Brokaw Fonda. His first wife had been the actress Margaret Sullavan, who had also been briefly married to Wyler.

EXECUTIVE OFFICES
321 WEST 44TH STREET
NEW YORK

TELEPHONE
EXCHANGE
HOLLY 1251

WARNER BROS.

PICTURES, INC.
WEST COAST STUDIOS
BURBANK, CALIFORNIA

12/31/37

JAYNE SIMONE FONDA
c/o HENRY FONDA
WARWICK HOTEL
NEW YORK NY

MY DEAR MANY THANKS FOR YOUR KIND WIRE ~~AND~~ HEARTY CONGRATULATIONS
on YOUR ARRIVAL AND HEARTFELT CONDOLENCE ON YOUR ~~INDISCRIMINATE~~
CHOICE OF ~~PARENTS~~ *father* HOWEVER WE FEEL IT OUR DUTY TO CORRECT ANY
ILLUSION YOU MAY HAVE BEEN UNDER IN THE PAST AS WE FEEL YOU ARE
OLD ENOUGH NOW TO BE TOLD THE HAPPY NEWS YOUR FATHER NEVER WAS
AN ACTOR STOP WE ARE SMOKING TO YOUR HEALTH WYLER WANTS TO MAKE
A TEST OF YOU SOON AS POSSIBLE UNDER CERTAIN PROVISIONS YOUR
CONTRACT AND HEREWITH REQUESTS YOU CALL HIM UNCLE ~~DUE TO THE FACT~~
Because ~~THAT~~ HE FEELS THERE IS AN UNDEFINABLE BUT NONE THE LESS DEFINATE
RELATIONSHIP SOMEWHERE SOMEHOW LOVE TO YOU AND YOU KNOW WHAT TO
YOUR FATHER

THE JEZZIES *and your mother*

and good wishes

Greta Garbo to Marion Davies

MARCH 12, 1938

In this plea for help to her friend, actress Marion Davies, Greta Garbo makes it clear that she really did just want to be left alone. After a dozen years in Hollywood and more than twenty films, the publicity-shy Garbo was attempting to take an extended European vacation with her companion, the conductor Leopold Stokowski, but the press was not cooperating. Davies had retired from the screen by 1937 but was still an important and popular figure in the Hollywood community. The longtime mistress of powerful media mogul William Randolph Hearst, Davies not only knew how to navigate unwanted attention, but also had the means to call off at least some of the dogs. In the end, though, it doesn't seem like Davies was able to offer much help; Garbo's European trip was covered exhaustively by reporters and photographers, who followed her to every destination.

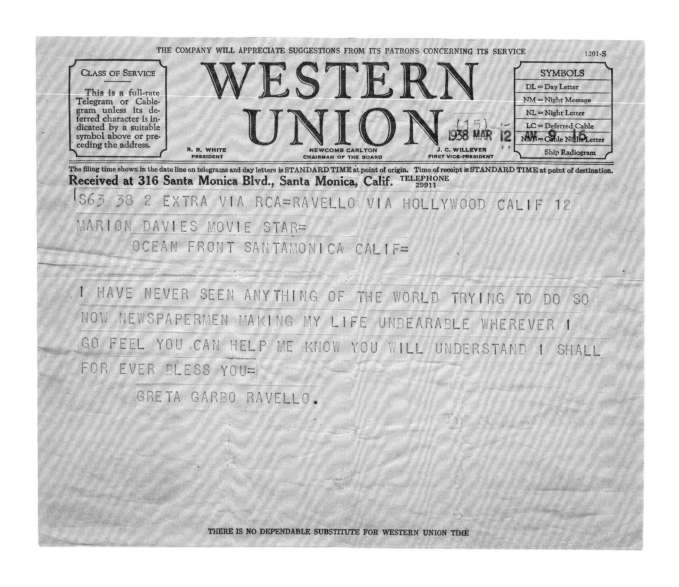

Mark Sandrich and Ginger Rogers during production of *Carefree*, 1938.

following spread

Pandro Berman to Mark Sandrich

APRIL 21, 1938

As head of production at RKO, Pandro Berman was used to putting out fires, and he does so expertly in this letter to Mark Sandrich, the director of five films starring Fred Astaire and Ginger Rogers. In 1938, the team's penultimate RKO film, *Carefree*, was getting off to a rocky start because Rogers was refusing to again work with Sandrich and finally had enough clout at the studio to stand up for herself. To make matters worse, Sandrich had also upset Lela Rogers, Ginger's mother, who was closely involved in all aspects of Ginger's career. Fred Astaire and Ginger Rogers were the most popular stars on RKO's roster, and if Rogers was refusing to work because of Sandrich, that could spell trouble for

the studio. Berman was finally able to negotiate a truce between Rogers and Sandrich, but not before production was delayed while the dispute was settled. Sandrich had been a top director at RKO for years, but *Carefree* was his last film at the studio. Rogers, however, stayed on and began to be given the opportunity to play serious as well as comedic roles, winning an Oscar in 1940 for her dramatic performance in *Kitty Foyle*. The diplomatic Berman, who oversaw a number of RKO's most memorable 1930s productions, moved to MGM in 1940, where he became a producer of prestige pictures directed by such filmmakers as Vincente Minnelli, Richard Brooks, and George Cukor.

OFFICES OF
Pandro S. Berman

April 21, 1938

Dear Mark:

After a great deal of difficulty, the Studio has persuaded
Ginger Rogers to return to work tomorrow morning.

Strangely enough, the major reason – in spite of what you
may have heard to the contrary – for her reluctance to report for this picture, has been her aggravation at the fact
that she is being asked to work under your direction. This
is not because she has ever had, or has now, any feeling
insofar as your abilities are concerned as a director, or
insofar as you are concerned as a person except that you have
undoubtedly been guilty of certain acts which have caused her
great anguish.

You must realize that Ginger Rogers, like every other actress,
is a person who will respond most completely to careful
attention and generous pampering, and you have made certain
statements to her and to her mother with regard to her, which
may have been meant in the best of faith but which antagonized
her to extremes. I refer specifically to a conversation you
had with Lela in which you told Lela that if Ginger did not
learn to improve her singing and dancing she would at some
future date find herself in great difficulties in the picture
business. I refer also to the numerous times in which Ginger
has been made to feel that she is of considerably less importance to any given picture than Fred Astaire. This feeling
can be transmitted in many ways, but mostly in your attitude
toward the two people. Ginger has every right to believe
that she is as valuable and as important to RKO and to the
picture as any other person in the set-up, and when she is
sometimes made to feel that her opinions, her clothes, her
dancing and her parts are to be given less consideration than
those of any other member of the cast, she naturally reacts
as a woman and an actress is bound to react. More flies are
killed with honey than with swatters, and I think you should
make it your business, on the company's behalf on this
production, now that she has consented to go ahead with it,
to make her feel that she is getting the complete respect of
the organization from top to bottom, and that she is being

Page 2.

given as careful attention and treatment as is humanly
possible for the Company, the producer and the director to
give to her.

It would be impossible to detail all the little points of
grievances that Ginger has had; but for example, just to
show you the kind of thing that has aggravated her, when the
rumpus was aroused over your reported inverview in London,
it seems that you went to some pains to correct the false
impression that had been créated in Astaire's mind as to what
your words had been, but at that time you ignored Ginger completely and made no attempt to make her feel that you had not
said what it was reported you had said. These may seem like
very minor things, but they are important to the person concerned, and I think it is only fair of me, for both your sake
and hers, that I give you now this review of what may have
been in her mind,so that you will know how to approach the
situation on this picture so as to promote harmony in the
unit rather than let any slight thing occur which might make
Ginger feel that the Company was not living up to its promise
to treat her with the utmost consideration. Let me assure you
that I am very sincere when I say that consideration from all
of us has been her main issue in this series of discussions,
and it seems wrong to me that any business which is so
dependent on so few outstanding personalities, should fail to
give that consideration which is so cheap to give and so
important to receive.

Don't take this in the nature of a criticism of you, because
as I said before you may have been entirely unconscious of
many of your actions and you undoubtedly were only for Ginger's
interests in your discussions, but it has not had a happy
effect and I am sure you would want to know about it rather
than have any false impressions. You must know, for example,
how important it is to a girl that great interest be taken
in what she wears, and how she looks, and how a few kind words
on this subject can often make a person break their neck to
accomplish something you wish in return.

Best regards.

Sincerely,

Mr. Mark Sandrich

S t u d i o

psb/b

SAMUEL GOLDWYN INC.

729 SEVENTH AVE.   NEW YORK

INTER-OFFICE COMMUNICATION

TO   Mr. Samuel Goldwyn

FROM Miriam Howell

RE: <u>ORSON WELLES</u>   DATE <u>July 12, 1938</u>

Dear Mr. Goldwyn:

I have just had a long talk with Orson Welles.

In the first place, he is not available for picture work and
cannot consider doing anything in pictures until June of next
year. The definite plans for the Mercury Theatre, his commitments to his backers, his associates and his actors, etc. make
it impossible for him to consider any picture activities until
the end of the coming theatre season.

I gathered that he is definitely interested in pictures as a
medium. He is, in fact, very excited and enthusiastic about
pictures - a real fan - but as far as he, himself, is concerned
he is least interested in the acting end. He would take an
acting job only if he and the company were completely agreed
that he was the only person who was ideal for the suggested
part.

What he is interested in is getting into pictures on the
producing and directing end -- and this presents a further
difficulty.

What he really wants is to have a picture company, or preferably
an independent producer like yourself, finance him and give him
a release and let him make a picture himself. He feels that
this is the only arrangement under which he could have as free
a hand as he insists on before he will do pictures. His reason
for this is that he has demonstrated successfully in the theatre
and on radio that he has definite and original conceptions in
producing and directing, and he wants to be free to bring the
same kind of individual conceptions to the production and direction
of pictures. Also, he would want the final say on script, cast,
etc.......In other words, Mr. Welles wants to be <u>you</u>, as far as
I can make out.

There was a lot more to the same effect, but this will give
you an idea of what his present frame of mind is, and in view
of his commitments for the immediate future I don't think
there is any point in our going further with him at this time.
However, I should be glad to keep in touch with Mr.Welles if
you continue to be interested.

With kindest regards, as always, believe me,

Cordially yours,

Miriam

Miriam Howell to Samuel Goldwyn

JULY 12, 1938

Miriam Howell's report to Samuel Goldwyn on a meeting with Orson Welles, written a year before Welles signed with RKO to make *Citizen Kane*, is a fascinating look at the evolution of the young filmmaker's career. Welles had made a name for himself with his Mercury Theatre stage productions and radio shows, and many producers in the movie industry were starting to take note. Interest in Welles became even more intense when the Mercury Theatre's *War of the Worlds* broadcast on Halloween eve in 1938 captivated, and in some cases terrified, audiences. But while Howell, the story editor in Goldwyn's New York office, observes that Welles "wants to be" Goldwyn, it's unlikely that a deal between the two would have worked out. In 1939, RKO's ambitious studio president, George Schaefer, agreed to give Welles complete creative control over his first film, an unprecedented agreement that Goldwyn, and the heads of the other major studios, would have found too financially risky to undertake. In the 1940s, Howell struck out on her own as a New York talent and literary agent who represented a small but devoted clientele.

From left: William Wyler, Carl Laemmle, an unidentified man,
and Paul Kohner pose at Universal in the early 1930s.

Carl Laemmle to William Wyler

OCTOBER 6, 1938

In 1938, Carl Laemmle, the film industry pioneer who founded Universal Pictures, should have been enjoying his retirement. Instead, spurred into action by the rise of Hitler, he, for several years, dedicated himself to finding a way to save as many persecuted European Jews as possible, both by sponsoring refugees personally and by asking his friends, family, and associates in Hollywood to step up and offer their help. In this letter to the director William Wyler, Laemmle spells out what can and should be done to help those who are trying to find sponsors in the United States and urges Wyler to complete as many affidavits as possible.

In his reply to the letter, Wyler assured Laemmle that he would do all that he could, but that he had also already reached his maximum number of sponsorships. Hollywood has been accused of ignoring the threat posed by the Nazis, but this effort, and the formation of groups like the Hollywood Anti-Nazi League in 1936, show that many in the movie industry were not only aware of the situation that was developing overseas but were willing to do something about it. Laemmle died on September 24, 1939, just a few weeks after war was declared in Europe.

CARL LAEMMLE
1051 BENEDICT CANYON DRIVE

BEVERLY HILLS, CALIFORNIA

October 6, 1938

Mr. Willy Wyler,
1115 San Ysidro Drive,
Beverly Hills, Calif.

Dear Mr. Wyler:

I want to ask you a very big favor.

The Jewish situation in Germany has been getting on my nerves for a long, long time. I feel that these poor, unfortunate people need help the worst way. I have been over there recently and know what they are going through.

I have issued so many personal affidavits that the United States government won't accept any more from me excepting for my closest blood-relatives. Nevertheless, while I was over there, I was worried so much by these distressed people that I promised about 150 of them I would move heaven and earth to find sponsors for them. And that's why I am writing you this letter.

If you want to do something really big -- something that will give you an immense amount of pleasure -- issue one or more affidavits, as many as your means permit. I am not only writing to Jews but to Gentiles as well -- to all those whom I have the honor and pleasure to call friend.

Of the younger generation -- those around 40 to 50 years -- if they do not get affidavits in the near future, they will be called in by the German government to help make public improvements. This is the hardest kind of work to do and the Jewish people are not accustomed to it because, as you all know, they have been making their success in mercantile lines and not through hard manual labor.

I predict right now that thousands of German and Austrian Jews
will be forced to commit suicide if they cannot get affidavits to come to
America or to some other foreign country. My heart goes out to them. As
a matter of fact, night after night, I lose many hours of sleep thinking of
their fate and how fortunate I am that I came to this country 54 years ago.
My own brother who will be 76 next February, will sail for America in a few
days hence. About ten or twelve more distant relatives of mine, two or
three cousins, will leave within the next six to eight months. They cannot
get their visas any earlier.

I wish I could talk to you face to face and explain the situation if you do not already understand it. I feel that every person in
America, Jew or non-Jew, with a heart, should do his bit, and thereby get
an immense amount of satisfaction and possibly save one or more lives.

I cannot write a brilliant letter but I am pleading now as I
never plead before in my whole life.

For your guidance, I am enclosing herewith a copy of the regula-
tion affidavit form together with a printed sheet of instructions to help you
properly execute an affidavit. As quickly as I hear from you that you are
interested in issuing one or more affidavits, I shall lose no time in sending
you the name or names of the persons who are so anxiously waiting for this
valuable document.

Of the countless number of affidavits that I have issued in the
past three years, I have only been called upon three times to help; once to
a girl who was operated upon for appendicitis. I loaned her $50. which she
is now paying back at the rate of $5. a week. To a man, 53 years old, and

his wife and child, I gave once $25. outright and at another time when they
had a fire and all their clothing burned, I gave them $50. additional. I
don't expect them to return this money; in fact, I don't want it. The man
in question is now earning a good living. To the third person who recently
came over from Germany -- a woman of 45 and her daughter of 14 -- I gave $25.
That was all she needed and she is now working while her daughter is being
taken care of by a Jewish family. That's all I have been called upon to
help up till now.

    The chances of your being called on for help is probably about
one in a hu dred because I do not intend to give affidavits to anyone excepting to those who can satisfy me that they will be self-sustaining.

    I am almost counting the hours until I hear from you. I hope
your answer will be favorable. I thank you a thousand times in advance for
what you are going to do.

    Kindest personal regards.

                                  Sincerely yours,

                                  Carl Laemmle

Alfred, Alma, and Patricia Hitchcock arriving in Los Angeles with Joan Harrison in 1939

Alfred Hitchcock to Daniel Winkler

JANUARY 27, 1939

After years as the biggest name in the British film indus-try, Alfred Hitchcock moved to Hollywood in 1939 to work for David O. Selznick. Hitchcock's longtime agent, not coincidentally, was David's brother Myron Selz-nick, who ran one of the most powerful agencies in the business. This letter to Daniel Winkler, one of Myron's associates, puts Hitchcock's dry sense of humor on full display. From his reference to the sexy French movie star Danielle Darrieux in his salutation to his tongue-in-cheek request that the entire office staff be dispatched to help him find the perfect piece of real estate, Hitchcock's letter delighted its recipient. In his reply to the director, Winkler reported that he took the letter around the office to show

it to all of his fellow staffers and that it was so funny that "his secretary had to call a physician to take care of the fourteen cases of hysteria that resulted." The family, which included Hitchcock's wife and collaborator, Alma Reville; their ten-year-old daughter, Patricia; and two dogs, arrived in Los Angeles in April 1939. Also joining the Hitchcocks in Hollywood was the director's assistant, Joan Harrison, who, like Alma, worked closely with Hitchcock on the scripts for his films and was credited as a writer on several of his early Hollywood productions, including *Rebecca*, *Foreign Correspondent*, and *Suspicion*. Harrison went on to become a successful film producer, and later produced the television anthology series *Alfred Hitchcock Presents*.

January 27th, 1939.

My dear Daniel Darrieux, (I mean Winkler),

If I may interrupt you a moment, and if
you will please take your hands away from
Miss Rogers, you could attend to a little
matter of business on behalf of the Myron
Selznick Agency Company Ltd. or Inc.

Would you please get Nat Deverich to
start punting around and find us a house.
We want a nice one with a pool because Pat
wants to swim during the summer. We want it
as near to the office as possible so that I
shan't have far to go for my fun. Would you
please get Noll Gurney to go around to the
Grosvenor Apartment House and get a price for
a very small nice flat for Joan? If
Townshend (James) isn't busy, could he take
over when Deverich gets tired and send us a
list of places with photographs. If the
agency hasn't any photographs, please get
Sig Marcus to go with a camera and take a
few shots of likely places. We don't want
to be so far away as Bel Air, but Collier
Young might run down there on his bicycle
and decide definitely for us that we shouldn't
go there. Meanwhile get Myron to run through
the small advertisement columns of the "Examiner"

153, CROMWELL ROAD,
S.W.5.
FROBISHER 1339.

and the "Times" to see if any houses are
on offer there.

Dear Danny, I hope you don't mind my
troubling the office like this.   Naturally,
I wouldn't dream of asking you to do anything
personally, but, if you could persuade all
those mentioned above to whip themselves
into a fury about this house matter, I might
get some results, but I doubt it.

Incidentally, we shall need this house
from April 15th onwards.

Dear Daniel, is there anyone in the
office who could help us in this matter?
Thank you.

Looking forward to seeing you on March
30½th.

With love

from *Hitch*

P.S.   Is there anyone in the office with any sense
who could pick up the phone and tell the
Beverly Wilshire that we want the same suite
as before but with an extra double bedroom;
and also in the same hotel a double bedroom
and bath for the two maids. Will you choose
somebody in the office to do this who has a
sense of economy, high finance and monetary

153, CROMWELL ROAD,

S.W.5.

FROBISHER 1339.

restraint - in other words, cut the price to
the bone.   Will you find somebody in the office
who can cable me about this? We shall want
the Beverly Wilshire rooms from March 30th till
April 15th.

cc * Messrs Selznick,Marcus,Deverich,Gurney,Townsend,Young,
    Johnson,Williams, Wolff and Brickley.

Lewis Meltzer to Daniel Taradash

In 1938, the noted theater and film director Rouben
Mamoulian chose Lewis Meltzer and Daniel Taradash,
two young playwrights with no screenwriting experience,
to adapt Clifford Odets's play *Golden Boy* for the screen.
After months collaborating on the project, Taradash
returned to New York to work on a play, but Meltzer stayed
on in Hollywood, battling it out with "Mam" (Mamoulian) as they finished up "G.B." (*Golden Boy*) and settling
in as an overworked contract writer at Columbia Pictures.
Meltzer's letter perfectly captures the fragmented life of a
young, irreverent screenwriter in 1930s Hollywood, especially one with literary aspirations and a healthy disregard
for authority. Mamoulian did not get a writing credit
on the film, but Meltzer and Taradash did have to share
screen credit with Victor Heerman and Sarah Y. Mason, a
married writing team that had worked on an early, unused
version of the script. Taradash and Meltzer, members of
the embattled Screen Writers Guild, attempted to appeal
the decision, but at that time studios unilaterally decided
credits, and their request was overruled. To make matters
worse, Heerman and Mason belonged to the conservative Screen Playwrights, a company union set up by the
studios to undermine the Screen Writers Guild, which
was still fighting for recognition. Not surprisingly, Meltzer
and Taradash went on to be committed, lifelong Guild
members, with Taradash eventually serving as president of
the Guild from 1977 to 1979.

COLUMBIA PICTURES CORPORATION
OF CALIFORNIA, LTD.
1438 GOWER STREET
HOLLYWOOD, CALIFORNIA
HOLLYWOOD 3181

Mar 30
1939

You sun-uv-sunouva-sun-uva-sunuva bitch -- in the book of etiquette
it says, "when one half of a collaboration leaves it writes the
other half upon reaching its destination. And did you --? No.
A telegram, that's all. And I couldn't answer that, unless I sent
it collect. But Buddy says you're angry, so I'm writing.
Ruthie is here. More about that later. I've settled down. Yeah.
I worked, all in all, some three weeks on Blind Alley, did about
forty to fifty pages and am entitled to screen-credit, but doubt
the getting of it. Mess. Am now working on side for Perberg "Super-
Clipper" -- only a title, and I'm supposed to write original for
it. In the meantime, Mam and I are taking out what littles left
of Odets -- what little remains that gave the script distinction.
By the way -- Flroence is now in the office, and just a few minutes
ago I had interesting chat with her. Hold your breath, kid, this
will knock you off your feet -- BUT MAMOULIAN EXPECTS SCREEN CREDIT!
Yep, the armenian put a fast one over on us. He told her -- and
for gods sake keep this under your hat -- that he saw no reason
why heshouldnt get credit as long as he was teaching us how to write
a screenplay. However, this he said sometime ago. I'm going to try
to indretly discourage him. If I dont -- well, it only will bear
out what I've always thought -- dont trust anyone out here. Jesus.
I'm working day and night on G.B. -- still rewriting. If Mam meets
a kid on street, a kid with i.q. of -72 -- moronic -- illiterate --
and what not, and if said kid says, Mr. Mamoulian, I don't like this
scene -- you can be certain that that night, one Lewis Meltzer will
be rewriting that scene. I'm doing all I can to keep him away from
people with suggestions. He doesn't turn down a one. Otherwise
things are about the same. I'm still leaving him flat in cafes,
and he still gets his periods of vicious bitchiness and continental
humor, and I wish I were back in New York with you, collaborating on
cornbeef sandwich in sardis. Oy, I'm so jealous of you.
My sex-life has reached a happy pedestrianism, my financial condition
can still be smelled in Hong-Kong, and my literary work is in line
with Moss Harts dictum -- and "I'm not writing a good line" -- and
never will, I believe until I get out of G.B. I believe, and this
firmly, that I ould be better off, creatively (what's that?) if I
were working on some junk, them on this apparently "good" script,
which saps energy, and deludes one into thinking he's writing good
stuff, whereas its the same old pulp-crap, but with much more effort.
Oy, I'm so jealous of you. Write me. You're forgiven. Love.

Lewis (SP)

11125 Charnock Road
Palms, California
April 14, 1939

H.N.Swanson Incorporated
8523 Sunset Boulevard
Los Angeles, California

Dear Mr. Swanson:

Whenever someone says that the only way to become an
agent is to be an agent's nephew, I become angry with
my uncles. But just being angry dosn't seem to help,
you see Mr. Swanson, I want to be an agent.

If I were asked "What professional experience would be
most advantageous to a fellow contemplating an agency
career?", I would answer, in my most naive way, "The
legal profession." Maybe my answer would be a bit in-
fluenced because of my contemplations along agency lines,
or maybe it's because I am an atorney or maybe both.

A good agent must be able to buy and sell people or
their work by first selling himself. A good agent must
be able to deal with people, handle them, cajole them,
wheedle them, gain their confidence, gain their business.
Come to think of it, a good lawyer must do that too.

During my six months stay in Hollywood, I've learned to
be an assistant director, I've learned to be a reader,
I've learned to gain the confidence of good client possibilities, I've learned to get three or four home cooked
dinners a week, I've learned that the agency business is
a little lopsided and above all I've grown determined to
be a part of it if I have to straighten it out myself.

Mr. Swanson, you have a reputation for being one of the
best agents in Hollywood but more important you're a
fine man. In my selfish, calculating way I turn to the
best for help, for advice---I turn to you. Ten minutes
with a young personable attorney,with years of drama
and screen criticism experience, and with a living desire to imitate you and your position might not prove
boring. Please see me?

Very truly yours,

Jennings Bently Lang

Telephone number
Culver City 9601

Jennings Lang and Joan Crawford
at the Mocambo in 1954.

Jennings Lang
to H. N. Swanson

APRIL 14, 1939

When Brooklyn-born Jennings Lang arrived in California in 1938 with dreams of finding fame and fortune
in Hollywood, he was twenty-four years old and had
fifty dollars in his pocket. Without any contacts in the
movie industry but with a strong will to succeed, the brash
young lawyer took a chance and wrote this letter pitch-
ing himself to H. N. Swanson, the top literary agent in
the business. It is unclear if Swanson answered this letter,
or if it earned Lang a meeting or interview at Swanson's
office on the Sunset Strip. But less than two years after
writing to Swanson, Jennings Lang and his wife started
their own agency, and a few years after that Lang joined
the Jaffe Agency, which was later acquired by MCA. After

rising through the ranks to become one of the most
powerful agents in Hollywood, with clients including Joan
Crawford and Humphrey Bogart, Lang became a studio
executive, creating the television wing at MCA-Universal
and developing the idea for the first "Movie of the Week."
In 1965, Lang set his sights on features. He went on to
produce thirty-five films, including *Earthquake, Airport 75,
Slaughterhouse-Five,* and *The Front Page.* In the 1970s, Lang
gave Steven Spielberg his first feature assignment, *Sugar-
land Express,* and Clint Eastwood his first chance to direct
with *Play Misty For Me.* His instincts paid off. Over the
years, Lang's productions for Universal earned over a
billion dollars for the studio.

Bette Davis to Jack L. Warner

SEPTEMBER 1, 1939

By September 1939, Bette Davis already had two Academy Awards under her belt and was the undisputed queen of Warner Bros., where she had been under contract since 1931. For several years, however, she had been battling with her employers over the terms of her studio contract. In 1936, Davis had refused to accept a role that she considered substandard and was put on suspension without pay, so she went to England and announced plans to make films there with a British producer. Warner Bros. took her to court in London, and the judge rejected Davis's argument that her long-term contract was unfair and that actors should have more control over their own careers. After she lost the case and went back to the studio, her parts did begin to improve, but by 1939 she was once again going head to head with Jack Warner over the terms of her contract, as she makes perfectly clear in this letter to the studio chief. Working strategically with her business managers (the Wood brothers) and arguing that a more reasonable contract would lead to better performances, Davis did manage to get some concessions from Warner Bros., and in the next few years she made some of her most indelible films, including *The Letter*; *Now, Voyager*; and *Mr. Skeffington*. She continued to work at Warner Bros., and fight for better and more interesting roles, until the end of the 1940s. Davis was not the only Warner Bros. actress who chafed under the star system. Olivia de Havilland also clashed with the studio, and in 1943 she took a page from Davis's book and sued in the State of California over the terms of her long-term contract—and won.

Dear J. L.,

Have just finished talking to Hal. I must explain one thing—for the first time in my life I don't care whether I ever make another picture or not. I am that overworked. I have given you a lot of honest effort in the past eight years. The time has come when I feel I have earned some privileges in writing. These I must have.

My contract is ridiculous. I have no protection whatsoever. I must have limited pictures—I must have time off between. I think two is all I should make with a possible third if all conditions are favorable. The Wood Bros. know all the conditions—and were given to understand some weeks ago that you were willing to write a contract for me that would not be very far from what I wanted.

It is up to you. I am very serious about all this because I must be for my own good. If necessary I am even willing to stand the gaff of unemployment. Health is one thing that can't be manufactured. I am very serious about mine—and willing to go to any length to protect it. And staying in Hollywood working almost forty weeks of the year does not make sense—from your standpoint—box-office can be ruined by too many pictures—as you well know.

Would appreciate your not communicating with me—it upsets me very much. I must be allowed to completely forget business. The Woods know everything there is to know. Also arguing with me is no use—nor do I want to come back until it is settled.

Sincerely
Bette Davis

Dear J. L.

Have just finished talking to Hal. I must explain one thing — for the first time in my life I don't care whether I ever make another picture or not. I don't say that overworked. I have given you an awfully honest effort into the past eight years, & the time has come when I feel I have earned some further halt in writing. These I must have —

My contract is ridiculous. I have no protection whatsoever. I must have limited pictures — I must have time off between — I think two is all I should make with a possible third — if all conditions are fair — & The Wood Bros know all the conditions and were given to understand some weeks ago — that you were willing to write a contract for me —

that I would not a better

very far beyond what

wanted. It is up to you.

I am very serious about

all this because

he for my ... food.

Necessary I am

to stand the ... of

employment — Health is

one thing that can't

Manufactured. I am very

serious about

And willing to go to any

length to protect it. And
staying in Hollywood working
almost forty weeks of the
year does not make sense —
from your standpoint — Box
office can be ruined by too
many pictures — as you well
know —

I would appreciate your
not communicating with me —
it upsets me very much —
must be allowed to com-
pletely forget business. The
Word's know everything there

is to know. Also arguing
with me is no use —
nor do I want to come
back until it is settled —
                Sincerely
                    Bette Davis

David Niven to Samuel Goldwyn

SEPTEMBER 1939

The dashing actor David Niven had been in the British Army before coming to Hollywood, and when England declared war on Germany in September 1939, Niven was the first major British star to announce that he would return home to join the war effort. In this letter to his boss, the independent producer Samuel Goldwyn, Niven reflects on his years at the studio, his career in Hollywood, and his hopes to soon return to his life in Los Angeles. He also mentions completing *Raffles*, his final pre-war film, and sends his regards to Frances, Mr. Goldwyn's wife. Over the six years that followed, Niven would serve in various posts in the army, including the rifle brigade and a commando unit. He also appeared in British Army training films and, with Goldwyn's permission, made two British war-themed feature films: *The Way Ahead*, directed by Carol Reed, and *A Matter of Life and Death*, directed by Michael Powell and Emeric Pressburger. Niven returned to Hollywood in 1946 and went back to work for Goldwyn before striking out on his own in the 1950s and eventually winning an Academy Award in 1958 for his work in *Separate Tables*.

~~Thursday~~ Sunday

My dear Sam

I understand that I shall be finished in the picture today; so that appears to be the end of our association for the time being.

I am finding this letter very hard to write but I am just trying to tell you how truly sad I am to be leaving you and your great organization, where I got my start and where I have been so happy working during the last five years.

I am deeply grateful to you for your belief in me at the start and for your help and guidance throughout the rest of the time.

I have been treated <u>most</u> generously and considerately in these last few weeks, and believe me I shall long for the war to be over so that I can come back and repay you by doing some really good work under your banner.

Your personal friendship and the sweetness and kindness of Frances toward me will always be remembered.

We have had our moments of not exactly seeing eye to eye, but that I know will be cement that will make our friendship endure all the longer.

If, when I get home, I am told that they definitely have nothing for me to do, then the streak of light half way across the world will be Niven returning to Goldwyn!

In the meanwhile please accept my deepest thanks for everything you have done for me.

I shall miss you all <u>terribly.</u>

Yours ever
David

SAMUEL GOLDWYN INC., Ltd.
STUDIOS-7210 SANTA MONICA BOULEVARD
LOS ANGELES, CALIFORNIA

[1939]

~~Sunday~~
Thursday.

My dear Sam

I understand that I shall be
finished in the picture today ; so that
appears to be the end of our association
for the time being.

I am finding this letter very
hard to write but I am just trying
to tell you how truly sad I am to be
leaving you and your great organization,
where I got my start and where I
have been so happy working during
the last five years

I am deeply grateful to you
for your belief in me at the start and
for your help and guidance throughout the
rest of the time.

I have been treated most generously
and considerately in these last few weeks,
and believe me I shall long for the
war to be over so that I can come back
and repay you by doing some really
good work under your banner.

Your personal friendship and
the sweetness and kindliness of Frances
toward me will always be remembered.

We have had our moments of
not exactly seeing eye to eye, but
that I know will be cement that
will make our friendship endure all
the longer.

If, when I get home, I am told that
they definitely have nothing for me to
do, then the streak of light half
way across the world will be
Niven returning to Goldwyn!

In the meanwhile

SAMUEL GOLDWYN INC., Ltd.
STUDIOS-7210 SANTA MONICA BOULEVARD
LOS ANGELES, CALIFORNIA

please accept my deepest thanks
for everything you have done for me.
I shall miss you all
terribly.

Yours. ever

David.

1121 SUMMIT DRIVE
BEVERLY HILLS

Monday
Apr. 8

Dear David —

Phyllis and I have just seen "Rebecca" and really I had to write this note to express how really great we think it is. We thought nothing could ever follow "Gone", but this one certainly can, and does, as you know.

The picture is so magnificent in every possible way that it is hard to say much more than that. The casting was so wonderful and Joan Fontaine's performance absolutely amazing. She was marvellous + so was Olivier and all of them and — oh — I give up!

All the best —

Fred A

Fred Astaire to David O. Selznick

APRIL 8, 1940

Fred Astaire and David O. Selznick first crossed paths professionally in 1933, when Selznick, then head of production at RKO studios, decided to invite the elegant dancer and musical comedy star to do a screen test, which led to a contract with the studio. In this letter to his friend seven years later, Astaire expresses the feelings of many in Hollywood who were astounded by Selznick's remarkable success as one of the industry's top independent producers. Not only had Selznick produced *Gone with the Wind*, which was released in December 1939 to great acclaim, but that year

he also signed Alfred Hitchcock to a contract and brought him to Hollywood to make *Rebecca*, his first American production, which would win Selznick his second consecutive best-picture Oscar. Astaire had appeared opposite Joan Fontaine in the musical *A Damsel in Distress* in 1937, but her role in *Rebecca*, which earned her an Academy Award nomination, was much more in keeping with her talents as a dramatic actress. "Phyllis" refers to Astaire's first wife. They were married from 1933 until her death in 1954.

Monday
Apr. 8

Dear David,

Phyllis and I have just seen "Rebecca" and really I had to write this note to express how really great we think it is. We thought nothing could ever follow "Gone," but this once certainly can, and <u>does</u>, as you <u>know</u>.

The picture is <u>so</u> <u>magnificent</u> in <u>every</u> <u>possible</u> <u>way</u> that it is hard to say much more than that. The casting was so wonderful and Joan Fontaine's performance absolutely <u>amazing</u>. She was <u>marvellous</u> & so was Olivier and all of them and—oh—I give up!

All the best—
Fred A.

Constance Collier to Hedda Hopper

OCTOBER 21, 1940

Constance Collier was an esteemed actress and acting coach who had a wide constellation of famous friends and acquaintances, from Katharine Hepburn to Mary Pickford. In this letter to actress turned gossip columnist Hedda Hopper, Collier writes about her precarious finances and describes attending the New York premiere of Charlie Chaplin's *The Great Dictator* with Chaplin and his wife and costar Paulette Goddard. Chaplin had defied some of Hollywood's most powerful forces in order to complete his brilliant comedy lampooning Hitler and warning of the dangers of Nazism, and Collier's appraisal of Chaplin's accomplishments shows that many in Hollywood were acutely aware of the significance of the film. The second part of the letter recounts the experiences of a group of children who had recently been relocated to New York from London due to the outbreak of war in Europe. The children were sponsored by a British organization called the Actors' Orphanage, a venerable charity funded by British entertainers and headed, in 1940, by Noël Coward. This certainly must have been a memorable time for these youngsters. In a handwritten postscript, Collier writes, "Charlie was wonderful with the orphans. He made a speech to them & did tricks for them & they adored him. He went as a surprise & nobody but me & you & the children know." It's interesting that Collier seems to be suggesting in this letter that Hopper was friendly with Chaplin. In fact, the gossip columnist frequently attacked Chaplin in print and was one of the ringleaders in the campaign to brand him as a subversive in the years following World War II.

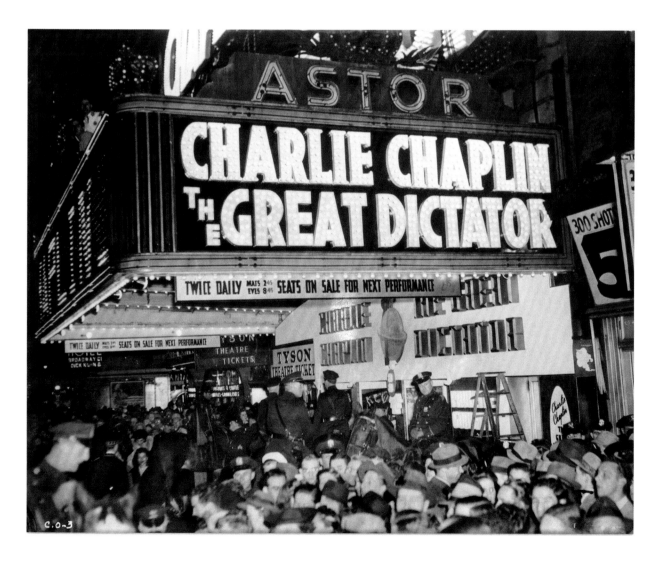

CONSTANCE COLLIER.

Meurice Hotel.
145 West 58
New York.

October 21st.

My very dear Hedda.

I had a letter fron Arthur Taylor
today, explaining that **several** of my friends, you included,
suggested paying a certain sum of money a month for me. I
can never tell you ,darling how deeply I appreciate it and
how wonderful I think it of you, but I don't need it and
I could not accept it. I have been very hard up, but I
shall weather this storm , as I have many others. I didn't
tell anybody about it except Paulette and Mary knew, but
dear Paulette out of the kindness of her heart, suggested
she and Charlie would make me an allowance, but I didn't
know she intended to ask other people to join. Of course
I would not have dreamt of it. Don't tell anybody about
all this , it is entirely between you and me. I made some
money in the summer theatres, where I had a great success
with "Our Better's" and can hang on for a bit and I know
a job will turn up soon.

I will never forget this gesture
of yours and I hope life will give me an opportunity to
repay your great kindness. You have always been a wonder-
-ful friend, ever since those early days in Hollywood when
we first met. Throuout the years you have never failed in
friendship and kindness. There are no words to express
to you my deep and grateful thanks.

We had a wonderful opening with
Charlie and Paulette. I have never seen such crowds. We
were nearly killed at the Astor and C harlie was forced
to his knees and my arm was nearly broken, inspite of
being surrounded by mounted police and with a wall of
police pushing their way ahead of us to get us into the
A stor. I have never seen such love as the public have
for C harlie, they simply adore him. The crowds went from
Broadway right down the side streets to 8th Avenue, four
and five deep on each side. He is the uncrowned kind of
the world and I think the message of the picture will
have a deep and vital effect on every one who sees it.
He is the first person to have the courage to throw
laughter in the face of the tryant. Paulette looked lovely
and was very sweet and she and Charlie have been all over
the town together. Now she is on her way for the opening
of the picture in Chicago. I was to have gone with her,
but there were several things I had to do in New York and
so shall come out and stay with them later on. H.G. Wells
and Charlie and Paulette and me went to the picture.

C harlie is a great human
being. He couldn't have made a techincally perfect picture

CONSTANCE COLLIER.

in these days. He had to burst out on the screen some-
-where and tell the world what he feels and his last
speech will have a tremendous effect I am sure. It is
so wonderful of him to have the courage to say what we
all feel, instead of conciliating and pandering and
making a neat little end to the picture that's all right
for ordinary times, but there isn't a writer or great
artist, or a man in the street, who isn't shaken to his
very roots by the wanton destruction of every nation in
the world. Poor little human beings how can we stand up
against these great forces of hate and fear ! Who was
it who said, " It isn't life itself, but the courage we
bring to it that matters."

            Are you all right,darling ? Please don't over-
-work. I don't see how you ever get through all the jobs
you have to do. I listen to you three times a week on the
radio, so you don't seem so far away.

            The A ctor's Orphans are here. I had a divine
day with them and took the whole 54 to the Fair. I can't
tell you the excitement, as it was their first glimpse of
America since they landed. Harvey Gibson was kind enough
to make arrangements for me and they gave us the whole day
free. We started at eleven and went to the British Pavilion.
Then we went to Swifts for a magnificent lunch. An exact
replica of the lunch given to the King and Queen at Hyde
Park by the President. The Boy Scouts cooked the hot dogs
for them and one little girl ate eight. Then we telephoned
to Mary in Hollywood and they thanked her on behalf of the
committee for bringing them over. Then we went to a puppet
show and to see the Pandra and on to Jubilee. I wish you
could have seen the children laughing, particularly at
Jackson, the clown with the bicycle. He must be about 80
now, I have seen him all my life, but the children were
hysterical when his bicycle dropped to pieces. It was
difficult to get them past the parachute jump, they all
wanted to go in one, because they had seen parachutes coming
down in England. It was divine to hear those children laugh,
but of course we couldn't allow them on the parachutes, as
there was too much risk for the tiny ones. Then we went to
Wonder Bread and have the most enormous tea of cake and
ice-cream. I think they had about six ices each. Then we
went in the midway and at 7.15 we went home. I have never
been so tired in my life, as it must have walked twenty miles.
There manners were exquisite, there wasn't a tear shed or
a squabble and they behaved beautifully.

            The children are living at the Gould Foundation
and you have never seen anything so magnificent in your life.
It is perfectly run. They have playing fields, swimming
pools, children's clothes, everything a child could

CONSTANCE COLLIER.

possibly need and they are as happy as larks. I must say
the American millionares did magnificent things, Carnegie
with his libraires, Rockefeller with Radio City and Edwin
Gould with this foundation. There are other children in
the different houses and there is one for tiny tots.
Children of two and three years old. The whole place is
done in minature, little tables and t iny little chairs and
those lost babies are as spotless and good and happy as if
they were in their own homes with a mother for each of them.
America is a wonderful country. I have known it always, but
somehow the kindness and warmth and friendship and the
gfeat things they are doing, seem to stand out in high relief.
This foundation isn't an emergency thing. It is a gift
to the world long before this horrible war started and that
anybody should have thought of the lost children like this,
is a magnificent tribute to a nation. I have never seen
anything like it in any other part of the world. Charlie
is going out with me this afternoon, to see the Orphanage.

All love,darling and again thanks.

All all love

Constance

*P.S. Charlie was
wonderful in the orphanage.
He made a speech to them &
did tricles for them &
the adored him. He went
as a surprise & nobody
informed him & run & the children
where*

Hedda Hopper to Aileen Pringle

JANUARY 27, 1941

Hedda Hopper was an aging character actress with a vast network of friends and connections when she decided to change careers and become a syndicated gossip columnist in 1938. By 1941, her daily column and a radio show had made her a household name, and her reporting on Hollywood was read by millions of people every day. As she explains in this letter to her friend, the actress and socialite Aileen Pringle, Hopper had talked her way into an early press screening of *Citizen Kane* and had quickly spread the word that it was a thinly veiled hatchet job on William Randolph Hearst, scooping even her rival columnist Louella Parsons, who had only heard rumors about the film up to that point. Hopper was unofficially friendly with Welles, however, so after initially relishing

her position as the first person to denounce the movie, she backed off and left the heavy lifting to Parsons and her boss Hearst, who used everything in their arsenal to destroy the film or at least keep it from being seen. Of course, despite Hopper's prediction that the film might never be released, RKO defied calls to shelve *Citizen Kane*, though many theater chains succumbed to pressure and refused to book the film. The gossip in the first part of the letter refers to Barbara Bennett (nicknamed Dick B.), who had recently divorced and was soon to marry the cowboy actor Addison "Jack" Randall. Hopper also mentions media magnate William Paley, who was involved in a long-term relationship with the actress Louise Brooks.

January 27, 1941

My dear "Pringle",

Thanks so much for your note and the latest information about Dick B. Yes, Ad Randall has the inside
track, and of course he hasn't a dime, not even to
bless himself with. She's such a fool, but then she
always was. But isn't it a wicked shame that five
children have been brought into the world and have
that kind of a girl for their mother? However,
maybe things will be patched up, but it will be a
cat-and-dog life, if it ever is. I'm surprised
there was nothing in that rumor about Paley and
Brook. It was current all over Hollywood. I
wish you could find out who he is attentive to.
Itwould be mighty interesting.

The town is so excited over the Orson Welles -
"Citizen Kane", and its being based on the life
of Mr. Hearst. They talk about nothing else.
I've seen the picture, and it's foul. It
doesn't leave Mr. Hearst with one redeeming feature. Nobody but Orson would have dared do a thing
like that, and I personally hope it will never
be shown on the screen, although they're going
right ahead making plans for its release in
February. But don't miss the opening - you may
not have another chance to see it, because if
they do open it, it may be stopped after the
first night. It's a foul thing to have done,
and if it's successful, it will only be because
of the publicity his enemies give him, which
will attract people to the box office.

Do write again soon and tell me any news you
have. I love having letters from you, and I
love you very much, "Pringle". I hope one of
these days you get the job and the chance that
you deserve. God knows, you've worked hard
enough for it. Bless you.

                    Always,

HHPR
Miss Aileen Pringle
111 East 56 Street
New York City

Thursday, Feb 12Th, 1942.

Dear Preston:-

(Continuing my conversation from where I left off on the phone last night):

Your dialogue sparkles, crackles, and explodes with brilliance;- the sociology as expounded by the butler is made deliciously palatable by the underlying humor and deft touches, those wonderful touches you showed me in McGinty; - you change the most brutal sadist I've ever seen on stage or screen in the person of the "Mr." into an angel when he takes the men to the church to enjoy the movies, the contrast is terrific; - the personification of Devine Love in the character of the negro preacher was superbly moving and inspiring; - the chuckles, the laughs, the guffaws were sprinkled throughout the picture as are the wines at a gourmet's din- ner, the subtleties for the discriminating, the broad comedy for the morons; - Sullivan (the best thing Joel ever did in my estimation) the prototype of everything that is sincere but muddling in Hollywood, he is believable to the Nth degree as is everyone of your characters, particu- larly little Veronica whom you have molded into the very essence of the heartbreak, the sophistication, the faith, the childlikeness that is also Hollywood; - Preston you have done yourself and the industry proud in giving us entertainment for the masses and the classes in this picture, for the thoughtful and the superficial, for the astute and the dull! More power to you - may you go on and on along these lines and let no thing or nobody sway you in your own good judgment.

For a while I was deathly afraid you were going commercial (but brilliantly) and that you would be persuaded to smother that bubbling originality that is Preston Sturges and put you in the groove - for God's sake don't let them! Sullivan has convinced me otherwise and I am grateful! Preston you have a soul as deep as the ocean and you've only begun to take out the gold that is there - there still remain tons and tons of it.

I may be a bit incoherent in the above, but oh how sincere.

Always your friend,

Vic Potel

Victor Potel to Preston Sturges

FEBRUARY 12, 1942

In this letter to his friend, the writer-director Preston Sturges, actor Victor Potel is surprisingly eloquent at explaining why Sturges's latest film, *Sullivan's Travels*, is so much more than just another screwball comedy, and what makes Sturges one of the most creative voices working in the movie business. A former vaudevillian who made his first screen appearance in the silent days, Potel was a fixture in Hollywood who played bit parts in hundreds of movies, including all of the films Sturges directed at Par- amount. That vantage point as one of the industry's band of anonymous working actors perhaps gave Potel a unique perspective on *Sullivan's Travels*, an inside-Hollywood tale that recounts the story of a comedy director who sets out to make a serious film and ends up falling headfirst into the real world, where he comes to realize the value of making audiences laugh during times of trouble. The stars of the film were Joel McCrea and Veronica Lake, but the cast also included Sturges regulars William Demarest, Franklin Pangborn, Eric Blore, and of course Potel, who appeared in one scene, as a waiter in a coffee shop.

Peter Ballbusch to Charles Laughton

OCTOBER 1942

This illustrated letter from the montage director Peter Ballbusch to the actor Charles Laughton offers a glimpse of the unlikely friendships that sometimes blossomed in Hollywood. The Swiss-born Ballbusch was responsible for the montage sequences in dozens of films at MGM and other studios but was also an artist and aspiring writer. *Tales of Manhattan*, the movie that Ballbusch discusses, was an anthology film featuring five different stories linked by one formal men's coat. It was directed by Julien Duvivier, a notable French director who had moved to

Hollywood because of the war, and starred Charles Boyer, Rita Hayworth, Edward G. Robinson, Henry Fonda, and Paul Robeson, among many others. Laughton's episode was about a composer who has a chance to conduct one of his pieces at Carnegie Hall but who is humiliated when the secondhand tailcoat hastily purchased by his wife (played by Laughton's wife, Elsa Lanchester) splits apart at the seams during the performance. The home that Laughton shared with Lanchester, and which Ballbusch was so delighted to have visited, was located in Pacific Palisades.

Dear Mr. Laughton,

I carried your precious "FUCHSIA-BALLERINAS" home to my wife. She let them glide over the satin surface of a silver tray—and enjoyed them, like a child enjoys a holiday.

But dear sir—I warned you—she wants a holiday of her own, in the form of a FUCHSIA BUSH. I don't think they grow on our sun-drenched hill.....but you know how women are.....always reaching for the [moon].

I hope that I shall not inconvenience you too much by asking to bring my wife over some day, to look at and study your FUCHSIA GARDEN. Poor dear—I have an idea she is headed for trouble with her FUCHSIA WISHES. But then, let each man or woman find her own GOLGATHA!

. . . .

The other night I went to see "TALES OF MANHAT-TAN" since you mentioned that your work in this film came closest to your own standard. Athough I did not enjoy the film as a whole—I was deeply moved by two sequences...YOURS + EDWARD G. ROBINSONS. If the tale and presentation of the other sketches would have reached the standard of those two—"TALES OF MAN-HATTAN" would be a great picture.

Reviewing your sketch on my way home I found only one incident which I would have presented differently... THE CRYING SCENE. It struck me like a wrong note in

a strong symphonie [*sic*]. I would never have made you kneel—but take the onrush of the tears standing, only gripping the music stand in front of you for support. And thus, like a tree in a tempest—the emotional storm of humiliation + defeat would have been much stronger, then [*sic*] in the bent position of the broken man, to whom the public could only react shamefacedly. But then DUVIVIER may have been striving for that very shamefaced pause—to heighten the leader's magnificent gesture, of taking of [*sic*] his coat. Yet—I still feel to be right, but then such differences make + mark the French-man DUVIVIER and the Swiss: BALLBUSCH.

. . . .

I don't know how to thank you for that afternoon of FILM VERSUS THEATRE and your god-given symbol of the great play as the house for the actor to live, eat, sleep, dream + rant in!

I don't know if I'll ever be able to write a great play— yet, if I succeed to write a couple of good ones, you have given me the first good shove in the right direction—and for that *JE VOUS EN REMERCIE*!

Cordialment
Peter Ballbusch

P.S. My wife would like so much to meet your wife—do you think it might be possible?

DEAR MR. LAUGHTON,

I carried your precious "FUCHSIA-BALLERINAS" home to my wife. She let them glide over the watersurface of a silvertray — and enjoyed them, like a child enjoys a holiday.

But dear Sir — I warned you — she wants a holiday of her own, in the form of a FUCHSIA BUSH. I don't think they'll grow on our sun-drenched hill ..... But you know how women are .... always reaching for the

I hope, that I shall not inconvenience you too much by asking to bring my wife over some day, to look at and study your FUCHSIA GARDEN. Poor dear — I have an idea she is headed for trouble with her FUCHSIA WISHES. But then let each man or woman find her own GOL-GATHA!

- -

The other night I went to see "TALES OF MANHATTAN" since you mentioned that your work in this film came closest to your own standard. Although, I did not enjoy the Film as a whole — I was deeply moved by two sequences ... YOURS + EDWARD G. ROBINSONS. If the tale and presentation of the other sketches would have reached the standard of those two — "TALES OF MANHATTAN" would be a great picture.

Reviewing your sketch on my way home I found only one incident, which I would have presented differently ... THE CRYING SCENE. It struck me like a wrong note in a strong symphonie.

I would never have made you kneel—
but take the onrush of the tears standing,
only gripping the music stand in front of
you for support. And thus, like a tree in
a tempest — the emotional storm of humiliation
+ defeat would have been much stronger,
then in the bent position of the broken
man, to whom the public could only react shamefacedly. But then DUVIVIER
may have been striving for that very
shamefaced pause — to highten the leaders
magnificent gesture, of taking of his coat.
Yet — I still feel to be right. but then
such differences make + mark the Frenchman
DUVIVIER and the Swiss: BALLBUSCH.

- -

    I don't know how to thank you for
that afternoon of FILM VERSUS THEATRE
and your god-given symbol of the great
play as the house for the actor
to live, eat, sleep, dream +
rant in!!

    I don't know, if I shall ever
be able to write a great play
— yet, if I succeed to write
a couple of good ones, you
have given me the first
good shove in the right
direction — and for that
JE VOUS EN REMERCIE!

        Cordialment

                Peter Ballbusch

P.S.   My wife would like so much to meet
          your wife — do you think it might
be possible?

IRVING BERLIN

November 2, 1942

Mr. Mark Sandrich,
Paramount Pictures Inc.,
Hollywood, Calif.

Dear Mark:

Thanks for sending me Mr. Reddin's letter. I had heard
of how big a hit 'Holiday Inn' was in London and was glad
to get some of the details first hand.

I spoke to Neil Agnew, last week, and he told me that the
picture is living up to all his expectations. You possibly
know that 'White Christmas' is the talk of the music
business and looks like the biggest hit I have had since
'Always'. That is, I haven't had a song, including 'God
Bless America', that sold as many copies in so short a
time. Last week, we sold over 92,000 copies and the week
before over 76,000 copies. The first mail today had orders
for over 12,000 copies.

The song seems to have a quality that can be applied to
the world situation as it exists today. I understand many
copies are being sent to the boys over-seas, and it is
just possible, while it isn't a war song, it can easily
be associated with it. Frankly, while we all felt this
was a natural hit, I personally didn't believe it could
be as much of a natural as the reaction to it shows. I
know you don't mind me going on about 'White Christmas'
in this manner. There are only so many of these kind of
songs in a songwriter's system. They are the milestones,
all the others are 'filler-ins', even if they become
popular.

'This Is The Army' continues to break records, so much
so that the only criticism we are getting is the fact
that people can't get in to see it. We just finished
the first week at the Mastbaum Theatre in Philadelphia
and will wind up, after the two weeks, with somewhat
over $200,000. We play Baltimore next week and the house
sold out the first day the boxoffice was opened. The
papers raised hell with us about so many people standing
in line who couldn't get seats. I am pretty tired but
manage to keep going. From here in, it's a tough job
and is going to be much tougher before the picture is
made. However, I am looking forward to California and
seeing a good deal of you.

Mr. Mark Sandrich - #2

I hope all is going well with your picture. It sounds
important and I am sure will be swell.

With love from us to you and Freida, I am

As always,

I
B
:
M
G

Irving Berlin to Mark Sandrich

NOVEMBER 2, 1942

By 1942, Irving Berlin was the most successful songwriter in the business, but even he seems surprised by the overwhelming popularity of his song "White Christmas," which had recently been introduced by Bing Crosby in the film *Holiday Inn*. In this letter to the movie's director, Mark Sandrich, Berlin marvels at the way the record has shot to the top of the charts and reflects on how it is resonating with men in the armed services. "White Christmas" earned Berlin his only Academy Award for best song, and it is still one of the most popular recordings of all time. The other project mentioned here is Berlin's musical revue *This Is the Army*, which was staged by and starred men from the military and served as a fundraiser for the Army Emergency Relief Fund. The patriotic musical opened on Broadway in July 1942 and later became a sold-out touring show and then a star-studded film produced by Warner Bros. The picture that Sandrich was preparing to direct at this time was *So Proudly We Hail*, one of two films that he made during the war about women in the military.

BY DIRECT WIRE FROM

WESTERN UNION

1225

CLASS OF SERVICE

This is a full-rate Telegram or Cablegram unless its deferred character is indicated by a suitable sign above or preceding the address.

R. B. WHITE
PRESIDENT

NEWCOMB CARLTON
CHAIRMAN OF THE BOARD

J. C. WILLEVER
FIRST VICE-PRESIDENT

SIGNS

DL = Day Letter
NM = Night Message
NL = Night Letter
LC = Deferred Cable
NLT = Cable Night Letter
Ship Radiogram

The filing time as shown in the date line on full-rate telegrams and day letters, and the time of receipt at destination as shown on all messages, is STANDARD TIME.

SB112 TWS PAID 5=CULVERCITY CALIF NOV 12 1942 657P

MR HAL WALLIS=

WARNER BROS PICTURES CORP=

DEAR HAL: SAW "CASABLANCA" LAST NIGHT. THINK IT IS A SWELL
MOVIE AND AN ALL-AROUND FINE JOB OF PICTURE MAKING. TOLD JACK
AS FORCIBLY AS I COULD THAT I THOUGHT IT WOULD BE A TERRIBLE
MISTAKE TO CHANGE THE ENDING. AND ALSO THAT I THOUGHT THE
PICTURE OUGHT TO BE RUSHED OUT.

KNOWING WHAT THEY STARTED WITH, I THINK THE FIRM OF
EPSTEIN, EPSTEIN AND KOCH DID AN EXPERT PIECE OF WRITING, EVEN
THOUGH RICKS'S PHILOSOPHY IS IN AT LEAST ONE INSTANCE WORD FOR
WORD THAT OF RHETT BUTLER.

I HAVE A FEW MINOR SUGGESTIONS TO MAKE, AND IF BY ANY
CHANCE YOU WOULD CARE TO HAVE THEM I WILL BE GLAD TO PASS THEM
ALONG. ALTHOUGH I AM SURE THAT YOU WILL FIND OUT THESE THINGS
FOR YOURSELF AT PREVIEW.

MIKE CURTIZ'S DIRECTION WAS, AS ALWAYS, SPLENDID. HE IS
CLEARLY ONE OF THE MOST COMPETENT MEN IN THE BUSINESS. I AM MOST
GRATEFUL TO YOU AND TO MIKE CURTIZ FOR THE SUPERB HANDLING OF
INGRID. THANKS TO YOU TWO, AND OF COURSE TO INGRID, THE PART
SEEMS MUCH BETTER THAN IT ACTUALLY IS; AND I THINK IT WILL BE
OF BENEFIT TO HER, AND THEREFORE OF COURSE TO ME.

I AM ALSO GRATEFUL, ON INGRID'S BEHALF AND MY OWN, FOR

BY DIRECT WIRE FROM

WESTERN UNION

1225

SB112 TWS PAID 5 SHEET-TWO.

ARTHUR ADESON'S SUPERB PHOTOGRAPHY OF INGRID. BUT THEN THE
JOB OF PHOTOGRAPHY ON THE WHOLE PICTURE IS EXCELLENT AND IS
TO NO SMALL EXTENT RESPONSBILE FOR THE PICTURE'S MOOD.
     AFTER "FOR WHOM THE BELL TOLLS" INGRID IS OBVIOUSLY GOING
TO BE WHAT I HAVE FOR SO LONG PREDICTED. ONE OF THE GREAT
STARS OF THE WORLD. THE DEMAND FOR HER SERVICES IS OF COURSE
TREMENDOUS. IN DECIDING WHO SHOULD HAVE OUTSIDE PICTURES
WITH HER IN THE FUTURE, AND SHOULD YOU AND MIKE HAVE A
REALLY IMPORTANT VEHICLE FOR HER, THE WAY IN WHICH YOU HAVE
KEPT YOUR PROMISES IN REGARD TO HER IS GOING TO BRING YOU
THE DIVIDEND OF SPECIAL CONSIDERATION.
     CORDIALLY AND SINCERELY YOURS=

          DAVID O SELZNICK.
               719P.

David O. Selznick to Hal B. Wallis

NOVEMBER 12, 1942

In this telegram to Warner Bros. production head Hal B. Wallis, the producer David O. Selznick weighs in on the merits of the studio's latest film, *Casablanca*, which would go into wide release in January 1943. With two best-picture Oscars under his belt and a background that included not only independent production but also stints at Paramount, RKO, and MGM, Selznick's opinion was a valuable one. But Selznick also had a vested interest in the film's success, because *Casablanca* starred Ingrid Bergman, one of the actors that he had under personal contract. In 1939, Selznick had produced Bergman's first film in America, *Intermezzo: A Love Story*, but since then she had worked exclusively at other companies. Loaning out talent to other studios was not only lucrative for a producer like Selznick but also allowed him to build up a star's value and persona without going to the expense of actually producing all of her films. It's notable that Selznick mentions debate about the ending of the film and whether it should be changed. The famous conclusion of the story was one of the last things written and filmed, and apparently there was a great deal of disagreement about it until shortly before the picture was released. The contributors whose work Selznick acknowledges in his telegram include the screenwriters Julius and Philip Epstein and Howard W. Koch; the director Michael Curtiz; and the cinematographer Arthur Edeson.

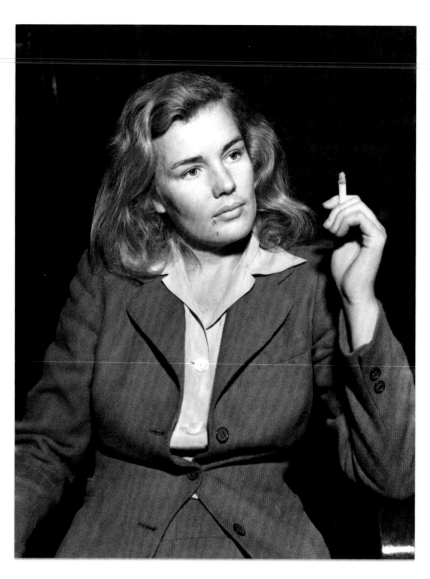

Frances Farmer after her arrest, January 1943.

Joseph M. Schenck to Charles K. Feldman

JANUARY 16, 1943

This telegram about Frances Farmer from Twentieth Century-Fox studio executive Joseph M. Schenck to the agent Charles K. Feldman is a fascinating, if cryptic, look at how friends and colleagues dealt with a celebrity breakdown. Two days earlier, the brilliant but troubled actress, who had been arrested on a parole violation, had been sent to county jail after she assaulted officers during a chaotic court appearance. Farmer had been battling alcoholism and mental illness for some time, but this well-publicized episode guaranteed that her struggles would become front-page news. After Farmer was transferred to the General Hospital's psychiatric ward, a judge agreed that she could be committed to a private sanitarium, a move that was, according to press accounts, subsidized by the Motion Picture Relief Fund. In September 1943, Farmer was released and left Los Angeles with her mother to return to her hometown of Seattle, essentially ending her connection to Hollywood. Farmer spent many years in and out of mental institutions, but she did eventually return to show business as an actress and local television host. When he wrote this telegram, Schenck had recently withstood a scandal of his own. A few months earlier he had been paroled from federal prison after serving four months for perjury, a conviction that was related to the Bioff-Browne extortion case that rocked Hollywood in the early 1940s. Schenck, who had been the chairman of Twentieth Century-Fox before his conviction, returned to the studio in 1943 as a production executive. His baffling references to home-raised chickens and eggs are most likely related to food rationing during World War II.

WESTERN UNION

NBZ225 TWS PAID 3=LOSANGELES CALIF 16 252P

CHARLES FELDMAN=   1943 JAN 16 PM 6 20

:SHERRY NETHERLAND HOTEL=

DEAR CHARLIE: WE ARE TRYING TO TAKE CARE OF FARMER, HER
MOTHER FROM SEATTLE, WHO IS BROKE, SHOULD COME ON THERE,
IT WOULD HELP THE CASE, ARRANGED FOR HER TRANSPORTATION,
ALSO SENDING A PHYSICIAN TO EXAMINE FARMER BECAUSE THE MAN
WHO DID EXAMINE HER WAS JUST TRYING TO GET PUBLICITY TO HER
DETRIMENT, WE CAN PROBABLY PUT HER INTO A PRIVATE
INSTITUTION FOR A PERIOD UNTIL SHE GETS WELL BUT NATURALLY

THAT WILL COST MONEY, I DONT WANT TO GET STARTED BECAUSE
ALTHOUGH THERE ARE MANY WHO WANT TO DO SOMETHING ONCE I DO
IT I AM SURE THE EXPENSE WILL FALL ON ME, LET ME KNOW
EXACTLY WHETHER BILL PALEY AND OTHERS WOULD GO THROUGH
TOWARDS THAT EXPENSE, WIRE ME IMMEDIATELY AND DONT WASTE
TIME IN NEWYORK, YOUR HOUSE IS READY FOR YOU AND YOU CAN
HAVE GOOD FOOD BECAUSE I HAVE A LOT OF CHICKENS YOU CAN CUT
THEIR NECKS AND COOK THEM FOR DINNER, IN A FEW WEEKS THEY
WILL LAY EGGS SO YOU CAN HAVE EGGS, MY LOVE TO YOU AND JEAN=
        :JOE SCHENCK,

Mar. 5, 1943

Dear Aunt Alice —

I received the lovely, lovely writing pad and thanks so much — I'm really rude for answering you so late.

Well I'm beginning to like it here immensely — At first I found it hard to find a place to live with everything occupied with defense workers, etc. but am now settled and like the place where I'm living —

I got a letter from Virginia Morrison — a very cute letter — and will answer it soon —

I'm studying hard with dramatic coaching every day and voice lessons three times a week — with the best coaches in town — Mr. Goldwyn plans to put me in a picture in about three months if I'm ready for it. So that's what I'm working towards. They started shooting on

Virginia Mayo to Alice Jones Wientge

MARCH 5, 1943

This letter from the aspiring actress Virginia Mayo to her aunt and acting teacher Alice Jones Wientge, who lived in Mayo's hometown of St. Louis, provides an inside look at how young performers were groomed for the screen during the studio era. Mayo's road to Hollywood started on the stage and eventually led to Samuel Goldwyn, who signed her to a contract in 1943 and began featuring her in small film roles a few months later. Mayo's description of studio filmmaking and life in wartime Hollywood is a fascinating window into a time when a newcomer could see Garbo and Dietrich out on the town or run across

James Cagney or Veronica Lake around the studio. Mayo's wide-eyed excitement over being in Hollywood cooled a bit over the next few months, however, as she waited to be cast in her first part. By July, her letters show that she was getting impatient with the slow pace at the studio and was unhappy about having to do a screen test with comic actor Danny Kaye, one of Goldwyn's biggest stars at the time. In the end, Mayo did five films with Kaye, though her greatest achievement at Goldwyn was the 1946 classic *The Best Years of Our Lives*, in which she was cast as the unsympathetic wife of a former bombardier played by Dana Andrews.

the Russian picture, "North
Star" on our lot. Monday,
and it will be one of the
good one's you must see –
The cast includes. Ann
Baxter, Walter Brennan, Ann
Harding, Walter Huston, Dana
Andrews, Jane Withers, and
lots of others. I go on the set
almost every day – it's so very
fascinating to watch them
work – although it is terribly
slow –

I saw Garbo in a Department
store the other day and didn't
even notice her – I mean recognize her – Have also seen
Marlene Dietrich close, also
Jean Gabin, the French star – James
Cagney, who is always on our
lot, and his brother who is
a producer – Saw Veronica Lake
at Paramount one day –
And Groucho Marx who I
simply didn't recognize. Will
keep you posted on who I
see –.

I, too, was sorry we could.

①n't have had more time together on my stopover in St. Louis – but was terribly pressed for time. Maybe you'll come out here –

I've a lot to learn about picture making – it's so different from the stage – One's voice has to be so soft and controlled – and can't do too much or it looks like over acting – there's a lot to screen technique – and it's like starting all over again –

Mr. Goldwyn is a swell person and really eager to help me – and said he'll give me every opportunity to make good – So it's up to me –

I'll be glad when the rainy season is over here – it's simply beautiful when it is sunshining –

Well, I'd like to see some of your pupils and friends and pupils out here but can't guarantee it will be soon – I'm so busy –

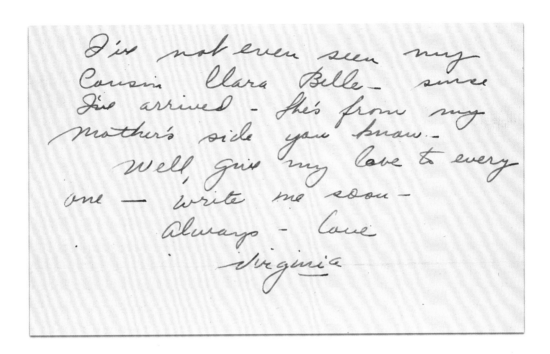

Mar. 5, 1943

Dear Aunt Alice—

I received the lovely, lovely writing pad and thanks so much. I'm really rude for answering you so late.

Well, I'm beginning to like it here immensely. At first I found it hard to find a place to live with everything occupied with defense workers, etc. but am now settled and like the place where I'm living.

I got a letter from Virginia Morrison—a very cute letter—and will answer it soon.

I'm studying hard with dramatic coaching every day and voice lessons three times a week with the best coaches in town. Mr. Goldwyn plans to put me in a picture in about three months if I'm ready for it. So that's what I'm working towards.

They started shooting on the Russian picture, "North Star," on our lot Monday and it will be one of the good ones that you must see—the cast includes Ann Baxter, Walter Brennan, Ann Harding, Walter Huston, Dana Andrews, Jane Withers, and lots of others. I go on the set almost every day—it's so very fascinating to watch them work—although it is terribly slow.

I saw Garbo in a department store the other day and I didn't even notice her—I mean recognize her. Have also seen Marlene Dietrich close, also Jean Gabin, the French star. James Cagney, who is always on our lot, and his brother who is a producer. Saw Veronica Lake at Paramount one day—and Groucho Marx who I simply didn't recognize. Will keep you posted on who I see.

I, too, was sorry we couldn't have had more time together on my stopover in St. Louis—but was terribly pressed for time. Maybe you'll come out here.

I've a lot to learn about picture making—it's so different from the stage. One's voice has to be so soft and controlled—and can't do too much or it looks like over acting. There's a lot to screen technique—and it's like starting all over again.

Mr. Goldwyn is a swell person and really eager to help me, and said he'll give me every opportunity to make good. So it's up to me.

I'll be glad when the rainy season is over here—it's simply beautiful when it is sunshiny.

Well, I'd like to see some of your pupils and friends and pupils out here but can't guarantee it will be soon. I'm so busy. I've not even seen my cousin Clara Belle since I've arrived. She's from my mother's side, you know.

Well, give my love to everyone—write me soon.

Always—love
Virginia

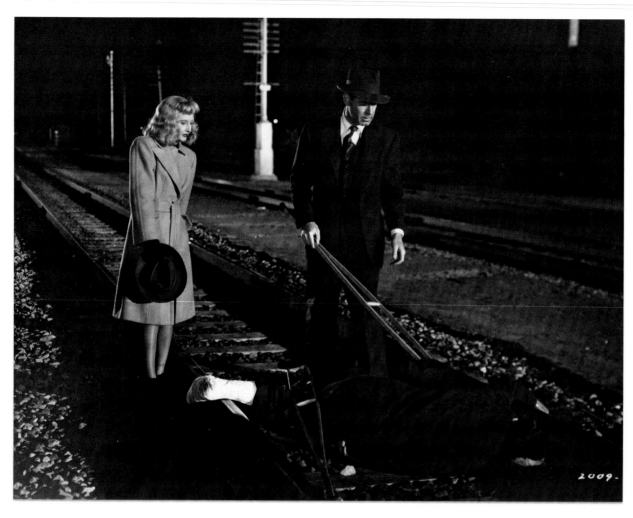

Barbara Stanwyck and Fred MacMurray committing murder together in *Double Indemnity*, 1944.

Joseph Breen to Luigi Luraschi

MARCH 15, 1943

The litany of seemingly unresolvable problems with *Double Indemnity* laid out in this letter from Production Code chief Joseph Breen to Paramount executive Luigi Luraschi illustrates exactly what made the Code such a bitter pill to swallow for Hollywood screenwriters, especially those who wanted to tackle stories about crime and corruption. Before Billy Wilder decided to adapt the story, James M. Cain's gritty novel had been floating around Hollywood for years, and studios that inquired about it were always handed this same flat-out rejection signed by Breen. This time, though, the project went forward, and fifteen months after this letter was written a film version of the novel was on its way to theaters. The fact that Paramount and Wilder were able to negotiate to a middle ground shows that in the 1940s the Production Code process was evolving in order to accommodate tougher stories, a development that would become even more evident in the years following World War II, when film noir became one of the most popular screen genres.

March 15, 1943

Mr. Luigi Luraschi
Paramount Pictures, Inc.
5451 Marathon Street
Hollywood, California

Dear Mr. Luraschi:

   With regard to the novel, DOUBLE INDEMNITY,
by James M. Cain, concerning which you requested a report, I regret to inform you that, because of a number
of elements inherent in the story in its present form,
it is our judgment that the story is in violation of
the provisions of the Production Code, and, as such,
is almost certain to result in a picture which we would
be compelled to reject if, and when, such a picture is
presented to us for approval.

   As we read it, this is the story of the murder
of a man by his wife and an insurance agent who is, apparently, her lover. The motive of the murder is to
collect insurance on the dead man, which the murderous
couple had first conspired to place upon his life. At
the end of the story, the crime is confessed by one of
the murderers to the officers of the insurance company,
who proceed thereupon to withhold this information from
the proper legal authorities and successfully effect a
gross miscarriage of justice by arranging for the escape of the two murderers from this country. The pair
later commits suicide.

   The first part of the story is replete with
explicit details of the planning of the murder and the
effective commission of the crime, thus definitely
violating the Code provisions which forbid the presentation of "details of crime". This part of the
story is, likewise, seriously questionable, when it is
not definitely offensive, because of the cold-blooded
fashion in which the murderers proceed to their kill.

The second part of the story has to do with the successful efforts of the criminals to avoid arrest and punishment, and culminates in the decision of the man to kill his accomplice. The attempt is frustrated when the woman shoots him, whereupon the wounded man, in love with the stepdaughter of his accomplice, confesses the crime to save the girl he loves, against whom a mass of circumstantial evidence has been piled up.

This story violates the provisions of the Production Code in that:

(1) The leading characters are murderers who cheat the law and die at their own hands. They avoid successfully the consequences of their crime through a miscarriage of justice, even though, subsequently, they commit suicide. It may be argued, too, that one of these criminals is, in a sense, glorified by his confession to save the girl he loves.

(2) The story deals improperly with an illicit and adulterous sex relationship;

(3) The details of the vicious and cold-blooded murder are clearly shown. These details are definitely and specifically in violation of the Production Code.

The general low tone and sordid flavor of this story makes it, in our judgment, thoroughly unacceptable for screen presentation before mixed audiences in the theatre. I am sure that you will agree that it is most important, in the consideration of material of this type, to avoid what the Code calls "the hardening of audiences, especially those who are young and impressionable, to the thought and fact of crime."

It is our considered judgment that the story under discussion is most objectionable and, unless it can be materially changed, both in structure and in detail, all consideration of it for screen purposes should be dismissed.

Cordially yours,

Joseph I. Breen

2/mw

following spread

Sam Fuller to Al Cohen

SEPTEMBER 2, 1943 & OCTOBER 7, 1944

Sam Fuller had already lived a couple of lifetimes as a reporter, writer, cartoonist, and screenwriter before he joined the US Army in 1942 and was assigned to the Sixteenth Regiment of the First Infantry Division, known as "The Big Red One." Fuller and his fellow soldiers were engaged in brutal campaigns in North Africa and Sicily, landed in Normandy on D-Day, and marched into Germany and Czechoslovakia. In his autobiography, Fuller wrote that soldiers were encouraged to keep their letters home upbeat and positive, and that certainly seems to be the case in these V-mails to his friend Al Cohen, a producer at Republic Studios. And yet Fuller's letters are also revealing, especially in the way they capture the fact that he is storing up his experiences to use in his later work. Fuller's observation that "Hollywood has never even brushed the surface of what war is really like," could be a primer on his future career, during which he wrote and directed a series of remarkably authentic war films, as well as low-budget westerns and crime dramas.

In 1980, Fuller completed *The Big Red One*, his brutally realistic long-planned film about World War II, based to a great extent on his own experiences as a member of the famed infantry division. *The Dark Page*, referenced in one of Fuller's missives, was a pulp novel published in 1944, while Fuller was in the service. Ving was one of Fuller's brothers, and Alex Gottlieb was a producer Fuller had worked with before the war. *Ice-Capades Revue*, the innocuous Republic picture that was screened for the soldiers in Fuller's unit, was a low-budget musical starring Ellen Drew and produced by Robert North. Both of the letters reproduced here are examples of V-mail (short for Victory Mail), a system used by the US government during World War II to drastically reduce the volume of mail being sent home by G.I.s. Service members wrote their letters on special forms that, after passing by military censors, were then photographed and shipped to the US on microfilm. The letters were then printed out and delivered stateside in a reduced size.

No. 591995

To

Mr. Al Cohen

Republic Studios

No. Hollywood, Calif.

U.S.A.

From

Cpl. Samuel Fuller, 39532377
(Sender's name)

Regt.Hq. 16th Inf.
(Sender's address)

1st U.S.Inf.Div. APO#1,NYNY

2 September 1943 Sicily
(Date)

(other day, swimming bareass in Mediterranean, we experienced stern-end of a sirocco...what a hot,strong,
biting wind)

Dear Al:

We had three things on the program last night. A talk on sex and how to

avoid it (!) Malaria pills. (again). And movies.

The pic. was ICECAPADES REVUE, and only credit title, other than cast,

was Bernie Vorhaus'...production, tech and writer titles were snipped.

Somehow I figure you produced it, for it was musically reminiscent of

Times Square Lady that you pounded with Shannon for MGM. Remember that

one? Soon as she inherited a racket, I figured Al Cohen was compelled

to pull one of his old ones out of the battered hat ...Am I right?

Sure they liked it. They like anything here. We're training for our

next assignment and it's anybody's guess as to where we'll go...Last time

I saw Ellen Drew she was at a party given me when I was leaving for the

Army. Understand her husband is a Capt. in Wash.D.C....Well - I did expect

an answer from you to my last letter...That was written during the battle

of Randazzo...even wrote one from Troina right after we took that town...

Understand Ving worked for you? On what? What happened? Haven't heard

from him yet. Perhaps a delay in the mail ...Am working, in spare moments,

on original for Hollywood based on actual invasion, beach-head hold and

push battle of Sicily up to its fall. Have a lot of stuff, and believe me

Al, Hollywood has never even brushed the surface of what war is really like,

and that goes for What Price Glory, Big Parade, all of them...The closest

was "All Quiet ..." What are you on now? Best to the gang. Good luck

V-MAIL

Sammy.

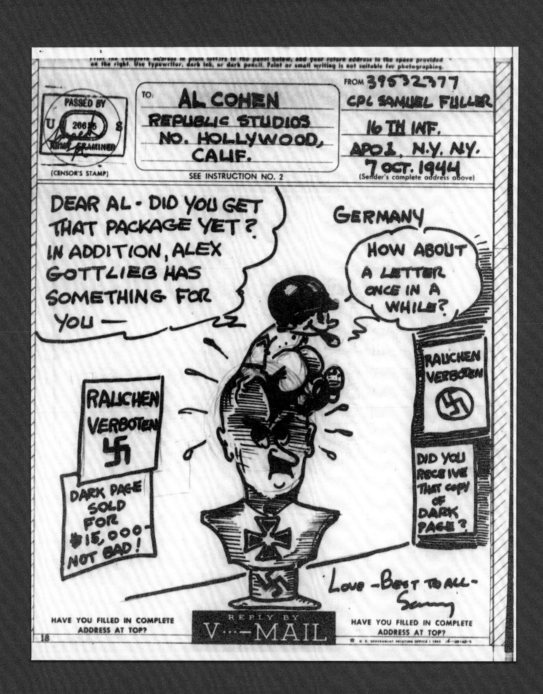

Dorothy Arzner to Preston Sturges

CIRCA 1944

During the silent era, women were active in all areas of Hollywood filmmaking, and many of the period's most accomplished directors were women. By the end of the 1920s, however, the opportunities for women directors started to disappear. The exception to the rule was Dorothy Arzner, the only woman who regularly worked as a director in Hollywood in the 1930s. After starting as a top film editor and scenario writer at Paramount in the 1920s, Arzner went on to direct twenty features, including *The Wild Party, Christopher Strong, Craig's Wife,* and *Dance, Girl, Dance.* And yet by 1944, directing offers had dried up, leading Arzner to send this letter to Preston Sturges, who had recently left Paramount to set up an independent production company. Her letter is intriguing not only because of the never-realized possibility of a Sturges-Arzner collaboration but also because of the way Arzner frames her background and experience at the studios, emphasizing her strong relationships with writers and below-the-line personnel and focusing on craftsmanship more than on the subject matter of her films. Arzner did not become a film executive, nor did she direct another feature film after 1943. However, she did produce a radio show, direct some short films and commercials, and teach cinema courses at UCLA. In the 1970s, Arzner was rediscovered by a new generation of women filmmakers and rightfully celebrated for her distinctive body of work as a director. In 2018, a building on the Paramount studio lot in Hollywood was dedicated in her honor.

From Dorothy Arzner
2249 Mountain Oak Dr
Hollywood, Calif

Tel. Glad. 5978

Preston Sturgis,
California Studios
5255 Clinton Street
Hollywood, California

Dear Mr. Sturgis:

I am acting on a hunch - seems a bit
egoistic to me - but I don't know any better way to
approach you and make it brief.

I am wanting an active executive place in the
picture business.   Being a free lance director
and not having the instruments in my character to
push or sell myself, I find that waiting for an agent
has not been very condusive to action

I have had much personal satisfaction as far
as attainment and credit - so my ambition is not one
that would take anything from anyone.

I should like to function as part of a
growing project and give whatever values I have from
a rather long and varied experience.

I have had very long years of experience with
very real men in this business and from those men
I'm sure you would get the best reccommendation for
my ability to coordinate with a whole company
Eddie Chodorov "Craig's Wife - Eric Pommer "Dance Girl
Dance" - Bud Lighton "who knows me from Paramount days
With Jim Cruze for Five years - Walter Mayo at Goldwyn
could tell you about "Nana" - Jack Backman could tell you
about My history at Paramount

Writers: Zoe Akins - I did five of her plays
           Mary McCall "Craig's wife
           Eddie Chodorv
           Edwin Justus Mayer "Merrily"

I don't know what kind of a reccommendation
Harry Cohn or Ben Schulberg would give me - both producer's
I did successful pictures for - or do I know about actresses'
reccomendation. But men like Paul Lukas - Fredric March -
assistant director's,camera men, and crews - they know
You know enough about this business to know that the
history should tell something.

Would you be interested enough to telk
with me - providing you have any desire for such a person

Sincerely,

Mary C. McCall Jr. to
Screen Writers Guild Board

JULY 3, 1944

Soon after writer Mary C. McCall Jr. moved to Hollywood in 1933, she joined the Screen Writers Guild, and
over the next nine years she dedicated herself to standing
up for the rights of writers as they fought the studios
for recognition. In 1942, after serving two terms on the
Guild's board and being instrumental in negotiating the
organization's first contract, McCall was elected president
of the Screen Writers Guild, the first woman to hold that
position. McCall was reelected to a second one-year term
but stepped down in July 1944 because she was pregnant with her third child. In this humorous resignation
letter to the board, McCall explains that she is leaving
the presidency due to "the November premiere of a

major production" with her husband David Bramson but
reiterates her staunch support for the Guild and its ideals.
It's notable that McCall singles out the Motion Picture
Alliance, the right-wing anticommunist group formed
in Hollywood in 1944, as one of the dangers that the
Guild is facing. When she again served as Guild president
from 1951 to 1952, her tenure and her writing career were
undermined by the blacklist enforced by the Alliance and
other anticommunist groups. The handwritten notations
on the original letter were most likely made by the Guild's
newsletter editor, who published the text of McCall's
resignation and the note about the board's recognition of
her service in the *Guild Bulletin.*

Telephone HOllywood 3601

Hollywood Center Building
1655 NORTH CHEROKEE AVENUE
HOLLYWOOD 28, CALIFORNIA

SCREEN WRITERS' GUILD, INC.
AFFILIATED WITH THE AUTHORS' LEAGUE OF AMERICA, INC.

July 3, 1944.

President
MARY C. McCALL, JR.
☆

1st Vice-President
LESTER COLE

2nd Vice-President
SHERIDAN GIBNEY

3rd Vice-President
JAMES HILTON
☆

Secretary
TALBOT JENNINGS
☆

Treasurer
HUGO BUTLER
☆

Executive Board
HUGO BUTLER
LESTER COLE
MARC CONNELLY
SHERIDAN GIBNEY
JAMES HILTON
TALBOT JENNINGS
MICHAEL KANIN
RING LARDNER, JR.
GLADYS LEHMAN
MARY C. McCALL, JR.
JANE MURFIN
MAURICE RAPF
BETTY REINHARDT
ALLAN SCOTT
JOHN WEXLEY
☆

Alternates
RICHARD COLLINS
DELMER DAVES
GORDON KAHN
EMMET LAVERY
WALDO SALT
ADRIAN SCOTT
☆

Counsel
MORRIS E. COHN
☆

Executive Secretary
ANN ROTH MORGAN

The Executive Board
Screen Writers' Guild
1655 North Cherokee
Hollywood, California

Ladies and Gentlemen:

Because I am readying for a November premiere a major production, in collaboration with David Bramson, I must ask the Board to accept my resignation as President of the Screen Writers' Guild.

I've served the Guild with pride. I'm in debt to it for great satisfaction. To be introduced as President of an organization which bore the main responsibility for the meeting last Wednesday night, salved all the smarts which a screen writer contracts in her daily work. Nine years ago next Fall, I was chosen to be a teller at the annual meeting. I set more store by the good opinion of screen writers than of any other group on earth. I was glad then that enough of them knew me to choose me to count votes. To be twice elected President of the Guild meant that the whole membership knew me and trusted me. That warmed my heart and will always keep it warm.

I shall miss active work in the Guild much more than the Guild will miss me.

A murrain on the Alliance and all the forces of disunity and retrogression. To the Board and the membership, to Counsel, and to the staff, my respectful affection.

(Signed)   Mary C. McCall, Jr.

In accepting Miss McCall's resignation, the Executive Board voted a resolution in recognition of her valuable service to the Guild inscribed in the minutes.

Saturday;

Dear Darryl;

It has indeed been a long time since we have had correspondence of any kind, but lately you, and the studio, and all that part of my life have been much in my thoughts, and so I thought I would sit down, and drop you a little line.

In the first place, I want to say how happy I was for you, when I read all the rave reviews of Wilson......they were really the most marvelous that I have ever seen, and I know how proud you must have been, to see a dream like that finally materialize. I have not seen it as yet, nor am I likely too, from all I hear, as long as I am on a military post. That is going to have to be just another of those things which I am saving up until this bloody mess is over.

My life is really pretty dreary, and I miss you all like hell, and wish that I were back there. This all seems so pointless, somehow. Though I guess there must be a reason back of it someplace. I am not doing a damn thing. Oh, flying yes, and a lot of that, but doing nothing that fifty thousand other fellows could do as well as I......and probably a lot better in most instances. But here I sit, grinding out some kind of a shoddy existence, and seemingly to no point.

I really have to laugh when I think of how ironic the whole thing is. Here I am, an Officer in the Marine Corps, having come up from an enlisted man, getting in to this whole thing anyway because I thought there was something I could do.....some place I could fill, and on top of that, wanting to see something of the war and what the hell was going on outside. I was going to be the Knight in Shining Armor....Oh, Yes! So what happens? I run my bloody guts and heart out, and my legs off in San Diego and Quantico, and sit on my ass in Corpus Christi, Atlanta, and Cherry Point! BUT.....that's only half of it.....All those who didn't go into the service have been to South America, Africa, India, Egypt, England,the South Pacific, Australia, New Zealand, China.....the list could go on forever....... that is the part that really get's me.

Oh, well. I know this must sound like the eternal gripe....the age-old 'beef'.....the usual 'bitch'......and you know......it is. But I guess it will all be over soon, and then who the hell will care?

As I look back over that last page, that
is probably the gloomiestthing I have ever seen in my
life. I didn't mean it to be like that, but at least
it tell you a little of what I feel. I still think that
I was right to do it, however.

Now that the deal has finally been completed,
with the Government, it looks like I will be with you
for some time to come, and I would like to tell you
now that I am very happy about the whole thing. There
are a hell of a lot of exciting things that we can do,
after this is all over. And while I see from the Bill-
boards that you are not suffering any acute man-power
shortage, I trust that there is still a place for me.
But girls, Darryl....girls. We really have to get some
damn good girls on the lot. Can't you do something
about finding another Loretta? I mean someone of her
type. I think we could surely use one, don't you?

Annabella id still in New York, suffering
through the heat that they have been having. I talk
to her quite often, and have been able to get up there
a couple of times. That, I must say, is the one advantage of this place....it's proximity to New York.

I hope that Virginia, and the children are
well, and as happy as one can be, under the present
circumstances. Please give her my love, and tell her
I hope to see her soon.

Again I say, Congratulations! And when you
have a moment, I would certainly like to hear from you.

Always Sincerely,

Tyrone

Tyrone Power to Darryl F. Zanuck

AUGUST 26, 1944

Tyrone Power was one of the most popular movie stars in the country when he enlisted in the US Marine Corps in November 1942. Power was trained as a pilot and became an officer, but instead of shipping overseas he was posted at a series of stateside bases, ending up in Cherry Point, North Carolina. That was where he was assigned when he wrote this frustrated letter to his friend Darryl Zanuck, the man who had made him into Twentieth Century-Fox's biggest star and who was counting the days until he could put his leading man back to work. Ironically, Power felt that his civilian colleagues at the studio who were touring with the USO, raising money for war bonds, or visiting hospitals were seeing more of the world than he was. Everything changed in December 1944, however, when Power was assigned to fly supply missions in the Marshall Islands and at Okinawa and Iwo Jima. Power was decorated for his heroic actions during this time and continued to serve honorably until he was discharged in January 1946. The actress Annabella, whom Power mentions toward the end of his letter, was his wife at the time. They were married from 1939 to 1948.

July 16.1945

Dear Charles:

A brief note of appreciation and thanks for the privilege
of seeing The Lost Weekend. I haven't the slightest doubt that it
is the best picture I am likely to see this year. The writing
and directing are superb, the performance of Milland is absolutely
to me the finest piece of sustained acting I have seen in ages,
and I never expected to see him bring it off. I have heard it said
that this picture is adult, which means nothing to me. No picture
made in Hollywood is or canbe adult in any absolute sense, because
the moment the question of whether a guy gets over being a drunk
becomes important because of some girl, it—in one sense—ceases to
be important at all. I know you must have had a great deal of
praise and flattery over this job. I am one of those who feel quite
sure it will be a hit, if there is any possibility of intelligent
exploitation. I wouldn't care for myself whether it was or not. It
is still a distinguished picture and cannot be less.

I don't remember the book awfully well, but who the hell cares
about a book. The scenes between the Milland and Da Silva are just
about perfect. The performance given by Dowling in this showed compared to (or with) the cheesy exhibition in the last picture I
worked on just go to show you have to have a director. I don't know
just what this dame was doing in the bar, but there was a wistful
tough quality about the wayshe behaved that was wonderful. I liked
the brother very much except when he confessed to being the family
drunk. I was sorry that the bag stealing episode had to hinge on
(Don't)
his need for money to pay the check rather than on his alcoholic
sublimation; but I can see how the latter would be tough to put

over even to intelligent people—of whom there must be hundreds, but not enough to make a success. I thought the race between Milland trying to get to the door andbolt it before the janitor reached the outside to unlock it was rather too contrived, but Loretta Young will probably say it is the best moment she ever saw in a picture.

What to say about the ending I don't know. No doubt a completely insolubleproblem. Nothing you could do with hope in it could fail to be slightly unreal, since it takes about three years for that kind of drunk to get normal, even if he wants to. I expected to be let dax down. Frankly, I wasn't. Perhaps because I expected to be. I didn't believe the ending in the least, but I accepted it because there was no percentage in the ending in the book.

As you know I know nothing about pictures. I think this one is over-cut. I never saw anything that was left out but I feel absolutely sure things were left out which should not have been. Altogether my deepest congratulations, and if any decent pictures are made in Hollywood, Brackett and Wilder will probably have to make them.

Which leaves me having said no nice thing adequately and half a dozen things I probably should not have said at all.

Ray

Raymond Chandler to Charles Brackett

JULY 16, 1945

Raymond Chandler had fought bitterly with Billy Wilder when they worked together on the screenplay for *Double Indemnity*, but this didn't stop Chandler from contacting Charles Brackett, Wilder's writing partner on *The Lost Weekend*, in order to praise the team's success at bringing Charles R. Jackson's bestselling novel to the screen. One of the first serious films about alcoholism, *The Lost Weekend* charts the downfall of a writer, played by Ray Milland, who is struggling to beat his debilitating addiction to booze. Chandler, who had created the ultimate gumshoe Philip Marlowe and featured him in a series of popular detective novels, had battled

alcoholism for years. Two months before this letter was written, shooting had wrapped on Chandler's first original screenplay, *The Blue Dahlia*, starring Alan Ladd. According to the autobiography of its producer, John Houseman, when Chandler was having trouble finishing the *Blue Dahlia* script on schedule, he convinced Houseman and the studio to allow him to write the rest of the screenplay during a supervised eight-day drinking binge. Doris Dowling, whose performance as "the dame" in the bar impressed Chandler, was also in *The Blue Dahlia*. She played Ladd's philandering wife, who is murdered early in the film.

Circle 5-7930

The Playwrights' Company

MAXWELL ANDERSON • S. N. BEHRMAN • ELMER RICE • ROBERT E. SHERWOOD • JOHN F. WHARTON • *Directors*

630 FIFTH AVENUE • NEW YORK 20
VICTOR SAMROCK • *Business Manager*
WILLIAM FIELDS • *Press Representative*

August 27, 1945

Mr. Samuel Goldwyn
1041 North Formosa Ave.
Los Angeles, Calif.

Dear Sam:

I have been thinking a great deal about "Glory for Me" and have come to the conclusion that, in all fairness, I should recommend to you that we drop it. This is entirely due to the conviction that, by next Spring or next Fall, this subject will be terribly out of date.

The vast majority of men in the armed forces will be demobilized by then, and included in that vast majority will be virtually all of those who have had actual combat experience, with the exception of the men who are going to stay in the services, as a permanent career.

MacKinlay Kantor's story is fundamentally concerned with men who have had medical discharges, who got out before the end of the war and were, therefore, somewhat lonely figures as veterans in a civilian community. The situation will be radically different when every American city has tens of thousands of soldiers and sailors who have returned to civilian life and who will already have passed through the first stages of readjustment before this picture can be released.

I do not believe that more than a small minority of these men will still be afflicted with the war neuroses which are essential parts of all of the three characters in "Glory for Me", and I, therefore, think that this picture would arouse considerable resentment by suggesting that these three characters are designed to be typical of all returned servicemen.

Willy Wyler said one thing which impressed me tremendously when the three of us were talking in Hollywood a month ago: that this picture could prevent a lot of heartaches and even tragedies among servicemen who were confronting demobilization and return to civilian life. However, the sudden end of the Japanese war has changed all that because, by the time the picture is released, the demobilization process will have been completed in many millions of cases.

I, therefore, urge that you consider very seriously whether
you want to go ahead with this picture. It isn't merely a
question of my reneging on a job that I agreed to do ---
it is the major problem of your investing a lot of money in
a picture which, in my opinion, will be doomed to miss the
bus. I shall be glad to work on some other story if you
have something which is up my street.

Please let me know immediately how you feel about this.
Perhaps we could talk it over on the telephone.

All is apparently going well with my play. The casting is
virtually complete, Garson Kanin is very much on the job and
we start rehearsals by next Monday. We certainly hope that
you and Frances will be here for the opening.

Madeline sends her love to you both,

Yours,

Bob

RES:GM

Robert E. Sherwood to Samuel Goldwyn

AUGUST 27, 1945

Robert E. Sherwood was a distinguished critic, playwright, and screenwriter who had served as head of the overseas bureau of the Office of War Information when he was approached by producer Samuel Goldwyn about writing a screenplay based on *Glory for Me*, a blank verse novel by MacKinlay Kantor about the challenges faced by three traumatized military veterans. Writing to Goldwyn in August 1945, as the war was drawing to a close, Sherwood expresses a belief, shared by many Americans, that the millions of returning servicemen, even those with physical or psychological scars, would quickly adjust to the postwar world, and that a story like the one told in Kantor's novel would soon be irrelevant. As one of those injured veterans, however, the director William Wyler was convinced that the trauma and dislocation of war would not be so easily forgotten, and he and Goldwyn convinced Sherwood to help them bring the story to the screen. Despite his misgivings, Sherwood crafted a timely and moving screenplay that became, under the guidance of Goldwyn, Wyler, and the cinematographer Gregg Toland, one of the most important and influential works of American cinema. The play that Sherwood refers to later in this letter was a drama called *The Rugged Path*, which was also about World War II. It was directed by Garson Kanin and starred Spencer Tracy, and opened on Broadway on November 10, 1945. *The Best Years of Our Lives* was released to universal acclaim in December 1946. It won eight Academy Awards, including one for Sherwood's screenplay.

Frank Sinatra and kids in a scene from *The House I Live In*, 1945.

Frank Sinatra to Albert Maltz

AUGUST 31, 1945

In this letter to Albert Maltz, Frank Sinatra praises his acclaimed screenplay for *Pride of the Marines*, which was being released just as the war in Japan was coming to an end. Maltz's script was based on the true story of Al Schmid, a Marine who was blinded at Guadalcanal after singlehandedly killing two hundred Japanese soldiers. *Pride* was among the first films to tackle the issue of physical and mental rehabilitation for veterans and to frankly address problems that returning soldiers might face, such as unemployment and racial and religious discrimination. The fight against bigotry was an important issue for both Maltz and Sinatra, who had recently collaborated on a short film called *The House I Live In*, in which

Sinatra sings the title song in order to preach tolerance to a group of boys who are tormenting a Jewish classmate. The RKO short was released widely in theaters in November 1945 and earned a special Academy Award the following year. In 1947, Maltz was called to testify before the House Un-American Activities Committee and later was blacklisted and imprisoned as one of the Hollywood Ten. In 1960, Sinatra attempted to break the blacklist by openly hiring Maltz to work with him on an adaptation of *The Execution of Private Slovik*, but Sinatra was forced to abandon the project under pressure from powerful industry and political forces.

THE *Frank Sinatra* PROGRAM

August 31, 1945

Mr. Albert Maltz
RKO Radio Pictures, Inc.
780 N. Gower St.
Hollywood, Calif.

My dear Albert:

This is probably the first letter I've written anyone in
quite a few moons. However, in every instance there's an exception
to the rule and in this instance, you're it!

I have just seen "Pride of the Marines" and throughout my
entire chaotic existence, I have never been so emotionally moved
by anything - whether it be a film, a book or a story. Honestly,
Albert, I was genuinely awed.

You see, you must first understand -- excuse me, I know you
do understand -- that my anxiety and interest in our social and
discrimination (or what have you) problems have been hungrily
awaiting such valuable assistance. When I think of the tremendous
amount of Americans who will see and hear and be made aware of
this deplorable problem, I tell you, Albert, it's wonderful. A
thousand guys like me could talk to kids in schools and people in
auditoriums for a year and we'd still only reach a small amount in
comparison.

Please don't think I'm going overboard on this thing; it's
just that I'm completely convinced that the greatest, most effective
weapon has suddenly come to life for the millions of bigoted, stupid,
anti-everything people. I'm sure that they have read it in books and
newspapers and I'm sure they've heard it on their radios, and I'm also
sure that they have been talked to -- but I tell you, Albert, this is
it -- just plain movies. You've got to hit 'em right in the kisser
with it and, baby, you really did.

So there - I've said my piece and unlike the Arab and his tent
and his silence, I will very loudly fold up my soap box and make
a helluva lot of noise on my way out.

Fondly,

Frank

P.S. If you haven't already guessed how I feel - just for the record,
I know that you're the best goddam writer around. And believe me, it's
a big "around".

Frank Sinatra/b

Oscar Hammerstein II to Alfred Newman

SEPTEMBER 20, 1945

Just a few months after their groundbreaking musical *Carousel* opened on Broadway, Richard Rodgers and Oscar Hammerstein II turned their attention to the release of *State Fair*, the Twentieth Century-Fox movie featuring the pair's first and only musical score written directly for the screen. Despite Hammerstein's doubts, the nostalgic film was a great success, and one of its songs, "It Might As Well Be Spring," won the team an Oscar and became a standard. In this letter to Alfred Newman, the celebrated

composer and longtime musical director at Fox, Hammerstein marvels at how important the art of scoring is to motion pictures and how skillfully Newman handled the assignment. The Newman family is one of the most notable dynasties in Hollywood history. In addition to Alfred, the talented clan included his brothers, the musical directors Emil and Lionel Newman, as well as Alfred's children David, Thomas, and Maria, all composers, and his nephew, the composer and songwriter Randy Newman.

OSCAR HAMMERSTEIN, 2ND

September 20, 1945

Mr. Al Newman
20th Century-Fox Studios
Beverly Hill, Calif.

Dear Al:

I was in California for only four days last week and
spent all of them auditioning people for "Show Boat".

One of the things I had hoped to find time to do was
to see you and thank you in person for the brilliant
job you did on "State Fair". You will remember that
when I ran the picture without the scoring, I was
quite depressed. It was an eye-opener to me to find
how depression could be converted to elation by the
mere addition of background music. This is a poor
phrase to describe it because, without intruding too
dominantly, you have brought the music into the foreground and made it a part of the story and character
structure. All I can say is that when I ran the
picture in the New York projection room, I had the time
of my life.

I still maintain some reservations about the casting
and direction. These can't be cured, but you have
certainly smoothed them over. I am happy that the
picture is such a great success and I know that you
are a very important part of this.

Dick's feelings on this subject are the same as mine.

All good wishes to you.

Sincerely,

Oscar Hammerstein, 2nd

OH/lz

Twentieth Century-Fox Film Corporation

STUDIOS
BEVERLY HILLS, CALIFORNIA

OFFICE OF
DARRYL F. ZANUCK
VICE-PRESIDENT
IN CHARGE OF PRODUCTION

March 5, 1946

Dear Joe:

At a story conference today on MY DARLING CLEMENTINE, we very carefully studied your letter of February 28th in reference to this script. The conference was attended by the authors, Mr. John Ford, and myself.

We have no intention of offending the morals of anyone, and many of the ideas in your letter will be automatically taken care of.

However, I wish to point out to you that MY DARLING CLEMENTINE is in its way just as historical as WILSON or any other film which deals with the picturization of an era. The characters in our story come out of history just as much as did Clemenceau or Lloyd George. Wyatt Earp, Doc Holliday, and Kate Nelson are well-known figures and many books have been written in which they play prominent parts.

MY DARLING CLEMENTINE is not intended to be just another western picture which relies upon gunplay and the usual melodramatics. As Remington captured on canvas the genuine spirit of the early west, so we are endeavoring to portray on the screen early Arizona and life as it actually was in Tombstone. We cannot avoid the inescapable fact that whiskey drinkers, gun toters, and prostitutes were as much a part of this era as singing waiters and dance hall gals were a part of the Bowery.

The point I wish to make to you is that we have no desire to offend anyone, or violate the Code, but at the same time when you read the new version of the script I request that you study it in the light of what I have said, and take into consideration that we are sincerely endeavoring to portray a period, and the rules and regulations that apply to ordinary HOPALONG CASSIDY films and films of like nature should not apply to an historical picture such as we hope to produce.

When we last met on FOREVER AMBER you were quick to permit certain elements to enter into the story that could not possibly

have been retained in a modern picture. You realized that we
were attempting to faithfully capture the spirit of an era.
The same is entirely true about MY DARLING CLEMENTINE. As a
matter of fact, it is actually far more historical than FOREVER
AMBER, and you can rest assured that we will approach it with
good taste.

Sincerely yours,

Mr. Joseph Breen
Motion Picture Association,
5504 Hollywood Blvd.,
Hollywood -28- California.

P.S. Dear Joe: It would be very easy for us to cheat (as they
cheated in THE HARVEY GIRLS, SAN ANTONIO, AND FRONTIER GAL) and
call our girls hostesses in the saloon, but just between the two
of us nobody is fooled, and I think that if for once we treat
the matter with honesty and avoid anything that is in bad taste,
there cannot possibly be an complaint from anyone.

D.F.Z.

CC: Col. Joy

Darryl F. Zanuck to Joseph Breen

MARCH 5, 1946

As head of production at Twentieth Century-Fox, Darryl F. Zanuck had negotiated with the Production Code Administration enough to know that historical accuracy in movies was far from a priority under the Code. Nevertheless, Zanuck decided to play the history card when he wrote this response to a five-page letter from Production Code chief Joseph Breen that eviscerated the first script for John Ford's *My Darling Clementine*, a dramatic retelling of the gunfight at the O.K. Corral. Not surprisingly,

Zanuck's plea fell on deaf ears, and Breen and the boys at the PCA continued to insist that the prostitution, drinking, lawlessness, and brutality that were all part of the real Tombstone be toned down or eliminated in the film. Of course, despite Zanuck's claim that *Clementine* was aiming to be historically accurate, the storytelling in the movie plays fast and loose with the facts. In the end, like most Westerns, Ford's brilliant retelling of the famous gunfight is more myth than history.

EXECUTIVE OFFICES
321 WEST 44TH STREET
NEW YORK

TELEPHONE
EXCHANGE
HOLLY 1251

PICTURES, INC.
WEST COAST STUDIOS
BURBANK, CALIFORNIA

June 10, 1946

Mr. Oscar Levant
180 W. 58th Street
New York, New York

Dear Oscar:

    Right off I'm going to tell you that this is a "Fan Letter"
for if I don't you'll probably get mad at me even before you finish
reading this. As a matter of fact, Oscar, you will recall that
during the time we made "Humoresque" I always told you how wonderful you were and that you should not have any worries as far as
the picture went. However, it was not until I saw the picture
all put together that I fully realized what an asset you were to
our story not only because of your superb performance but also
for the many countless suggestions you made and all the splendid
dialogue you wrote for it.

    During all of our association there was something about
your general attitude toward me and some of the others that, frankly,
annoyed me. It was not that you actually didn't give us consideration as far as our time and schedules were concerned but rather
your unhappy and hurt manner toward me and the picture as a whole.
You always seemed so disgruntled over the way we handled the shots
and their sequence and in my own very stubborn mind I believed that,
I, only, was right and you were really crabby and uncooperative and
were, not in the least way, trying to be "one of the boys" among
us. I have felt this way all along until just the other night when
something happened that has changed my entire view-point in your
favor.

    Dusty (we are going to get married in a couple of weeks)
and I were arguing over her career and I was telling her that I
could not understand how any intelligent human being could work
in pictures and keep their self respect with the kind of treatment they receive. How could anybody get up at such ungodly hours,
check into the makeup department - wait around, then go to the
set - wait around again for one shot, go to lunch, come back and
probably wait around again in a stinking little dressing room
for one more shot to be taken before the day is over and you can
go home. I continued this arguing - in my own behalf - regarding

Dusty and her own career and ambitions when I suddenly realized that there I was arguing your case; and Oscar, you were right! Coming to this sudden realization and remembering many of the "kicks" you had voiced I vowed that I had to write you how I felt before "Humoresque" was previewed this week. Forgive me for not understanding you - for I do now.

Everyone, at the Studio, who has seen the picture thinks it is great but I still have a funny feeling in the pit of my stomach which I probably won't get rid of until it meets the public and has been proven so. Whatever happens we know that everyone did their best and I hope that all the assurances I have received from people here will prove right. No matter what the ultimate results are I want you to know that I am very grateful for everything you did and more than that - this lucky foreigner is one of your ardent "fans".

Dusty, in spite of the fact that you insulted her the first time she met you, thinks you are wonderful. Believe me that is quite a compliment coming from a woman who worships only one man (I don't blame her thought, it's me)!

I am working hard on my house and starting preparations on another story, "Deep Valley" the Dan Totheroh novel which is quite an exciting thing. Remember me to your very charming wife and here is love and kisses from your tyrant and your victim.

JEAN

ljc

Jean Negulesco to Oscar Levant

JUNE 10, 1946

This letter from director Jean Negulesco to the multi-talented performer Oscar Levant, whom he directed in *Humoresque*, is surprisingly insightful about the challenges of film acting and the tensions that can arise between a director and his cast. A composer, conductor, pianist, and noted wit, Levant appeared in a number of films, usually playing a composer or musician, and inevitably sitting down at the piano at some point for a musical interlude. Famously neurotic and curmudgeonly, Levant was nevertheless a respected figure in the Hollywood community, and he and his wife June had a wide circle of devoted friends. The stylish Negulesco was a contract director at Warner Bros. who found some success with glossy melodramas like *Humoresque*, which starred John Garfield and Joan Crawford, along with Levant. Negulesco, a noted painter and caricaturist in his own right, and his wife, Dusty, were also art collectors and world travelers who were well known in the movie colony.

2203 S. Harvard
Los Angeles,7,Calif.
29 March 1947

Miss Hedda Hopper
Los Angeles Times
Los Angeles, California

My dear Miss Hopper:

First, let me thank you for speaking so kindly of me in
your column.   I do appreciate your speaking of my not
being ashamed in playing the part in Gone With The Wind
that got me an Oscar.

I, for one, feel as other actresses do, that the part is
the thing. So I do not feel that I have disgraced my race
by the roles that I have played. I'll close this issue by
saying that I am trying to fathom out in my mind as to just
what an Uncle Tom is. People, who can afford it, certainly
have maids and butlers. Yet, are these people who work as
maids and butlers called Uncle Toms? Truly, a maid or butler in real life is out making an honest dollar, just as we
are on the screen. I only hope that the producers will give
us Negro actors and actresses more roles, even if there will
be those who call us Uncle Toms. Which, I am sure that when
they so speak, they are doing so, because of their frustrated
minds. And so be it.

In regards to the Laura Slayton Youth Guidance League, I ,
myself, would appreciate it, if there is any way that you
see fit to let the League have some of your hats. Or, would
you give one or two of them to be auctioned off to help this
Youth Guidance League ?

Thanking you again, for all of your past kindnesses to me,
I am

                              Most sincerely,
                              Hattie McDaniel
                              Hattie McDaniel

HM/a

Hattie McDaniel to Hedda Hopper

MARCH 29, 1947

During and after World War II, the NAACP and other civil rights activists began pressuring the Hollywood studios to eliminate black stereotypes from the screen, particularly the maid and mammy roles like those usually played by Hattie McDaniel. In this letter to gossip columnist Hedda Hopper, McDaniel seems to be honestly trying to understand the actions of the protesters, though she clearly has another point of view. Hopper was virulently opposed to the NAACP's campaign, however, and quickly published an edited version of McDaniel's letter in her column to bolster her own position. A few months later, Hopper took the issue even further, writing a lengthy Sunday profile of McDaniel that painted her as a victim of a left-wing movement that was destroying the careers of black actors who had long made their living playing servant roles on screen. As a result of these stories, many readers wrote to Hopper admonishing her for defending stereotyping, but of course none of those letters were ever mentioned in Hopper's column. Instead, Hopper focused on praising McDaniel's latest film, Disney's problematic *Song of the South,* and advocating—successfully—for a special Oscar for McDaniel's costar James Baskett, who played Uncle Remus. McDaniel appeared in only a few more films after *Song of the South,* but continued to act on radio and television until her death in 1952. The Laura Slayton Youth Guidance League mentioned in the letter was an organization in South Los Angeles supported by McDaniel, who was a leader in the city's black community.

Dalton Trumbo to Harry Tugend

FEBRUARY 2, 1948

Dalton Trumbo was a successful screenwriter under contract to MGM when he was subpoenaed by the House Un-American Activities Committee in October 1947 and subsequently blacklisted by the movie industry. A few months after the hearings, Trumbo was targeted for nonpayment of dues by Screen Writers Guild treasurer Harry Tugend, leading to this letter and several more tense and increasingly personal exchanges between the two writers. Their feud was a microcosm of what was going on in the Guild at the time, as different factions argued about whether to fight the blacklist and defend the Hollywood Ten or focus on keeping the Guild running and supporting its non-blacklisted members. Trumbo's suggestion that Tugend was in favor of a "political test" for Guild officers refers to the fact that the Guild board had decided to abide by the recently passed Taft-Hartley Act, which included a requirement that union leaders sign noncommunist affidavits. The Guild did file a lawsuit against the motion picture industry attacking the legality of the blacklist, but it was never resolved, and after losing another case in the early 1950s that undermined the Guild's right to determine credits for all writers, the Guild found itself powerless to fight the blacklist, which claimed many more victims once the committee reconvened in 1951. Nevertheless, Trumbo and many of his fellow writers continued to work, using pseudonyms or fronts, creating a thriving black market for scripts that lasted throughout the 1950s.

February 2
1 9 4 8

Dear Harry:

I have received a notice, presumably from
you as treasurer of the Guild, warning
that I am now in jeopardy of being placed
in bad standing for non-payment of dues.

Please be informed that my contract with
M-G-M has been abrogated, my work has been
proscribed and that I myself have been
banned from employment in my profession
until such time as I perform an act of political purification hitherto characteristic
of Fascist states.

I am sure you understand the situation in
which I find myself, since you may take
credit for being one of its architects by
reason of your advocacy of the same political test for Guild officership which
the producers have taken over as a test
for employment.

In consequence, my income has ceased and
I have no money with which to pay dues.
After thirteen years of membership---years
during which some members of the present
board resigned in terror lest they dis-
please the producers---I am therefore ob-
liged to go into bad standing.

Attached herewith my card.

                              Cordially,

Lazy T Ranch
Frazier Park
California

My good friend Hedda —

At the risk of having you regard me as a simpering sentimentalist — I must tell you how wonderful I thought it was to read the friendliest and warmest tribute you paid to Louella Parsons daughter Harriet — in your column this morning.

Honestly Hedda — it stirred great tears of joy as I read how fairly — and how genuinely you revere Harriet.

I hardly knew the young lady in question but this I do know — that it could be a very easy matter to dismiss the subject of the opposition's daughter — or to find fault with vengeance! Neither of these things could you be guilty of. That is why this note. — Yes, Hedda, more love — like this that you have expressed is what the world is crying and yearning for. Wars and

My good friend Hedda—

At the risk of having you regard me as a simpering sentimentalist—I must tell you how wonderful I thought it was to read the friendliest and warmest tribute you paid to Louella Parsons' daughter Harriet in your column this morning.

Honestly Hedda—it stirred great tears of joy as I read how fairly—and how genuinely—you revere Harriet.

I hardly know the young lady in question but this I do know—that it could be a very easy matter to dismiss the subject of the "opposition's daughter"—or to find fault with vengeance! Neither of these things could you be guilty of. That is why this note. Yes, Hedda, more love—like this that you have expressed, is what the world is crying and yearning for. Wars and even the rumors of wars would cease if every man in his turn would regard his brother with such fairness—and in my book you are to be highly congratulated for doing as your heart tells you.

With much affection,

Ginger
March 12, 1948

116 North Gale Drive,
Beverly Hills, California,
April 1, 1948

Dear Ernie,

The above is my new base of operations. It consists of two and one-half rooms plus a copy of the Kinsey report.

I had dinner with Jerry Wald last night. He drove me home and as we sat shooting the excrement in his car in front of my place, Wald boasted to me that he was bringing talented new writers out from New York. He mentioned Norman Rosten (a poet), Jerome Weidman and others. I thought that this would be a great opportunity to get in a preliminary punch on your behalf and told him that you would fit into that setup very nicely. I told him that I would speak to him again about you in a week or so when the Colliers story came out. He seemed favorably disposed and, anyway, I had him hoist on his own verbal petard.

I am going to have lunch with him next week and will keep you informed with a late bulletin. Who knows, you may become a successful Hollywood writer and I may be able to live in a corner of your swimming pool.

I hope to be getting a brand-new convertible this week, plus a wire recorder for recording what goes on in the apartments of some of my neighbors. Meanwhile, I am doing quite well. I have had dinner on the cuff at LaRue's through the kind courtesy of Leo and Warners and Leo also took me to Ciro's and Mocambo. I even had a glimpse of a list of new talent that Leo got from Irving.

Let me hear from you and by that time I should have a collection of grisly stories to relay.

Ezra

Ezra Goodman to Ernest Lehman

APRIL 1, 1948

With a talent for schmoozing and an eye for detail, Ezra Goodman headed to Hollywood in 1948 to break into the movie business. In this letter to his friend Ernest Lehman, a writer and former press agent who wanted to be a screenwriter, Goodman recounts his efforts to get a foothold in Tinseltown by mingling with producers like Jerry Wald and hanging out at hot spots like Ciro's and the Mocambo. Goodman joined the Hollywood press corps as a self-described "publicist, free-lance writer, columnist, correspondent, and critic," but in 1961 he burned most of the bridges he had built by writing a scathing indictment of the movie business, called *The Fifty-Year Decline and Fall of Hollywood*. When it was published, the *Los Angeles Times* said it was "just about the most merciless expose of Movietown's mores and morals ever to appear outside fiction covers." The "Collier's story" that Goodman mentions to Wald is "Hunsecker Against the World," which was the first Lehman story to feature the columnist Harold (later J. J.) Hunsecker, the toxic figure at the center of Lehman's novella *Sweet Smell of Success* (originally published in 1950 under the title "Tell Me About It Tomorrow!")

FINNICH MALISE,
DRYMEN STATION.
STIRLINGSHIRE.

TEL. DRYMEN 288

20th. August 1948.

My dear Hume,

    I spent a week in London and things
seemed to be going very well. On our side
of the picture there are only (D.V.) the
narration and the tag to do. Oddly enough,
my dialogue sounds terribly deliberate in
the mouths of the two American actors and I
have had to do a lot of cutting and gingering
up with their lines. The English actors with
their more theatrical pace come over very
well.

    This has come as rather a surprise to
me and may partly account for the dismal
notices my plays get in New York. I had always
associated the American Theatre and screen
with tremendous speed and slickness, but the
speed is evidently in the writing and production and the actors themselves seem to be
more concerned to point the dialogue and make
it intelligible. Perhaps you could tell me
about this.

    Both Ingrid and Cotten are honies with
very little nonsense about them at all and
they have given me a new regard for American

film stars. Hitch's first seven minute take in England came off at the thirteenth try and was greeted by loud cheers all through the studio. Sidney is off to America tomorrow for a week.

This is rather scrappy news but the last few weeks have been very scrappy and I hope to give you a fuller account later.

The "Black Eye" people have failed to come along with their latest renewal so I take it that the whole thing is off. I wish you would ask Dickie Madden to let you have a look at my "Daphne Laureola". In many ways I think it is the best thing I have done.

Rona says that she would like a parcel, but don't bother yourself if you are busy.

We are off to Edinburgh for the Festival and shall spend two or three weeks at the N.B.Station Hotel there. The house will be shut.

Please give madam my warmest regards.

Ever yours,

OH.

James Bridie to Hume Cronyn

AUGUST 20, 1948

James Bridie, whose real name was Osborne Henry Mavor, was a Scottish doctor and playwright who moved into screenwriting in the 1940s and worked with Alfred Hitchcock on three films produced in England. In this letter to Hume Cronyn, Bridie discusses the shooting of *Under Capricorn*, a period mystery starring Joseph Cotten and Ingrid Bergman, which Cronyn had adapted for the screen. *Under Capricorn* was one of several films that Hitchcock did in the late 1940s with the producer Sidney Bernstein, who is mentioned briefly in Bridie's letter. Not only does Bridie make some interesting observations about the differences between British and American actors, he also provides a first-person account of Hitchcock's use of the long take, a technique that the director had explored even more extensively in his previous film, *Rope*. Cronyn, who had also adapted *Rope*, was an actor and writer who had recently appeared in the Hitchcock films *Lifeboat* and *Shadow of a Doubt*. Cronyn's wife, Jessica Tandy, referred to by Bridie as "madam," later played a key role in Hitchcock's *The Birds*. Bridie's wife's request for a "parcel" from the United States most likely was in response to the strict rationing that was still in place in Great Britain in 1948.

SANTANA PICTURES
1438 NO. GOWER STREET
HOLLYWOOD 28, CALIFORNIA

March 21, 1949

Mr Joseph I. Breen
Motion Picture Association
5504 Hollywood Boulevard
Hollywood 28, California

Dear Joe,

Here is the book that we are going to use as
the basis of a picture for Mr Bogart.   From
your point of view, I realize there are several
things wrong with the story basically.   First
of all, the fact that the protagonist kills a
series of women.   Second, the fact that he
has a glaring, illicit relationship with Laurel,
one of the women.

Both of these objections can and will be taken
care of in our treatment of the novel.   We
intend to have the protagonist kill only one
person within the framework of the story.   He
has killed another person before the story
begins.   He is caught and brought to justice
for his crimes.   As for the relationship between the protagonist and Laurel, I am positive
we can handle this so that it will not violate
either the Code or the canons of good taste.

Anyhow, would you be kind enough to have your
boys read the book, and let me know if there
are any other pitfalls in it which I may have
overlooked?

Thanks, and all best wishes.

Sincerely yours,

Robert Lord

RL:ba
Enclosure

MAR 23 1949

"In A Lonely Place"

Publicity still of
Humphrey Bogart for
In a Lonely Place, 1950.

Robert Lord to Joseph Breen

MARCH 21, 1949

Robert Lord was a Warner Bros. screenwriter and unit producer who joined forces after the war with Humphrey Bogart in Santana Films, an independent production company named for Bogart's yacht. In this letter to the Production Code head Joseph Breen, Lord shows that in postwar Hollywood even producers well-versed in the restrictions of the Code would pursue censorable material that was unlikely to be approved in its raw form. Interestingly, Breen left the door open for this "unacceptable" story, and Lord and his writers were able to reshape *In a Lonely Place*, a novel by Dorothy B. Hughes, into a riveting film noir about a Hollywood screenwriter whose paranoia and violent temper destroy his relationship with the woman he loves. In a subsequent letter to Breen, Lord apologized that the story was so tough, but pointed out that finding film projects for Bogart was no easy task, writing that "I wish Mr. Bogart were Shirley Temple so that we could do tales of sweetness and light with him. But since he is not, we will have to push the steam roller uphill to make pictures of this type with him." *In a Lonely Place* was released in August 1950, the same month as *Sunset Boulevard*, another dark film about the downfall of a cynical screenwriter.

Gloria Swanson to Barron Polan

APRIL 15, 1949

Although legend has it that Mary Pickford, Pola Negri, and Mae West were all considered for the leading role in Billy Wilder's *Sunset Boulevard* before Gloria Swanson was cast, it's hard to imagine another actress embodying Norma Desmond the way Swanson did. In this letter to her friend and publicist Barron Polan, Swanson shows how she collaborated closely with the costume designer Edith Head and the makeup and hairdressing team to bring Norma Desmond to life. Swanson was fifty when she played the role, roughly the same age as the character, so it's interesting that she had to be vigilant to make sure that Wilder and his crew didn't needlessly age her for the camera. Of course, Swanson was not the only silent screen personality

in *Sunset Boulevard*. Wilder also convinced director Cecil B. DeMille and actors Buster Keaton, Anna Q. Nilsson and H. B. Warner to appear as themselves, and cast Erich von Stroheim, who had directed Swanson in the uncompleted *Queen Kelly* in 1928, as Norma's devoted butler Max. This and many other references to Swanson's own life and career that Wilder incorporated into the story, along with Swanson's completely believable performance, led some viewers to think that Swanson was "playing herself" in the film. In reality, Swanson had a fulfilling professional career that included a radio show, pioneering work on television, stage appearances, and business enterprises.

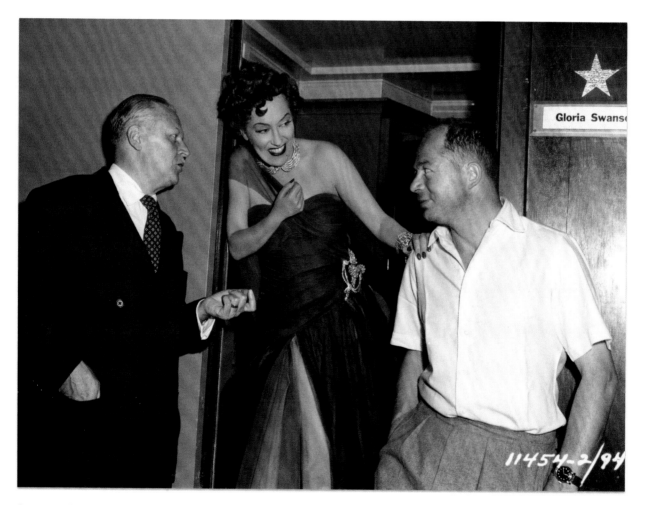

Cowriter and producer Charles Brackett, star Gloria Swanson, and cowriter and director Billy Wilder during production of *Sunset Boulevard* in 1949.

1131 Horn Avenue
West Hollywood
California

April 15, 1949

Mr. Barron Polan
18 Beekman Place
New York 22, N.Y.

Dear Barron:

Hi! Picture officially starts Monday. I tested
all day for clothes today. Have something like
twelve changes. Edith Head and I have gone crazy
creating things out of this world. The part is
fabulous. It has been somewhat changed since
they saw my test and I blinked my pretty blue eyes
at them. But today while testing they crept up
on me and put some gray streaks in my hair, hoping
to make me look a little older that way. The director has had the camera man and make-up man in conference and while they admit they are in my camp
and are not going to make me look a snitch older
than I do, I am still watching them with an eagle
eye. So you see there is always something to contend with. However, it cannot help but do me a
lot of good and I might add, according to the
script so far it is a woman's story. In fact there
is no premise but that it is only a character sketch.

I am most certainly interested in a television show
providing it can be national with the possibility
of allowing it to emanate from here if it should
be necessary. It really should be flexible enough
to be able to come from New York or California.

I have a charming apartment, brand new, overlooking the Gala, Dolores Drive-In and the "Utter"
Mortuary - beyond that, of course, is a twinkling
carpet of lights. I have just (knocking wood) got
over my smog allergy sore throat and cannot wait
to get back to the cinders of New York. They agree
with me much more than smog, smudge and fog.

I did not mean this to be a letter, so will close
with some love to you,

Sherry-Netherland

FIFTH AVENUE AT 59TH STREET · NEW YORK 22, N.Y. · VOLUNTEER 5-2800

May 24, 1949

Dear Mr. Hal,

Please forgive me for not writing sooner
but we've been so busy that we can't see
straight. How are you and Mrs. Wallis
and Brent? I hope this finds you all
well.

I've been speaking with Mr. Hazen con-
stantly -- he's a real wonderful man and
he's been very nice to me.

We sure can't wait to get back home.
Well, only five more weeks and we'll be
there. Do you think you can find some
work for me? After New York I'll do just
about anything to stay in California.

I called Paul Nathan but couldn't reach
him as yet, but I'll probably speak with
him soon and take him out to lunch one
day. (I'll see "21" yet)

There isn't too much more to say except
that the reports on "Irma" are wonderful.
We keep getting phone calls and letters
from people who have seen it either in
Peekskill or at the 72nd Street Theater.
It's a real big thrill.

Well, I guess that's all for now, boss..
Hoping to hear from you real soon and
with warmest personal regards from Dean,
I am

                    Sincerely yours,

P.S. I hope you don't mind my dictating
this letter but, honestly, I'm too tired
to pick up a pen -- I hope you'll understand.

          'Bye   Child Star

opposite

Jerry Lewis to Hal B. Wallis

MAY 24, 1949

When he sent this letter to the producer Hal Wallis, Jerry Lewis and his partner, Dean Martin, were the hottest nightclub act in show business and were also starting to make a name for themselves in radio and television. In 1948, Wallis had signed the pair to a contract with his independent production company, which was headquartered at Paramount, and in February 1949 the team started shooting their first movie, an innocuous comedy called *My Friend Irma*. Martin and Lewis had small roles in the film and in its sequel, *My Friend Irma Goes West*, but within a couple of years they would be among Wallis's most profitable stars. It's interesting that in this letter to Wallis, Lewis writes like one of the shy, naive characters he played on screen, addressing Wallis as "Mr. Hal" and calling himself "Child Star," a frequent sign-off in his early letters to the producer. In reality, Lewis was an ambitious, driven professional, even at this stage in his career, and before long he and Martin would start to clash with an infuriated Wallis over the terms of their movie contract and their many other performing commitments, which included nightclub appearances and a television series. Joseph Hazen, whom Lewis describes as a "real wonderful man," was Wallis's business partner who handled the company's affairs in New York, and Paul Nathan was Wallis's right-hand man in Hollywood. *My Friend Irma* was not released until October 1949, so the reports that Lewis says he is getting from "people who have seen it" must be referring to trailers for the upcoming film.

following spread

Louis Calhern to Leonard & Sylvia Lyons

OCTOBER 30, 1949

In this humorous dispatch from the wilds of Los Angeles, the veteran actor Louis Calhern expertly skewers some of Hollywood's sacred cows for his friends, the columnist Leonard Lyons and his wife, Sylvia. A famous Broadway leading man, Calhern also appeared in dozens of films, usually in supporting roles, and in the late 1940s and 1950s was under contract to MGM, which cast him in a handful of musicals including *Annie Get Your Gun*. Despite his insistence on lampooning his movie acting, and Hollywood in general, Calhern was a versatile performer who earned high praise for his work in films like *The Asphalt Jungle*, *The Magnificent Yankee*, and *Julius Caesar*. The forgettable musical that he made with Carmen Miranda was *Nancy Goes to Rio*, a 1950 MGM release that also starred Jane Powell and Ann Sothern. The Garden of Allah Hotel was an elaborate estate on Sunset Boulevard that had been developed into a hotel in the 1920s by the actress Alla Nazimova. The hotel was a popular hangout for movie stars for more than thirty years. It was demolished in 1959.

Garden of Allah Hotel

Hollywood's Most Distinctive and Unusual Hotel
in a Truly Southern California Resort Environment

8152 SUNSET BOULEVARD · · HOLLYWOOD 46, CALIFORNIA
CABLE ADDRESS — GARDALLAH

Sunday
30th October 49

Dear Sylvia amd Len,
                    This is to acquaint you
with a change of address.
                    We have taken a house and
the ensconcing takes place on th. day after
tomorrow which is November 1st.
                    I have always thought I'd
never take a house out here. Little did I
know that I'd join the ranks of those who
bemoan the ~~dsii~~ dissappearance of the servant
class and are concerned with the bug that
bites the rose and sleep under a California
moon with no ready trunk in the room. We
haven't moved in yet and we've already had
servant trouble. A cook was engaged last Wednesday and closed out of town. She didn't
even open - she quit on Thursday early in
the afternoon and I guess that's the way it's
going to be.
                    I enjoy my work because
I have reached a sensible attitude toward it.
One starts out here wearing a necktie and
refusing to buy sports coats and suede shoes
and otherwise assuming lordly poses toward
the Industry. But the wise man conforms and
learns his place and stays in it. Lordliness
dwindles when you are told to tear your head
from an untimely pillow at 5:30 and scoot
through the clammy dawn to wark and you obey.
You ain't nothing but an employee and happy
is the man who knows it. Of course there are
subtle little ways of preserving selfrespect
and clingimg to individuality. For instance
I always sing flat. When they put me in a musical
and order me to raise my voice in song I sing
flat and I stick to it and that's my satisfaction
and my private revenge and please don't tell
anybody. Why just the other day in the
unforgatteble character of Buffalo Bill in
Wnnie Get Your Gun I rendered There's No
Business Like Show Business alongside of Miss
Betty Hutton and I rendered it flat which you

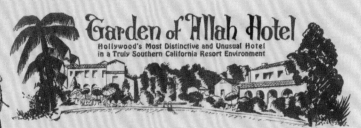

may notice when said rendition graces your
local silver sheet. John Green who is the head
of MGM's music department and all his staff
and a sixtyfive piece band and a man named
Mayer stood over me armed with batons and
other weapons but I was staunch and I sang
flat and you are the only two people
in all the world who know I did it on
purpose as a means of preserving my dignity
as an untrammeled American and to show MGM
that money simply cannot buy everything.

You two may be used to being in
on things but it tickles me to picture you
exchanging knowing glances in a darkened
theatre when I step up and start to yell
There Is No Business etc.

I'm telling my mother too.

Everybody else will believe that
I'm singing flat because I can't help myself.

I have other quiet small blisses
which I keep to myself. Viz. In immortal
cellulloid I played some pretty dam sexy
scenes with Carmen Miranda if I do say so
myself who shouldn't. This picture reached
it's completion on a Thursday and the
following Tuesday the press of the world was
agog with the announcement of the dissolution
of Senora Miranda's marriage. People sidle
up to me and ask if playing those scenes had
anything to do with the crash of Carmen's
matrimonial barge. I simply lower my eyes.
I lower my eyes and I change the subject
by asking what time it is. This gives the
impression that I am late for an assignation
with Carmen Miranda and steps up the talk.
This I haven't even told my little grayhaired
mother --- the stark facts are that Carmen
didn't know I was alive before during ob
after the performance of the sexy scenes and
she never even properly memorized my first
name. Used to call be Juan. Wan?

Like a lot of other even greater
men my joys are private and inner. I share
them with you because I love you.

Lou

PS — The new address is 1012 South Flenroy Ave West Los Angeles 24 California

Clara Bow and Gilbert Roland in the 1920s

Gilbert Roland to Clara Bow

DECEMBER 19, 1949

The handsome Mexican-born actor Gilbert Roland was one of the few Hollywood friends who stayed in touch with Clara Bow, the silent era's wildly popular "It Girl", after she retired from the screen. Roland and Bow first met when the young actor appeared opposite her in the 1925 film *The Plastic Age*. The couple embarked on a romance and soon became engaged, but they were prevented from marrying by her prejudiced father, who objected to both Roland's Catholicism and his Mexican heritage. In the late 1920s, Bow was a superstar at Paramount, where she was dazzling in films like *Dancing Mothers*, *Mantrap*, *It*, *Wings*, and *The Wild Party*. The victim of several tabloid-fueled scandals that damaged her image in the early 1930s,

Bow chose to leave the movie business in 1933. She wed cowboy star Rex Bell in 1931 and they had two sons together, but Bow suffered from mental health issues for much of her life, and when Roland wrote this letter to her she was undergoing treatment at a psychiatric facility in Connecticut. At the time, Roland, who had a solid career as a character actor and occasional leading man, was divorced from his wife Constance Bennett, the mother of his two daughters. Roland later remarried and lived to the age of eighty-eight, appearing frequently in films and on television well into his seventies. Bow, who had become a recluse, died in Los Angeles in 1965.

GILBERT ROLAND

Monday Morning.
December, 19th.

Hello Clarita Girl-
How happy I was to hear from you. I wrote
you and Rex from Tucson Arizona. We were filming
'The Furies' there with Barbara Stanwyck.
I might do 'The Crisis' at Metro next month
with Cary Grant if terms can be arranged.
You tell me., you long for your boys and for
California. I share your feelings.
My daughters are with their mother in Wiebaden,
Germany. And there is nothing I can do, except
cry a little once in a while.
They are showing some of your pictures around
in the silent theaters. I hope someday they
show Plastic Age. Whow!
It would be wonderful to see that dancing
scene, you and I, and I get into a fight with
Donald Keith, and knock him out, and the police
are breaking the doors of the 'Speak-easy' and
I rescue Don from the claws of the law. It would
be pleasant seeing how I looked when I was your
beau, and you were my dream girl. It would be
pleasant seeing that. And then it might be
very beautiful, and suddenly it might be very
sad.
" Turn backward, turn backward o time in thy
flight..."
I hope the treatments there alliviate your
illness, and that you can be with your boys
and Rex soon and that you are happy. I will
go to church and pray for that.
How is your Dad? I would like to see him.
I always had a warm spot in my heart for him,
even though many years ago he refused to let me
marry you because I was making seventy-five
dollars a week, and you three hundred--and when I
made three hundred, you made a Thousand, and when
I made a thousand you made more. ad infinitum,
and so it goes, and that's the way it is, and give
Rex my best, and your boys.
I am going to Texas to see my old school-
teacher. she is old and lonely.   G.R.

Errol Flynn to Lewis Milestone

JANUARY 24, 1950

In 1950, the great Warner Bros. swashbuckler and self-made rogue Errol Flynn was heading into the final decade of his life, and though he was still under contract to the studio, he didn't seem to be interested in spending much time in Hollywood. In this letter to the acclaimed director Lewis "Milly" Milestone, who had directed him in the 1943 wartime drama *Edge of Darkness*, Flynn offers what must have been welcome support to a fellow outsider. A committed liberal, Milestone had been working under a cloud since he was subpoenaed by the House Un-American Activities Committee in 1947, and though he had not yet been called to testify, the director was already planning a move to Europe, where he would live and work for five years. Like many actors during this period, Flynn was beginning to get interested in setting up his own production deals. He did make a film in France in 1951 with William Marshall, titled *Adventures of Captain Fabian*, but Flynn never did collaborate again with Milestone. Many years later, in an interview published in the book *The Celluloid Muse*, Milestone said, "Maybe not enough people knew Flynn well. I not only admired him as an actor, I liked him very much as a person. I knew him as a perfect host, a marvelous connoisseur of good food and wine, and as a beautifully behaved guest in my home. His faults harmed no one except himself." The brief reply to Flynn's letter scribbled at the top of the first page by Milestone was probably meant to be transcribed into a letter or telegram by the director's secretary.

Dear Errol,
I too am returning to Hollywood for one picture with Twentieth. ~~Will see you~~ I'm flying Sunday will see you there. Milly.

Jan. 24th

Dear Milly,

Many thanks for yours, and of course I must have missed the fucking script by no more than an hour, as I got your letter just as I got out of town in a hot hurry, an angry mother hard at heel. As usual, I was entirely innocent of ill-doing.

Will be back in Paris the 31st to leave for the U.S. the 2nd. Address 1 Bis RUE VANEAU, PARIS 7. Phone: Invalides 4770. Leaving here tomorrow for Kitzbuhel, Austria, staying Grand Hotel for several days.

I need hardly tell you I'm more than delighted at any prospect of an interesting story I could do with you. I'm going to do a Niven Busch yarn in France when I finish MGM's Kim and am quite frankly fed up with working in Hollywood and always being harassed by tax gatherers, ex-wives or mistresses-to-be. So I've put together a partnership deal with Bill Marshall for one picture only, the Busch story.

Let us therefore "get together", as the quaint saying goes, and see if we can't contrive some original device to fuck those who fuck us—d'accord?

Yrs
Errol.

DEAR Errol

I too am returning to Hollywood for one picture with twentieth — ~~will see you~~ I'm flying Sunday will see you there.

Jan 24th. Mitty.

Dear Milly

Many thanks for yours, and of course I must have missed the fucking script by just not more than an hour, as I got your letter just as I got out of town in a hot hurry, an angry mother hard at heel. As usual, I was entirely innocent of ill-doing.

Will be back in Paris the 31.st to leave for the U.S. the 2nd/ Address 1 Bis RUE VANEAU, PARIS 7. Phone: Invalides 4770. Leaving here tomorrow for Kitzbuhel, Austria, staying Grand Hotel for several days.

I need hardly tell you I'm more than delighted at any prospect of an

interesting story I could do with you.
Am going to do a Niven Busch yarn in France, when
I finish MGM's KIM. and am quite
frankly fed up with working in Hollywood
and allways being harassed by tax
gatherers, ex-wives or mistresses-to-be.
So I've put together a partneship deal with
Bill marshall. for one picture only, the Busch
story.

Let us therefore 'get-together', as the
quaint saying goes, and see if we cant
contrive some original device to fuck
those who fuck us — d'accord?

Yrs &

(ERROL FLYNN)

THE ACTORS' STUDIO, Inc.
1697 BROADWAY
NEW YORK 19, N. Y.

PLaza 7-4785

Dear Fred
    this is just a
note say I hope its all
going along well and
I wish I was with you
because my plans about
streetcar are very much up in
the air because they can't get
it past the Breen office and
Gadget (Kazan) won't do it

Marlon Brando to Fred Zinnemann

SPRING 1950

When he wrote this letter to Fred Zinnemann in the spring of 1950, the still relatively unknown Marlon Brando had recently finished making his first film. *The Men*, written by Carl Foreman and directed by Zinnemann, was a docudrama about a paraplegic adjusting to life after World War II that used both actors and real wounded veterans. Trained at the Actors Studio to immerse himself in his roles, Brando spent a month living at a veterans hospital and using a wheelchair to prepare for the part, and his hard work was rewarded with glowing reviews when the film was released in August of that year. Meanwhile, Brando was preparing to start on his second movie, the film adaptation of *A Streetcar Named Desire*, in which he had triumphed on Broadway. Producer Charles K. Feldman had secured the rights in September 1949, but Brando's *Streetcar* director, Elia Kazan, was digging in his heels with the Production Code in order to bring Tennessee Williams's play to the screen with as few changes as possible. Shooting finally got underway in the summer of 1950 but the film was not released until late 1951.

unless if they demand re-
vision. They have been fucking
around with it for about
three months now and I'm
getting kind of sick of it.

Oh well! The spring
has come and I'm astounded
how every year I'm so pleasantly suprised. The country is
sprinkled completely over with
spring flowers. I'm going to the
country this week to camp
for a couple days and I
thought of you hence this note

Dear Fred

This is just a note say [sic] I hope it's all going along well and I wish I was with you because my plans about Streetcar are very much up in the air because they can't get it past the Breen office and Gadget (Kazan) won't do it unless if they demand revisions. They have been fucking around with it for about three months now and I'm getting kind of sick of it.

Oh well! The spring has come and I'm astounded how every year I'm so pleasantly surprised. The country is sprinkled completely over with spring flowers. I'm going to the country this week to camp for a couple days and I thought of you hence this note.

There is a slight chance I can get over there so if it works out please let me know when you'll be where. Never mind I guess I can find out easily enough through your office.

Don't feel you must answer this note cause I know you'll be rushed for time.

Hope to be seeing you soon, Fred.

As ever
Marlon

Twentieth Century-Fox Film Corporation

STUDIOS
BEVERLY HILLS, CALIFORNIA

INTER-OFFICE CORRESPONDENCE ONLY   DATE _____ May 5 _____ 19 50

TO ___ DARRYL F. ZANUCK ___   FROM ___ JOSEPH L. MANKIEWICZ ___

SUBJECT ___ ALL ABOUT EVE ___

<u>PERSONAL</u>

Dear Darryl:

Just a few words about Time.

To begin with, you must know that I am most aware of the dire necessity, these days, for shooting a film in the shortest time possible. I appreciate, further, the circumstances that require you to be, if anything, particularly demanding time-wise on a film which you are personally producing.

I know also that I have never worked as hard before. And I write you this note because in addition to the exhaustion I feel, I find myself deeply depressed by my inability to make much better time than I am making at present.

In all honesty, I think you have been misinformed as to the "liberality" of our schedule. Forty days for a script of 180 pages, involving three female stars - two of whom are chores to photograph - and involving seven or eight major performances which are made up of painstaking bits of business, inflections and details.

The San Francisco location was under-scheduled by more than the two days we lost up there. The weird economy that sent us up there with three - and later one more - electricians for a set which would require at least fifteen down here, is one of those bits of production planning I will never understand. The stage electricians we used up there didn't know a lamp from a jock strap.

The sequence in Margo's dressing room which you liked so much ran 21 pages. It started with 4 characters, then went to 5 and then to 6 characters in a tiny room. To have staged it in a static manner would have destroyed it. Walls had to come in and out every time an angle was changed. These 21 pages were scheduled for 4 days! We did them in 5. Without the half day of rehearsal upon our return from San Francisco, it would have taken 6.

I am now involved in the party sequence - 28 pages involving every character in the script, extras, atmosphere - and extremely delicate characterizations throughout. These 28 pages have been scheduled for 6 days. I don't think I've got a chance of doing it in that time. Krasner is doing a superb job, not only in terms of quality but in concentrated work. I have never changed a setup - and he knows my setups well in advance. The cast is behaving admirably, on the whole.

The next sequence I shoot is the entire Sarah Siddons banquet. This is 16¼ pages. It is scheduled for 3 days! At Western Avenue.

Darryl, more than anything in the world I wish I could tell you the magic formula by which I can make up our lost time and finish this film in 40 days. I am sure that when I get into the more intimate scenes, I will pick up some of it. But not all.

I am doing the very best I can, and I am extremely unhappy about my inability to do any better. I wish I were calloused enough, and "big shot" enough, not to let it bother me. But it does. And I think it's only fair that I let you know it's got me down.

J.L.M.

Joseph L. Mankiewicz to Darryl F. Zanuck

MAY 5, 1950

Written more like a letter than a typical studio memo, this plea from Joseph L. Mankiewicz, the writer-director of *All About Eve*, to Twentieth Century-Fox production head Darryl Zanuck captures the challenges of making films within the strict budget and scheduling parameters of the Hollywood studio system. Mankiewicz had started to fall behind during the first few weeks of location shooting in San Francisco and was repeatedly called on the carpet by Zanuck, who did not seem to have much sympathy for the complications of working with talented but demanding actors and a complex, dialogue-driven script. By the time this memo was written, the company was back in Los Angeles shooting on the Fox lot, but clearly Mankiewicz was still feeling the pressure to stay on schedule. With

his proven track record, which included Oscars for writing and directing the previous year's *A Letter to Three Wives*, Mankiewicz might have thought he would get some leeway from the studio head, but Zanuck continued to demand that Mankiewicz and his crew pick up the pace. In the end, Mankiewicz did go a few days over schedule, but nevertheless he and film editor Barbara McLean delivered the completed film on time. In stark contrast to today's lengthy postproduction periods, *All About Eve* finished shooting in early June and premiered just four months later, in October 1950. At the Academy Awards the following March, Mankiewicz once again won Oscars for writing and directing, and *All About Eve* was also named best picture, an award that Darryl Zanuck was more than happy to claim.

Preston Sturges to Y. Frank Freeman

JULY 14, 1950

One of the wittiest screenwriters in Hollywood, Preston Sturges realized after years in the movie business that he wanted to direct his own material. In 1939, when Paramount gave him the green light to make *The Great McGinty*, he became one of the first, and most accomplished, writer-directors of the sound era. After his success with *McGinty*, Sturges embarked on a dazzling run of sophisticated hit comedies for Paramount, including *The Lady Eve*, *Sullivan's Travels*, *The Palm Beach Story*, and *The Miracle of Morgan's Creek*. In this eloquent and painfully honest letter to studio head Y. Frank Freeman, Sturges outlines the accomplishments and missteps of his time at Paramount and analyzes the events that led to his catastrophic break with the company in 1944 during production of *Hail the Conquering Hero*. Even years later,

it's clear that Sturges is still upset about the events that took place, including his showdown with executive producer Buddy DeSylva over the actress Ella Raines, whom the studio wanted to fire and Sturges insisted be kept on the film. Though Sturges had quickly landed on his feet and found some success as an independent producer, he clearly yearned to be back at Paramount, and this plea, six years later, seems genuine. Freeman, an unimaginative but genial Southerner who came from the exhibition side of the business and loved drinking Coca-Cola, claimed to appreciate Sturges's offer but turned him down. Sturges, who until the early 1950s also owned a Sunset Boulevard restaurant called The Players, continued to write but directed only one more film after 1950. He died in 1959 at the age of sixty.

July 14, 1950

My dear Frank:

Thank you very much for your letter and for saying
in it that you had always liked me. I have always liked you too,
as you know, and been everlastingly grateful for the opportunity
you gave me to try my wings at directing. As I remember it, we
pulled pretty well together; you were always available to answer
a question or set me straight on something, and I, on my part,
did my damnedest to knock out some good films as far as I could
for the company which had given me my start and had stood so loyal-
ly behind me in two of my illnesses. You will remember that I was
never interested in time off between pictures, that I was always
available to help with somebody else's script or picture, that I
read and recommended stories for the company to buy, that I tried
to develop new directors for you, such as Billy Wilder, to bring
you some famous ones, such as Rene Clair, to encourage young writers,
such as Robert Pirosh, to make you some new stars, such as Betty
Hutton, Diana Lynn, Veronica Lake, Eddie Bracken, Brian Donlevy,
Charles Coburn, and to revive some old ones such as Barbara Stanwyck,
Henry Fonda, Joel McCrea, Rudy Vallee and Betty Field. You will
further remember that I was extremely happy with twenty-five hundred
dollars a week and no contract except thirty days notice either way.
I told you I would probably stay forever on those terms and I very
probably would have.

The only reason for writing all the above is that you,
with whom I worked so closely, apparently also subscribe to a theory
that I am hard to get along with, and if you believe it there must
be something to it and I had better make haste to correct the matter
before I am completely prevented from practising my profession. A
dentist of whom everybody says "he hurts" might as well leave town.

So I have searched my memory and my inward heart and
there is no question but that I have given my friends and associates
some bad moments. That a few fools, crooks, drunkards and opportun-
ists were injured bothers me not. I was trying to make good pictures,
not win a popularity contest, but that men that I loved and respected were also hurt, I regret bitterly. The awful day about Ella Raines
will be with me always. It seems very unimportant now whether she
was kept in or thrown out. It seemed very important then. I had
read Cervantes. I should have known about tilling at windmills.
The dreadful hours with Buddy once the break, urged by his sycophants,

had occurred. The reasonable and depressing talks we had later,
both fond of each other, when it was too late to mend the break.
My leaving Paramount, which was my home, and settling as near its
gates as possible...the faces on the men...the goodbyes in the
commissary...the piano you sent me...all these things come back to
me...far from cheerfully. That I have broken some records for
earning power since my departure means nothing to me. Just plain
money never did. I did not care for the places I worked nor the
people I was working with. I grew up at Paramount and I was happy
there.

Now as to the degree of acquiescence and docility
the employee of a large corporation should have: It seems to me
that that depends a little on the nature of his job. Obviously
strict obedience is in most cases essential, but when a department
head like Harold Hurley told his directors to remember they were
making "B" pictures and under no circumstances to try to improve
them as they were sold by the mile and would not bring in an extra
dollar at the box office if they were twice as good, I believe the
directors who disobeyed him were entirely right and twice as intelligent as he was. I think that when my first producer at Paramount,
Mr. Maurice Revnes, told me 1936 was not the time for comedies and
wished to abandon the whole project, I was justified in taking the
script directly to Mitchell Leisen, which resulted in the picture
"Easy Living" and my staying on at Paramount. I believe that when
Arthur Hornblow decided to postpone the shooting of "Never Say Die"
with Jack Benny that I was right in trying to get him to reconsider,
warning him that we would lose Benny and a valuable star, which he
would have been, I sincerely believe, after that picture as it was
then written. Mistakes? I've made plenty of them. What I'm trying to say is that by the very nature of his art, which depends on
invention and inovation, a story teller must depart from the beaten
track and, having done so, occasionally startle and disagree with
some of his associates. Healthy disagreement we must have, it is
its aftermath which is sometimes dangerous and there, beyond question,
is where I erred.

If you believe that I have enough intelligence not to
fall in the same hole twice, enough awareness to realize the necessity for economy in these perilous times, enough ingenuity to have
found a method to combat high costs if I say I have, and enough
honor to be believed when I say that I will abide cheerfully and to
the letter by your decision in whatever difference of opinion might

arise, I would like to come back to work for you...the terms can
be easily arranged...because I am busting with ideas. I would
also like to have an occasional coca-cola with you as I used to.

                         Affectionately yours,

                         Preston Sturges

Frankank Freeman, Esquire
Paramount Pictures Inc.
5451 Marathon Street
Hollywood 38, California

PS/cw

Kirk Douglas to William Wyler

MARCH 28, 1951

In *Detective Story*, Kirk Douglas plays an uncompromising New York City cop who turns on his own wife when he learns she once underwent an illegal abortion. Based on a play by Sidney Kingsley, the film depicts one day and night at a tough New York City police precinct. The intense ensemble drama offered Douglas and his costars, including William Bendix and Eleanor Parker, the opportunity to work with filmmaker William Wyler, who was known for his perfectionism and the demands he put on his actors. In this letter to the director, Douglas provides some fascinating insights into Wyler's personality, as well as his directing style and the loyalty he earned from those who worked with him. Though Douglas did not receive an Academy Award nomination for *Detective Story*, two of his costars, Parker and Lee Grant, were honored, joining a long list of actors who were recognized for their work in Wyler films. Despite Douglas's enthusiasm for another chance to be directed by Wyler, this was the only film the two made together.

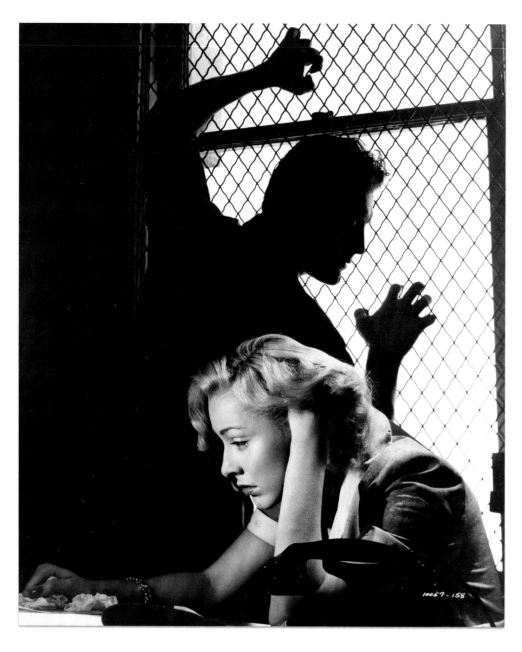

Kirk Douglas and Eleanor Parker in a publicity still for *Detective Story*, 1951.

8619 Vado Place
Los Angeles 46, California
March 28, 1951

Dear Willie:

You may not remember me. I'm the guy that worked
for you on a picture about detectives called, I
think, DETECTIVE STORY. It's been so long ago
that it may have been called something else.
Anyhow, I'm on my way to Florida tonight, and I
wanted to tell you before I leave how wonderful
it was working with you.

I didn't think so at the beginning. For the first
few days, you had me completely baffled. You
seemed to be wrapped in an impenetrable shell, and
I'm a guy who need a very personal contact. But
once, when you didn't know it, you had your guard
down, and I saw under it a very warm human person
with the sense of humor of a kid who likes to throw
bags of water from a second story window on the
unsuspecting pedestrian below. This won me over
completely, and for this I forgive all the whip-
lashes across the back that you gave me during
the course of the picture. As soon as the bruises
on my back have healed, I'll be ready to do it
again.

Thanks for a wonderful experience, and may all
your slalom be perfect ones. And, if your must
fall, don't fall on y ur head. We may both need
it again.

            Your devoted slave,

John Huston and Katharine Hepburn during production of *The African Queen* in 1951.

John Huston to Katharine Hepburn

APRIL 1, 1951

In this letter from the writer-director John Huston to Katharine Hepburn, the star of his next film *The African Queen*, the unlikely duo seems to already be on their way to a comfortable working relationship. Huston had trained as an artist, and this letter about the costumes for the film shows his tendency to convey his ideas using both words and images—and it also reveals that he was still working on the script just a few weeks before principal photography was set to begin in May. Connie De Pinna, the costume consultant Huston suggests to Hepburn, was an artist and fashion designer, and part of the family that owned the famed De Pinna department store in New York. Her meeting with Hepburn must have gone well, because she is credited on the film for "other costumes by," though Doris Langley Moore is also listed as a designer of costumes for Miss Hepburn. Famously, much of *The African Queen* was shot in Technicolor on remote river locations in the Belgian Congo and Uganda. The difficulties of the location shooting, which included everything from dysentery, extreme heat, and soldier ants to the accidental sinking of the main boat set, were later chronicled by Hepburn in her book *The Making of the African Queen: Or How I Went to Africa with Bogart, Bacall and Huston and Almost Lost My Mind*, published in 1988.

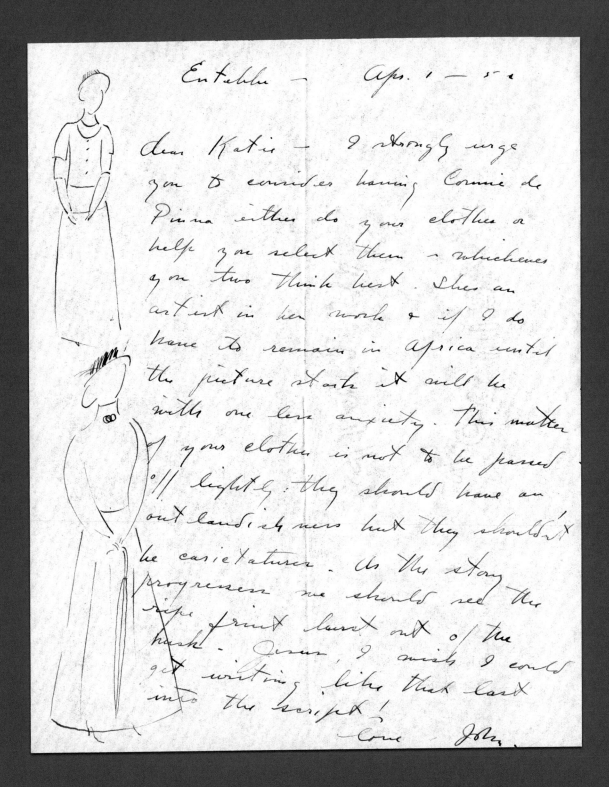

Entebbe—Apr. 1—51

Dear Katie—I strongly urge you to consider having Connie de Pinna either do your clothes or help you select them—whichever you two think best. She's an artist in her work & if I do have to remain in Africa until the picture starts it will be with one less anxiety. This matter of your clothes is not to be passed off lightly: they should have an outlandishness but they shouldn't be caricatures. As the story progresses we should see the ripe fruit burst out of the husk. Jesus, I wish I could get writing like that last into the script!

Love,
John

OFFICE OF
CHARLES BRACKETT

April 5, 1951

Dearest Gloria:

When I came out of Romanoff's about three o'clock
in the morning after the Academy Awards, a shabby
old fellow shuffled up to me and quoted, "We was
robbed." You know how dearly I was hoping that
Ralph Bunche would pull your name out of that envelope, but I also hope you know how unimportant I
think that final tinsel on the big Christmas tree of
your achievement. In the hearts of everybody, you'd
gotten it the year before, when you'd have walked
away with it had the picture had a 1949 release.
Never forget that a great many of our members had
seen SUNSET not in early 1950, but in late '49. All
sense of timeliness was gone.

Also remember, and I think it's important, that the
vote this year proved our members realize the superlative value of two or three years of rehearsal,
rehearsals in parts written out to the utmost comma.
When I reconsider the problem, I can only remember
you that first day, saying, "But I've got to know more
about her -- is she really nuts? Is her arrogance
genuine, or is she faking it? What's the line of the
part?" To this you got no answer, as we too were
feeling our way, and only reached our final conclusion
through you. Nobody can expect audiences to "make
allowances" for that kind of thing, but I find it
healthy for my soul to set it down clearly. And to
add that, despite the fogs of our uncertainty, you
were magnificent and "the greatest star of them all."

As President of the Academy, I can't be heard carping
about the choice of our members, so this has to remain
a confidential communication between us.

Devotedly,

Charlie

Charles Brackett to Gloria Swanson

APRIL 5, 1951

Charles Brackett, the cowriter and producer of *Sunset Boulevard*, was also the president of the Academy of Motion Picture Arts and Sciences in 1951, so he had a front-row seat to one of the most competitive races in the Academy's history. Along with a number of other nominees, *Sunset Boulevard*'s star Gloria Swanson was listening to the show at a special radio broadcast in New York, where she was appearing in a play. The surprise best-actress winner, Judy Holliday, was also at the New York event, as was the recipient of the best-actor statuette, José Ferrer. Brackett's comment that the voters rewarded "the superlative value of two or three years of rehearsal" refers to the fact that Holliday's winning role in *Born Yesterday* was one that she

had originated on the Broadway stage. In her autobiography, Swanson claimed that she was not expecting to win and so was not devastated by the loss. But it must have been good to know how disappointed Brackett was on her behalf and to read his kind words about her astounding performance. Ralph Bunche, the unusual presenter of the best-actress award that year, was a political scientist and diplomat who had won the 1950 Nobel Peace Prize.

(From left) Judy Holliday, José Ferrer, Gloria Swanson, George Cukor, and Celeste Holm celebrating after hearing that Ferrer had just won an Academy Award, 1951.

George Cukor to Garson Kanin

OCTOBER 2, 1951

George Cukor captures the Cold War zeitgeist in this amusing letter written in the style of a coded spy communique. Though it was done in jest, perhaps Cukor was reacting to the fact that the House Un-American Activities Committee had just completed a round of hearings in Hollywood, and the town was on edge. The letter is to Garson Kanin, the writer-director who with his wife and writing partner Ruth Gordon had penned the script for Cukor's latest film, *The Marrying Kind*, which starred Judy Holliday and Aldo Ray. Cukor and the Kanins were frequent collaborators, along with Katharine Hepburn and Spencer Tracy, also referenced here in "code" (along with the agent Abe Lastfogel). The friends had all worked together on *Adam's Rib*, and their next film together, also mentioned here, would be *Pat and Mike*. "Old Lady 31" refers to a play from the 1910s in which an elderly man is given that nickname because he goes to live with his wife (played by Emma Dunn) at a poorhouse for women. Bert Granet, who had the unenviable job of dealing with studio head Harry Cohn, was the producer of *The Marrying Kind*.

COLUMBIA PICTURES CORPORATION
1438 NO. GOWER STREET
HOLLYWOOD 28, CALIFORNIA
HUDSON 2-3111

October 2, 1951

TOP SECRET

To Operator 27 from Old Lady 31 (not Emma Dunn)*

The script of "P-- and M---" arrived late Sunday night. I was awful tempted -- but seein' as I was going to start shooting on "The M------- K---" early the next morning, I had the strenth of character to put it aside. The first moment that I'll be able to read it from cover to cover, and with concentration, I'll fall to. It usually takes me about two or three days to get over the new picture jitters. *I'm dying of curiosity —*

Operator Ab- -----fogel has reported that S----- T--cy and K--- -----rn are both mighty enthusiastic. So far so good.

Our first day's shooting here was a little rugged. The boy was scared, and it was pretty trying for Judy, who is behaving like an angel. This is being dictated to you at 10:43 Tuesday, and we've already shot a scene. He's much more relaxed and should be himself in a day or so. I'm very, very hopeful.

Bert Granet will see that the script changes reach you (including the Van Upp and Manheimer revisions). We won't bother to send you the rewrites we do on the set. We're just pepping it up, putting some jokes in here and there.

Bert will also try to get the stills from Harry Cohn. Generals Bradley and Ridgway have an easy job of negotiating with the Kwomintang, compared to this.

I'll call you as soon as I have read the script.

My love to you both.

George Le Guerre

* If you don't get this, contact Miss R. G. who was around in those days.

ALAN LADD

Dec 28 - 51

Dear George —

Thank you, thank you, thank you for the wonderful "Shane" pictures.

I can never tell you how thrilled I was to get them, because they fit perfectly in a certain spot in my drawing room here in town — a spot that we have been trying to fill with just the right thing ever since we completed the house.

Also, at this time, George — I would like to repeat again how honored I was being in your so capable hands during the making of "Shane". As long as I have been in the business, you taught me more in those few weeks than I would have learned in many years to come

Alan Ladd to George Stevens

DECEMBER 28, 1951

Known for playing tough-guy detectives in film noirs like *This Gun for Hire* and *The Glass Key*, Alan Ladd was cast against type in George Stevens's elegiac Western *Shane*, released in 1953. As a solitary gunman who decides to help a farming community stand up to a cattle baron and his sadistic enforcer, played by a menacing Jack Palance, Ladd created one of the most indelible Western heroes of the 1950s. In this letter of thanks to Stevens, Ladd echoes what many actors expressed about the taciturn director and his uncanny ability to elicit nuanced performances from his stars. Stevens was also known for his attention to detail, and he certainly brought that to the forefront in *Shane* as well. Photographed in Technicolor, most of the film was shot on location in Jackson, Wyoming, and Stevens worked closely with his production team to make the costumes, props, and settings as realistic as possible.

ALAN LADD

I can only say, that you are and always will be "The Top" in my book, and only hope that we can be together in the near future —

Do hope you enjoyed the Holidays and that the wear and tear was not too exacting.

Thanks again, George, and give our love to the family —

My best always,

"Shane"

P.S. Will call you after the first of the year —

A.

Dec 28-51

Dear George—

Thank you, thank you, thank you for the wonderful "Shane" pictures.

I can never tell you how thrilled I was to get them, because they fit perfectly in a certain spot in my dressing room here in town—a spot that we have been trying to fill with just the right thing ever since we completed the house.

Also, at this time, George—I would like to repeat again how honored I was being in your so capable hands during the making of "Shane." As long as I have been in the business, you taught me more in those few weeks than I would have learned in many years to come.

I can only say, that you are and always will be "The Top" in my book, and only hope that we can be together in the near future.

Do hope you enjoyed the Holidays and the wear and tear was not too exacting.

Thanks again, George, and give our love to the family —

My best always,
"Shane"

P.S. Will call you after the first of the year—A.

Hi, Freddie:

.Long time no write, but you know me, kiddo.

Well, I've had a wonderful time here, and I can't tell you
how glad I am I came. Never had more fun, or met nicer people. And the
air of all kinds is so fresh here, too.

Actually, I spent most of my time in and around London, altho I did make five brief trips to Paris and environs, and spent about a
week in Germany, where the bomb damage was magnificent. But all in all,
shortages or no shortages, weather or no weather, I like London the best.
In many ways it's the last bit of civilization left in this sad old world.
Everyone here has been extremely nice to me, ad it's been like a tonic.
Needless to say, I don't miss Hollywood at all.

But what I really wanted to write you about was to tell you
how happy I am "High Noon" has been received in the way it has, and how
wonderfully you have come off in all the reviews I have read. Not that
you don't deserve all the encomiums, because you do. But you of all
people know the conditions under which we made the picture from start to
finish, and surely we are both entitled to feel that its apparent success is a joint and individual justifixxtixx vindication. I have seen all
the New York reviews, as well as Time and the Saturday Review, and altho
frankly and honestly I feel that they have all gone xxxxd overboard considerably, they're very nice to read. I still think we had a chance for
a great picture, and that we came off with a near miss again, but by God
I don't know of any made under more difficult circumstances. You were
great throughout all of it, Freddie; you showed tremendous courage and
gallantry as well as skill, and I'm delighted it's turned out this way.
Or do I have to tell you? The picture did very well here, critically as
well as in a business way, and you certainly haven't harmed your prestige
here with it in any way. Naturally, I'm also delighted that Dmitri has
come off as well as he has. And I can't help wondering how Stanley and
George are reacting to the triumph of the poor little orphan they dis-
liked so much, the baby that Stanley - unconcsiously I'm sure - tried to
dismember in the cutting room. But I shouldn't be bitchey. I should be,
and am, very grateful it's turned out this way.

Please let me hear from you. I'M anxious to know how you
feel about "Member of the Wedding," and all about your state of mind and
health and future plans. I've had a number of discussions with Tony
Havelock-Allan (whom I like very much) about you, and I'm sure you could
do just about anything you wanted to over here. But about business, more
later.

About myself, I can't tell you anything definite just yet, but I may be able to in my next letter. Suffice it to say, it seems as if I can write my own ticket here if I want to. However, I want to see how Kate and Estelle get along here before making any committments. But I like it!

One of the reasons I didn't write sooner was that I really wanted to be ignati keep my trip as quiet as possible. I know it's no secret, but I want to keep out of the press, and the trade press particularly, as much as possible. It's better for me that way. So be a good boy and please keep it in mind. The less said about my presence here, the better.

Take care.

Love ---

Care

<- First fold here ->

Fred Zinneman, Esq.

1766 Westridge Road,

Los Angeles 49, California.

U.S.A.

following spread

Philip Dunne to Alexander Knox

SEPTEMBER 19, 1952

Philip Dunne, a highly respected liberal screenwriter at Twentieth Century-Fox, offers advice on navigating the treacherous political landscape in 1950s Hollywood to Canadian actor Alexander Knox. Eight years after starring in *Wilson*, Darryl Zanuck's epic biopic of President Woodrow Wilson written by Dunne, Knox found himself targeted by right-wing groups like the American Legion because of his support of liberal causes and opposition to the House Un-American Activities Committee. There were many like Knox and Dunne who were never subpoenaed by HUAC but who nevertheless had to submit to clearance procedures in order to avoid being blacklisted. Dunne's

trust in the virulently anticommunist Roy Brewer to help with that process is surprising, but given the dire situation it was probably wise of him to cultivate that connection in order to save the careers of a few of his friends. Knox did take Dunne's advice and attempt to clear his name, but his efforts were less than successful, and he ended up moving to England and continuing his acting career in the British film industry. Dunne continued to be a strong liberal voice but chose to work within the system. He was the screenwriter for a number of big studio productions in the 1950s, including *The Robe*, *Demetrius and the Gladiators*, and *Ten North Frederick*, which he also directed.

Thursday, Sept. 19, 1952

Dear Alex:

This is in haste to answer your letter and to suggest a course of procedure. I was heartsick to hear that you had found yourself on the index purgatorius. I had heard nothing about it and certainly there has been little if any talk about it in town.

From my own personal experience, let me tell you what has happened here. The Legion, along with other similar groups, sent the studio heads a list of about three hundred people, which has not been published, whom they consider questionable, i.e. too liberal. Those on the list employed by major studios were then requested by the studios to explain their past activities, "if they cared to." In my case, I had an extremely friendly call from Skouras explaining their dilemma: the threat that my pictures would be picketed, etc. Lamar Trotti was another at Fox, and perhaps it hastened his death.

I needn't tell you how degrading I found the whole procedure nor what I went through in making my decision. The upshot was that I finally decided to make the required explanation, and I did it without crawfishing or apologizing. In fact, I took the opportunity of expressing my own point of view as vigorously and eloquently as possible, in the hope that my letter might have some missionary effect.

Free-lance people, such as yourself, did not receive this opportunity, and as a result many have found themselves on a "gray" list, not exactly accused of being Reds, but somehow unable to get work.

Now there are three ways you can fight it. One is the out-and-out libel suit approach. Most lawyers agree that legally the position is very strong. Practically, given the present American climate, the position is not so good. You might be able to collect damages, but you would remain on the gray list. The second way is to write a letter to the board of the SAG, asking for their advice and help. They, I am sure, would then request you to write an explanatory letter and you would eventually be "cleared."

The third way is to let me first do some exploratory work for you. I am working had on the Stevenson campaign with a group of people, one of whom is Roy Brewer. He seems to be honestly anxious that no sheep should be slaughtered with the goats. Since it is no longer possible in this town to make any headway whatsoever in fighting the blacklist on straight moral grounds, I myself have been forced into the position of saving good men from ruin by calling his attention to their cases. In every such case, he has come through for me. If you would like me to explore the situation delicately with Brewer, cable me "yes" at Centfox, Losangeles. If you prefer some other approach, cable me "no." I have a hunch that I can do you some good, but I warn you that a letter from you may be required.

Much love to all.
Ph.

As you may gather from the above the motto for 1952 is not "Death before Dishonor" but "Sauve qui Peut."

Thursday, Sept. 19, 1952

Dear Alex:

This is in haste to answer your letter and to suggest a course of procedure. I was heartsick to hear that you had found yourself on the index purgatorius. I had heard nothing about it and certainly there has been little of any talk about it in town.

From my own personal experience, let me tell you what has happened here. The Legion, along with other similar groups, sent the studio heads a list of about three hundred people — which has not been published — whom they consider questionable, i.e., too liberal. Those on the list employed by major studios were then requested by the studios to explain their past activities "if they cared to." In my case, I had an extremely friendly call from Skouras explaining their dilemma: the threat that my pictures would be picketed, etc. Lamar Trotti was another at Fox, and perhaps it hastened his death.

I needn't tell you how degrading I found the whole procedure nor what I went through in making my decision. The upshot was that I finally decided to make the required explanation, and I did it without crawfishing or apologizing. In fact, I took the opportunity of expressing my own point of view as vigorously and eloquently as possible, in the hope that my letter might have some missionary effect.

Free-lance people, such as yourself, did not receive this opportunity, and as a result many have found themselves on a "gray" list — not exactly accused of being Reds, but somehow unable to get work.

Now there are three ways you can fight it. One is the out-and-out libel suit approach. Most lawyers agree that _legally_ the position is very strong. Politically, given the present American climate, the position is not so good. You might be able to collect damages, but you would remain on the gray list. The second way is to write a letter to the board of the SAG, asking for their advice and help. They, I am sure, would then request you to write an explanatory letter and you would eventually be "cleared".

The third way is to let me first do some exploratory work for you. I am working hard on the Stevenson campaign with a group of people, one of whom is Roy Brewer. He _seems_ to be honestly anxious that no sheep should be slaughtered with the goats. Since it is no longer possible in this town to make any headway whatsoever in fighting the blacklist on straight moral grounds, I myself have been forced into the position of saving good men from ruin by calling this attention to their cases. In every such case, he has come through for me. If you would like me to explore the situation delicately with Brewer, cable me "yes" at Centfox, Losangeles. If you prefer some other approach, cable me "no." I have a hunch

P.

As you may gather from the above, the motto for 1952 is not "Death before Dishonor": but "Screw Your First."

that I can do you some good, but I warn you that a letter from you may be required.

Much love to all

P.

Sept. 26, 1952

Dear Dad,

A number of things, good and bad, have occurred recently on the
movie front for me which you might be interested in. First, of
course, Pickford dropped out of THE LIBRARY. (Or Circle of Fire,
as it's now called.) She reported for rehearsal the first day
but not the second. I don't know many of the details myself but
apparently she got cold feet at the last minute. The enclosure
will tell you who Kramer got to replace her -- one of your favorite
actresses, Barbara Stanywck. She is by no means ideal casting and
we will have to rewrite some to make the character 10 years younger.
However, Kramer seems intent with a consuming passion to get this
film made, which is something. It is being delayed until she finishes
a picture she's about to start. So it will now go in December sometime.

On FROM HERE TO ETERNITY, the script was read yesterday in Quebec
by Montgomery Clift, who was in A PLACE IN THE SUN and is considered
one of the two great young American actors. He is crazy about it
and if we want him we can have him. First, though, he is committed
to a picture in Italy. So if we take him ETERNITY will probably be
shot in February. The other great young American actor is Marlon
Brando (who was in A STREETCAR NAMED DESIRE). We are going to think
about getting him for the other male part. If we wind up with these
two guys, this may well be the biggest picture of the year. Certainly
one of them. As far as the director goes, Zinnemann (High Noon) will
direct it if Clift is taken by Cohn. Monday or Tuesday should tell
the details on this.

As far as I am concerned here, I have asked for $2000 a week starting
Monday, with a guarantee of 4 weeks. They said okay if I would give
them a free week after that and then go on at $1500 a week -- but that
my official salary would be listed at $2000 a week. I told them I
would not give them a free week, since I had given them this one
now free and had been idle 3 weeks before that waiting for them. I
said if they gave me the $2000 a week for 4 weeks, I'd do any further
writing work at the rate of $1500 a week if it were put in the form
of a flat deal rather than as a weekly rate; then there would be never
any doubt that my established salary was $2000 a week. Cohn is out
of town for the weekend but I have a feeling that if they can sign
the director, Clift, and me on Monday, everything will work out.

We had a very pleasant dinner with Polly and Baron last night. We
showed them our house, then took them to Perino's. We finally were
introduced to Caesar, the wonder dog, and I must say he is very
beautifully trained. We are having Dorothy Fink over for dinner
tonight.

Oh, I forgot one of the most important developments on the movie
front. Before discussing any weekly deal with me, Briskin (the
Columbia negotiator and vice-president) spent over a hour offering
me a position with Columbia as a writer-producer.

2

COLUMBIA PICTURES CORPORATION
1438 NO. GOWER STREET
HOLLYWOOD 28, CALIFORNIA
HUDSON 2-3111

The interesting aspect of it is that he does not want a 7 year contract. He would be willing to do it on a one or two year basis. I told him I didn't know if I had the temperament to be a producer, that I didn't like to come in at 10 and leave at 6 and that I wanted to spend a good deal of time in Florida. Well, he said, if your requests in this respect are fairly reasonable, maybe we could work out a formula to cover them. Anything, he said, can be written into a contract. The theory seems to be that on a year deal a man should be willing to accept less than a weekly salary, so he mentioned the sum of $1500 a week or $78,000 a year. However, since he mentioned the money, I gather he'd be willing to go higher. He didn't say anything about a percentage but I had told him earlier I wanted $40,000 and 2½ % for a writing job on a new assignment.

Any way, I came back the next day and told him I couldn't decide overnight and I needed a few weeks to think about it. There are many aspects of the thing, good and bad, but it can hardly be dismissed lightly. The main feature is the fact that it isn't a 7 year proposition. This is a tremendous concession by one of these major studios. Apparently, Cohn is still in love with me.

The Army, incidentally, approved and passed the script practically lock, stock and barrel. They want about 10 line changes, only a few of them difficult. They have okayed the use of all their installations and men that we need in Hawaii. Not only will this mean a tremendous saving in money to the company but it will give a feeling of authenticity to the picture that you could not really ever quite get any other way. No wonder Cohn is in love with me.

I trust you found everything in Florida fine on your arrival. I'm sorry you didn't decide to come back here for a few weeks, however. Let me hear from you with all the news. We'll be talking every Sunday unless we go out of town. I think the best time would be either noon our time or six o'clock in the evening our time. With love,

Your loving son,

Dan

Daniel Taradash to William Taradash

SEPTEMBER 26, 1952

Though he studied to be an attorney, Daniel Taradash always wanted to be a writer, and by 1952, after years of hard work, he was at the top of his game. In this letter to his father, Taradash shares early casting and production details about *From Here to Eternity*, his adaptation of the James Jones novel about the intersecting lives of several characters at an army base in Honolulu in the days before the Pearl Harbor attack. Taradash, who was very close to his father and wrote to him often, also provides fascinating information about his salary and contract, and the possibility of becoming a writer-producer at Columbia studios. Taradash did not end up accepting this offer, but when *Eternity* was released to great acclaim he did become one of the most in-demand screenwriters at the studio, going on to work on such films as *Désirée*, *Picnic*, and *Bell, Book and Candle*. The other project that Taradash mentions, *The Library*, was a script that he had developed with the producer Stanley Kramer about a librarian who is persecuted when she refuses to take a book about communism out of the public library. Taradash and Kramer were thrilled because Mary Pickford had agreed to come out of retirement to play the leading role, but when she backed out the project fell apart. Finally completed in 1956 and renamed *Storm Center*, the revamped version starred Bette Davis and was the only film both written and directed by Taradash.

Humphrey Bogart to John Huston

The offbeat comedy *Beat the Devil*, released in 1954, would be Humphrey Bogart's sixth and final film with director John Huston. In this letter to his old friend, Bogart refers to himself as Huston's "timid employer" because the actor was bankrolling the project, having purchased the rights to the novel from its author, the journalist Claud Cockburn, aka James Helvick, a friend of Huston's. Despite the humorous tone of the letter, Bogart does raise some questions that show that he was taking his investment in the film's success seriously, making passing references to the casting (jokingly referring to Huston's overtures to Lauren Bacall about playing the lead), inquiring about the wardrobe that he should bring to Italy for his role in the film, and even suggesting an alternate title for the picture. In addition to giving insight into the friendship and professional camaraderie that Bogart and Huston shared, this letter also provides a fascinating snapshot of Hollywood in the fall of 1952, when fervent liberals like Bacall (and more realistic ones like Bogart) were hopeful that Governor Adlai Stevenson of Illinois might still have a chance of defeating Dwight D. Eisenhower in the upcoming presidential election. It is not surprising that Bogart would end his letter by reporting to Huston on the latest foray of the House Un-American Activities Committee into Hollywood. Bogart, Huston, and Bacall had all risked their careers when they condemned the 1947 HUAC hearings, and they all continued to be dismayed by the events that were wreaking havoc on the lives of so many in the film community.

HUMPHREY BOGART

232 S. Mapleton Drive,
Los Angeles, 24, Claif.,
Oct. 8, 1952.

Mr. John Huston,
Romulus Films,
27 Soho Square,
London, W. 1, England.

Dear Fly in the Ointment,

Because I always open my wife's mail, I read your
insidious and immoral proposals to my wife. It is perfectly safe to promise Miss Bacall a leading part in your
picture as soon as you are perfectly sure that she is
knocked up-by me, that is. I therefore instructed Miss
Bacall to disregard your blandishments and as your employer I request you not to further fuck up my home, which
has already been fucked up by Adlai Stevenson.

And now to more serious business. In talking around
the town I am informed by the people with know-how and
great vision that within a very few years there will be
practically no black and white pictures exhibited. Therefore with an eye to the future residuals of this epic upon
which we are about to embark, may I as a very timid employer, offer for your consideration, color. This they tell me
will immeasurably increase the value of the picture for
future play dates.It seems to me that if we are going to
all the places you plan to go, we'd lose a lot without it.
I repeat again, old boy, that this is entirely up to you
as since I've won the Oscar, I have tremendous respect for
your opinions, drunk or sober.

Got a long letter from Peter saying that everything
is going fine and the script is in wonderful condition,
which I presume means that somebody has written a title
on a piece of yellow paper. Incidentally would you think
The Lady Lies might be a better title than Beat the Devil?

HUMPHREY BOGART

Also could you give me the real scoop about the feud
between Tony Veiller and Romulus Films and also, as
soon as you know, could you let me know how little
wardrobe and what kind of wardrobe I have to bring
with me for the picture. I would say not too fancy
and not too much unless you want me to look like
Victor Mature, which I hope is impossible.

And now for some news about the local scene.
The country is teeming with the election. Everybody
is on the same side they've always been and everybody is campaigning to win somebody over from the other
side, which as you know is an impossibility. Stevenson
is making wonderful speeches, literate, intelligent and
intellectual. Eisenhower is saying what they tell him
to say, which is a sad spectacle because I thought he
was going to be a wonderful fellow. Miss Bacall supports
wholeheartedly, Governor Stevenson, up to the vomiting
point. The right people are on the other side, Jack Warner,
George Murphy, Y. Frank Freeman, etc. I of course am
supporting Stevenson because as Wilson Mizner once said,
"A single golden hair from the head of a beautiful woman
is stronger than the trans-Atlantic cable." However there
is a man running known as E. Darlington Hoops, on the Prohibition ticket, towards whom I lean slightly, especially
early in the morning. As you once said, old boy, and I agree
with you, it's a shitty world.

Our town has just been blessed with a visit from the
House Un-American Activities Committee-the usual well known
writer that nobody ever heard of bared his soul and exposed
members of the Communist party who have already done their
time in jail. They dug up a few doctors and lawyers, all of
whom told them to go to hell. In other words, situation normal.
The Committee for the First Amendment was conspicuous by it's
absence.

That's about all, John, except that I read this morning
that Sam Spiegel has sued Lynn for divorce naming divers
correspondents and Lana Turner has split up with Fernando

and the papers are full from time to time of your
amoral and immoral escapades, including black eyes
etc., etc.

Love to Ricky and when you get around to it,
please answer some of the questions I have asked.

Regards,

Bogie

Paul Kohner to John Huston

FEBRUARY 10, 1953

In this letter to his friend and client John Huston, the agent Paul Kohner reports on the upheaval sweeping through the industry as 3-D companies like Natural Vision and widescreen systems like Cinerama and CinemaScope were taking the movie business by storm. Huston, who was on location in Italy making *Beat the Devil*, may have inquired about whether they should jump on the 3-D bandwagon, but Kohner wisely predicted that the trendy new technologies still had some kinks to be worked out. It's interesting that the second part of the letter also relates to a major shift that was taking place in the movie business during this time. In the 1950s, the studios started shooting many films overseas, especially in Europe, mostly in order to take advantage of lower production costs and utilize frozen funds. This arrangement also appealed to directors

like Huston and William Wyler, who could not only work far away from the oversight of the studios but also benefit from loopholes in the US income tax laws. In fact, with Kohner's help, Huston was one of the first to embrace this new development in postwar Hollywood. Huston had moved to Ireland in 1952, and Kohner was always looking for international financing for his films, which is why they were planning to make his next movie, *Matador*, in Spain. That project never got off the ground, however, so Huston moved on to working on his adaptation of *Moby-Dick*, which would be his first widescreen film. The mention of an auto accident involving Huston and Bogart refers to a crash that occurred shortly after Bogart arrived in Italy for the filming of *Beat the Devil*, when their chauffeur drove their car off the road and into a ditch.

PAUL KOHNER, INC.

NEW YORK OFFICE
PETER WITT ASSOCIATES, Inc.
37 WEST 57TH STREET,
NEW YORK 19, N.Y.

9169 SUNSET BOULEVARD
HOLLYWOOD 46, CALIFORNIA
CRESTVIEW 1-5165

CABLE ADDRESS
PAUKONER, LOSANGELES

February 10, 1953.

Mr. John Huston,
Hotel Palumbo,
Ravello, Italy.

Dear John:

I gather from your cable that news of
Hollywood's latest Bugaboo has reached the shores
of Italy. Needless to say that Hollywood is once
again in utter confusion. People are running around
like chickens with their heads cut off. New processes
of 3-dimension stereo are bobbing up every day all
over town. Obviously, the industry sees a possibility
of getting in on something that seems to have caught
the public's fancy and desire for something new in
entertainment, and quite a few pictures will undoubtedly be done in various new processes. However, I
doubt very much that the entire industry will be converted to 3-dimension. Even if they should decide to
do so, it will be quite some time before theatres can
be properly equipped to show 3-dimensional films.
The industry has a backlog of close to 300 millions
in unreleased films and you may be sure they are not
going to let that go to waste. They simply cannot
afford it. So I think that, after the first flurry
is over, everyone will proceed slowly and methodically.
Some films will be made with the various new processes
but the great majority of theatres in America will
still be showing the regular old-fashioned "flatties".

As far as your picture is concerned,
even if we should want to do something, time would
be against us. I naturally contacted Morgan Maree
the moment the first item appeared in Hollywood about
the "financial success" of Gunzberg's process and we
discussed it at length. Then, when Fox announced
their Cinerama lens, Morgan contacted them only to
find out that there is one lens in existence and Fox
hasn't got it yet. They have had to postpone "THE
ROBE" which will be the first picture Fox will shoot
with this lens. I understand that the Fox process
is not a real 3-dimension process. It just conveys
a close similarity to a 3-dimensional effect. The

enclosed story in yesterday's L.A. Examiner will give
you a good idea of what is going on.

Naturally, I am thinking about the new
process for MATADOR. I just had a letter from Barnaby
Conrad of which I'm enclosing a copy. Please let me
have your comment on it.

Maybe the best thing to do would be to
plan on MATADOR, if we should actually find out that
it is possible to shoot in Sevilla in September. I
received a cable from Caesero Gonzales, the Spanish
producer with whom I discussed the collaboration for
the Spanish financing in Venice. He cabled me from
Buenos Aires that he would like me to meet him in
Mexico City to discuss the deal further. I may fly
down there the end of this month to meet him. But
before I do, I would like to have some expression from
you as to how you would like to do the picture in the
fall. By that time, we will probably know just what
process will generally be accepted and that will be
the one in which we can shoot the picture and we will
probably be among the first to shoot a 3-dimensional
picture in a foreign country.

We were worried in reading the first
newspaper reports about the automobile accident you
and Bogey had and were greatly relieved to find out
later that it was not too serious. I hope that Bogey
has fully recovered by now.

I received the copy of your letter to
Ralph Branton, today. As far as I am concerned, I
believe it is fine. If they should have any comment
to make, I will let you know. I hope, in the meantime, you have had a chance to talk to Willy who does
not seem quite to understand what it is all about. He
seems to have, or at least I gather that from a letter
Talli wrote to me, an idea that it is just a matter of
expediency for his picture. I am sure you have made
the situation clear to him but, if you have not seen
him yet, I wish you would talk to him as quickly as
you have the opportunity to do so.

Lupita joins me in sending our kindest
thoughts to you.

Sincerely,

PAUL KOHNER

PK/r

CC to you in c/o ROMULUS, LONDON.

following spread

John Wayne to Steve Trilling

JULY 7, 1953

John Wayne was more than a movie star. Between 1947 and 1951, he produced three of his own films at Republic, and in 1952 Wayne and his partner, Robert M. Fellows, formed Wayne-Fellows Productions and made a multi-picture deal with Warner Bros. Based on a story by Louis L'Amour, *Hondo* was the fourth film made under the agreement and proved to be a major undertaking for its producers. Not only was it shot largely on location in Mexico but it was made in 3-D, the popular technology that had recently captured the industry's attention by luring viewers away from their television sets. In this letter to Jack Warner's right-hand man Steve Trilling, a clearly frustrated and very involved Wayne makes it clear that the studio's unreasonable demands regarding the few available 3-D cameras are seriously undermining the production efforts in Mexico, and he reveals the many complications he is facing in trying to complete the location shooting for the film. In contrast to his screen persona as a taciturn cowboy, Wayne shows here that he was a committed producer and a fierce advocate who was willing to use his clout to stick up for his cinematographer Robert Burks, as well as the camera crew and the rest of the company. Ironically, by the time *Hondo* was ready for release in late 1953, the 3-D craze had started to die down. The movie was presented in 3-D during its successful first-run engagement, but many audiences in theaters across the country had the opportunity to see only the flat 2-D version of the film.

JOHN WAYNE

Camargo, Chih., Mexico
July 7, 1953

Mr. Steve Trilling,
Warner Bros. Studio,
Burbank, Calif.

Dear Steve:

I don't know whether it's your department heads, or Bob Fellows, or you, or Jack Warner, or who else, but I am goddamned sick and tired of everytime I come in from location to have my Production Department say that you want that other camera. We're spending around $30,000 a week down here keeping this troupe running – more than that, actually, because that's what we're spending in Mexico.

Your one camera got down just in time to save our butts. We would have lost four or five days if it hadn't been here. We now have the old camera fixed and we're holding it in case something goes wrong with this one. I don't know whose idea or who in their wildest stretch of imagination thinks we're going to send this camera back before I come back, but I don't want another message sent to me to send it back.

When we do the big exterior stuff we will probably use the other camera. At the present time it is here as a safeguard. The tripods have now broken down for the fourth time. If we hadn't had the extra tripod, our goose would have been cooked there. Even if we sent the camera back, we sure as hell wouldn't send any of the four motors we have here, and you can't run it without two motors, and we sure need two extra motors. We have had two days' work hurt by that; one motor blew up on us when we went to Red Rock Canyon to make the test; and if you have more motors up there and won't send them down to us, I know damned good and well you are going to pay all the salaries of the mechanics we had had working day and night and Sundays to keep these motors in shape, and I mean 24 hours a day.

We just shot a sequence in the rain that should be magnificent. We certainly couldn't take a chance of doing anything like that unless we had this extra camera – in fact, we couldn't take a chance of making the picture unless we have the other camera. If you don't want to cooperate in this, just call me up and tell me to bring the camera back, and I'll bring it back and cancel our relationship – I'm goddamned mad enough to.

I repeat - one of the tripods broke down for the fourth time today -
a mechanical defect held us up day before yesterday, and our little
camera is all we had to work with, because there isn't enough crew
and there isn't enough money to buy a crew to keep two of them going
at all times. So we shot with our little camera and took silent, long
shots while they fixed the big camera. We don't know whether the
little one works or not. We haven't seen any proof that it's good or
bad.

There isn't a man on this location that isn't batting his brains out
to get a picture, and there's not a damn one of them working any
harder than I am, and I'm not going to have that petty crap thrown
at me everytime I come: "When are you sending back the camera?" I
told you we needed the camera to make the picture with. I don't care
what anyone else in my organization said. I assure you that as far
as I'm concerned, I never intended to send the camera back. I can't
understand why we keep getting these calls. If you want the camera,
call up and say send it back, and the next time the camera is asked
to be sent back, I'm coming back with it.

Whoever the department heads are that are telling you that the camera
was ready to go, mechanically tested to where you should risk gambling
over a million dollars without insurance, you ought to fire.

I repeat, we have been told that there are no more motors up there,
and so the camera would be useless to you if you had it, unless somebody is lying to us, and if they are lying to us, those are goddamned
expensive lies.

I am sending this letter to you rather than Jack Warner (you can show
it to him if you want to) because I think some heads would fall when
he realizes what a foolish gamble they're wanting him to make. I
really shouldn't care whether he fires them if they are advising him
stupidly. They should pack a lot of them in a car and send them down
here and see what happens. Naturally the camera crews protect their
department head and take blame for things they are not really
responsible for, but I don't have to, so show this to Warner if you
want.

Hope this doesn't sound like a personal tirade against you - I don't
mean it as such at all, Steve, but it's against a situation that could
be damned expensive and because I feel you should have confidence in
the men you have in the field - at the moment I'm one of them - and
allow us to use our judgment. All I can say is that I asked Bob Burks
if we could get along without two motors, and he said "Oh, my god no!
We had one motor go out on our Red Rock Canyon test, and if we had two
and one blew up, that would be it." You know so far we've had trouble

with three out of the four, so I think someone should advise you as
to what's going on down here. That's why this letter.

Your Everloving, Easy-Living Friend,

Duke

Geraldine Page to Charles K. Feldman

SUMMER 1953

Geraldine Page was a young stage actress with a handful of TV and screen appearances on her résumé when she landed the female lead in *Hondo*, a 3-D color western starring and produced by John Wayne. Writing from Mexico to her agent Charles K. Feldman, Page sheds light on many of the challenges of remote location shooting, including long hours, isolation, unfavorable weather conditions, and technical breakdowns, and seems to be wistfully second-guessing her decision to choose this assignment over the glossy romance *Three Coins in the Fountain*, which was filmed on location in Rome. Page, who was associated with the Method school of acting, was considered an unlikely choice to act opposite John Wayne, but her description of working with him indicates that he was in fact a generous costar and receptive to her approach. Though *Hondo* was directed by John Farrow, it's clear from Page's letter that she was not impressed with him, and that the cast and crew looked to Wayne as both a leader on the production and as the main creative force behind the film. Page was nominated for an Academy Award for her performance but did not appear in another feature film for seven years, instead choosing to return to the New York stage and take on occasional roles in television. The "friend from N.Y." who visited her in Mexico might have been the violinist and conductor Alexander Schneider, whom Page married in May 1954.

MOTEL Baca

TELEFONO
PHONE **20**

SOBRE LA CARRETERA PAN-AMERICANA 45
KILOMETRO No. 1600
ON PAN-AMERICAN HIGHWAY 45

APARTADO
P. O. BOX **72**

C. CAMARGO, CHIH,, MEXICO

MODERNAS CABAÑAS
60 MODERN CABINS

BAÑOS
60 BATHS

RESTAURANT
DINING ROOM

ALBERCA
SWIMMING POOL

CANTINA
B A R

ESTACIONAMIENTO
INTERIOR PARA
AUTOMOVILES
PARKING SPACE
INFRONT EACH
CABIN

AGUA POZO PROFUNDO
WELL WATER

AIRE ACONDICIONADO
AIR CONDITIONED

CALEFACCION CENTRAL
CENTRAL STEAM HEAT

INFORMACION TURISTICA
FREE TOURIST INFORMATION

Tuesday

Dear Charlie —

Received your lovely letter saying the Immoralist can be gone ahead with! It really makes me so very happy. I can now settle down and work on the rest of this lovely picture without being fidgety, and look forward to other movies without turning a baleful eye upon them. Yippeee!

Did I leave the script, poor half-written little thing that it was, with you? The Immoralist I mean. I was sure I had it with me but I can't find it anywhere, so I thought maybe I had left it with you. If so would you be so kind as to have it slung in an envelope & mailed to me? Gracias señor!

From your description of things those stinkers in N. Y. might have at least answered your letter promptly & civilly be- fore the official communique. It was

UN CAMPO TURISTA DE PRIMERA CLASE EN UNA MAGNIFICA LOCALIZACION

FIRST CLASS COURT SITUATED IN A BEAVTIFUL LOCATION

probably my fault as I have been meddling them by mail and whining about my insecure state. I'm a worry wart.

You are wonderful and I can't tell you how much you're doing for me is appreciated by me although I behave like an ungrateful brat.

I'm very glad Dorothy McGuire has got the part in 3 Fountains. She could make it plausible. I think it's much better casting than Stanwyck or myself. I never did ask who the director was going to be. I think I did observe that even the craziest material can be good if consummately done. I must remember to enquire in future. In your next note can you tell me who the 3 Fountain director is & a little of what he's done? Gracias, muy gracias, señor. I wish I could learn some of this lovely Spanish but it evaporates from my memory at an alarming rate.

Here it is Tuesday and nobody is doing a lick of work. Yesterday we started out on a very distant location and left the equipment there. Last night there was a down pour and the lake bed which was our location + the roads leading to it are a mass of liquid adobe. We were to continue the filming of the finale with complete wagon train, cavalry, hundreds of Indians. It sure was a bitter blow to Mr. Wayne but we all need the rest after yesterday anyway and I've so many letter

3

MOTEL Baca

TELEFONO
PHONE 20

SOBRE LA CARRETERA PAN-AMERICANA 45
KILOMETRO No. 1600
ON PAN-AMERICAN HIGHWAY 45

APARTADO
P. O. BOX 72

C. CAMARGO, CHIH., MEXICO

60 MODERNAS CABAÑAS
MODERN CABINS

60 BAÑOS
BATHS

RESTAURANT
DINING ROOM

ALBERCA
SWIMMING POOL

CANTINA
BAR

ESTACIONAMIENTO
INTERIOR PARA
AUTOMOVILES
PARKING SPACE
INFRONT EACH
CABIN

AGUA POZO PROFUNDO
WELL WATER

AIRE ACONDICIONADO
AIR CONDITIONED

CALEFACCION CENTRAL
CENTRAL STEAM HEAT

INFORMACION TURISTICA
FREE TOURIST INFORMATION

to write that I don't mind a bit and
the rain has made it so cool I'm wearing
a sweater and blue jeans in complete
comfort today. From all they say I'll
be here about 3 wks or so more!

Thank goodness my friend from
N.Y. came to visit or those 2 wks off
I had a while back would have been
the death of me. Unfortunately he
had to go back but I guess I can
struggle along thru the next couple
of weeks without going beserk.

Publicity man say I must stop
a few days in L.A. before going to N.Y.
for publicity stuff so I'll see you
one of these days.

Oh! I meant to ask — we work
12 hrs. a day down here not including
my hairdressing + make-up call.
Week in and week out this gets a little
harrowing does SAG have anything
to say about such things or does one
shut up + be grateful for small favors?
I get wakened at 4:30 in the morning and
we come roaring home about 7:00 of the
evening. Its quite a chore.

So those 3 Fountain people left for
Italy, or will leave this Fri! And I'll be up

UN CAMPO TURISTA DE PRIMERA CLASE EN UNA MAGNIFICA LOCALIZACION

FIRST CLASS COURT SITUATED IN A BEAVTIFUL LOCATION

to my black stockinged thighs in Larmorgo mud or dust for 3 more wks. Ah well! Some-day I'll work there. It's got to be.

Considering how long I'll have to be here would I have been able to work in Fontainne even if an agreement had been reached? Oh that's done with anyway I mustn't harp on it.

As per "Hondo" as far as I could tell I've been pretty well satisfied with my work so far except one long days shooting that disgusted me beyond measure. This was scenes with Vittoro the Indian chief shot the one day Duke was away on another location shooting stepouts with Archie's camera. I firmly believe it was because Mr. Wayne was away and Mr. Farrow wanted to impress him with how much he could accomplish in one day that he rushed through everything in that barbaric manner. That sequence contained some of my most unnatural dialogue real difficult stuff and when Dukes around we stop and work out something com-fortable in the way of motivation or build-up or improvise around difficulties like that but this one day Mr. Farrow shot just as fast as he could yell action and I know the camramen were dissatisfied with the whole days work. I hate to think a handful of corny badly done scenes would ruin the careful work I've done of the other scenes. I can't think of anyone here who doesn't share my feeling that it would be nice to kick Mr. Farrow in his aging slats!

Thank you for everything tell Mildred I'm glad she likes the stills and give my love to Jenn & Dick Clayton & tell him I'll write him soon.
          Love, Berry

Tuesday

Dear Charlie—

Received your lovely letter saying The Immoralist can be gone ahead with! It really makes me so very happy. I can now settle down and work on the rest of this lovely picture without being fidgety, and look forward to other movies without turning a baleful eye upon them. Yippee!

Did I leave the script, poor half-written little thing that it is, with you? The Immoralist I mean. I was sure I had it with me but I can't find it anywhere, so I thought maybe I had left it with you. If so would you be so kind as to have it slung in an envelope & mailed to me? Gracias, senor!

From your description of things those stinkers in N.Y. might have at least answered your letter promptly & civily before the official communique. It was probably my fault as I have been needling them by mail and whining about my insecure state. I'm a worry wart.

You are wonderful and I can't tell you how much you're doing for me is appreciated by me although I behave like an ungrateful brat.

I'm very glad Dorothy McGuire has got the part in 3 Fountains. She could make it plausible. I think it's much better casting than Stanwyck or myself. I never did ask who the director was going to be. I think I did observe that even the craziest material can be good if consummately done. I must remember to inquire in future. In your next note can you tell me who the 3 Fountains director is & a little of what he's done? Gracias, muy grascias, senor. I wish I could learn some of this lousy Spanish but it evaporates from my memory at an alarming rate.

Here it is Tuesday and nobody is doing a lick of work. Yesterday we started out on a very distant location and left the equipment there. Last night there was a downpour and the lake bed which was our location & the roads leading to it are a mass of liquid adobe. We were to continue the filming of the finale with complete wagon train, cavalry, hundreds of Indians. It sure was a bitter blow to Mr. Wayne but we all need to rest after yesterday anyway and I've so many letters to write that I don't mind a bit and the rain has made it so cool I'm wearing a sweater and blue jeans in complete comfort today. From all they say I'll be here about 3 wks or so more.

Thank goodness my friend from N.Y. came to visit or those 2 wks off I had a while back would have been the death of me. Unfortunately he had to go back but I guess I can struggle along thru the next couple of weeks without going berserk.

Publicity man says I must stop a few days in L.A. before going to N.Y. for publicity stuff so I'll see you one of these days.

Oh! I meant to ask—we work 12 hrs. a day down here not including my hairdressing & make-up call. Week in and week out this gets a little harrowing. Does S.A.G. have anything to say about such things or does one shut up & be grateful for small favors? I get wakened at 4:30 in the morning and we come roaring home about 7:00 in the evening. It's quite a chore.

So those 3 Fountains people left for Italy, or will leave this Fri.! Well, I'll be up to my black stockinged thighs in Camargo mud or dust for 3 more wks. Oh well! Someday I'll work there. It's got to be.

Considering how long I'll have to be here would I have been able to work in Fountains even if an agreement had been reached? Oh, that's done with anyway I mustn't harp on it.

As per "Hondo," as far as I could tell I've been pretty well satisfied with my work so far except one long day's shooting that disgusted me beyond measure. This was a scene with Vittorio the Indian chief shot the one day Duke was away on another location shooting stunts with Archie's camera. I firmly believe it was because Mr. Wayne was away and Mr. Farrow wanted to impress him with how much he could accomplish in one day that he rushed through everything in that barbaric manner. That sequence contained some of my most unnatural dialogue real difficult stuff and when Duke's around we stop and work out something comfortable in the way of motivation or build-up or improvise around difficulties like that but this one day Mr. Farrow shot just as fast as he could yell action and I knew the cameramen were dissatisfied with the whole day's work. I hate to think a handful of corny badly done scenes would ruin the careful work I've done in the other scenes. I can't think of anyone here who doesn't share my feeling that it would be nice to kick Mr. Farrow in his aging slats!

Thank you for everything. Tell Minna I'm glad she likes the stills and give my love to Jean and Dick Clayton & tell him I'll write to him soon.

Love,
Gerry.

Elia Kazan to Steve Trilling

JANUARY 4, 1954

In this letter to Jack Warner's assistant Steve Trilling,
Elia Kazan lays out his approach to filming adult material
under the Production Code and tackles the subject of prostitution, an important element in *East of Eden*, his latest
project for Warner Bros. Like many filmmakers before him,
Kazan argues that the only way to condemn prostitution
is to show it realistically and without using euphemisms,
but despite his convincing argument and declaration
of principles, the Production Code staffers, Geoffrey
Shurlock (referred to here as Jeff) and Jack Vizzard, were
for the most part unmoved. Vizzard's response stated that
Kazan's protestations were "quite impressive" but that
they could not accept his argument for depicting scenes
inside a brothel. Considering how successful Kazan had
been in bringing *A Streetcar Named Desire* to the screen
nearly unchanged, the director must have been surprised
that he was not able to convince "the boys" to make an
exception. But in the end, Kazan did have to compromise
and make Kate, played by Jo Van Fleet, an "ex-madam"
in the story, though he also knew that anyone familiar
with Steinbeck's novel would read between the lines and
understand exactly who and what Kate was. Paul Osborn,
whose house Kazan was visiting when he wrote this letter,
was the screenwriter of *East of Eden*. *East of Eden* is also
notable as the first feature film starring James Dean, who
played Cal.

ELIA KAZAN

Dear Steve: I wrote you a letter yesterday in the country from
Paul Osborn's house. I've had some added thoughts. So this is
a second letter which,as in the other case,you are free to show
to Jeff and Jack.

The main point was that I do not want to make the
brothel attractive. The place in from here to Eternity was full
of dancing and music and had one very very pretty girl,Donna
Reed,and plenty of other that no one in the audience would ever
pass by. I think it would be really "moral" and uplifting if we
were to show oneof these dumps as they really are,drab,evil and
dull. Of course we would not label it as such,nor in other ways
show it to be a brothel except to an experienced eye. On the
other hand I dont like to label it a "club" or any such.

Now the next point is tht we would not show any
of its operation. We would rewrite the Anne scene to hinge on
her "entertaining" Cal. On the other hand here too I hope to do
it so that an adult would feel terribly sorry for the girl and
terribly tragic about her being in such a place and position.
Of course we would not show other customers doing anything except
lounging,sleeping,reading. No drinking. A whore house is an
incredibly dull place. No slamming of doors in this picture. No
towels,no negor maids,no cuteness,no humor.

The boys have had an experience with me on a delicate
issue.I'm speakingof Streetcar. I would ao make this picture so
that my daughter 17 and my daughter 6 could both go to it and
benefit. Neither would quite understand what was transpiring,but
they would not be DRAWN or ATTRACTED to what's going on. They would
NOT get an effect of gayety. Ask the boys to trust me again. Let
me as in STREETCAR do it as I wish,and if they dont like the
result,we will get together afterwards and make revision.s

As I said in the other letter Paul and I agree
completely about the Sheriff condonning the vice. This character
and his attitude is completely and almost precisely out of John's
book. We agree,and John agrees now,to change it.

We will also identify the neighborhood as a bad one.

Anyway,Steve,I've always had the feeling with Jeff
and Jack that they would allow a person who's intent was "honest"
to attempt things that they would not allow when the intent was
obviously sensationalistic.

I'll await their reaction. You are free to show them
my letters if you think them advantageous. The first was
kindof dictated to Paul on his machine. This is from the horse's
mouth itself,thatis me. A brothel is a brothel is a brothel. I
know where of I speak. Zinneman did not portray one honestly. It
was social,gay and pleasureable. Zinneman no doubt did what he had
to do. I couldn't do that in an honest venture. Kate is evil
and her place is evil and must be shown that way.

Happy New Year to all you hard working
Sunshine boys. See you not too soon,
which means when I'm rested. Signed

ESTABLISHED 1898

WILLIAM MORRIS AGENCY, INC.

202 NORTH CANON DRIVE
BEVERLY HILLS, CALIFORNIA
CRestview 1-6161

NEW YORK
CHICAGO
LONDON

March 8, 1954

Dear Joe:

I have your cable dated March 1st regarding "TWELFTH NIGHT".
We are discussing the matter with United Artists and will advise
you soon as to their interest.

You seem to be awfully interested in ~~Shakespeare~~ *Shakespeare*. I can understand
where doing "TWELFTH NIGHT" would, to a large extent, solve your
problem of having a summer picture in Europe - that you would
not actually have to write - but I am most dubious as to its
commercial possibilities. It just takes an awful lot of time
to get the money out of Shakespeare, as against a 'hit' picture,
less classical in nature. It seems that Shakespeare has just
got to go into the art houses and be given careful exploitation
and done practically on a road show basis, such "JULIUS CAESAR".
A major studio can stand this type of operation because they
have many other quick recouping pictures going forth, but for
an independent, it's a little different.

I wish you would let these thoughts bounce around in your head
while you're considering it. From personal prestige, I likewise
think that you should leave Shakespeare alone for a while.

I well understand your feelings on "THE END OF THE AFFAIR". It
was just a thought to pass on, predicated upon your seeming
urgency to get something into work this summer.

With reference to "GUYS AND DOLLS" - it looks like Goldwyn just
bought it. Paramount made a bid of $750,000 against 7-1/2 percent
of the gross, and had planned on starring Bing Crosby and Danny
Kaye; however, Goldwyn came up with a bid of $1,000,000 against
10 percent of the gross and while it has not been officially con-
firmed as yet, it looks like he will get the property. Undoubtedly,
he will not make it until 1955 and I don't know what his plans on
it are as yet, as he has been in Palm Springs. I am sure he would
love to have you write and direct it but it would be strictly
employment - even though on a salary and percentage basis - and it's
certainly nothing that could go through Figaro. Therefore, I wonder
how interested you would be. You might drop me a note or send me
a cable so that I will know whether or not to talk to him about it
as soon as he returns.

Mr. Mankiewicz

No more now, Joey. I guess you're on the home stretch and I'll
certainly be thrilled when I get a cable saying "the end".

Let me hear from you soon, please.

Love,

Mr. Joseph Mankiewicz
Figaro, Inc.,
Cinecitta
Via Tuscolana 1055
Rome, Italy

Bert Allenberg, 1956.

Bert Allenberg to Joseph L. Mankiewicz

MARCH 8, 1954

One of the most literary writers in Hollywood, Joseph L. Mankiewicz was no doubt bemused by his talent agent Bert Allenberg's opinions about the box-office prospects of William Shakespeare. Mankiewicz had already managed to convince MGM to let him make a screen version of Shakespeare's *Julius Caesar* with Marlon Brando, and it's intriguing to think what he might have done with *Twelfth Night*, which never came to fruition. However, Mankiewicz did write and direct *Guys and Dolls* for Goldwyn, again starring Brando along with Frank Sinatra and Jean Simmons, and it was a critical and financial success. The bidding war

for *Guys and Dolls* that Allenberg describes reveals just how far the studios were willing to go at this time to obtain rights to proven hits like Frank Loesser's Broadway smash. Though it seems incongruous now, Paramount's idea to costar Bing Crosby and Danny Kaye in *Guys and Dolls* indicates that those two stars were still box-office draws, and that the studio was anticipating a major hit for the duo in *White Christmas*, which was released later in 1954. When Allenberg wrote this letter to his client, Mankiewicz was in Rome making *The Barefoot Contessa*, which he wrote, directed, and produced through his company, Figaro Inc.

John Huston (left) and Ray Bradbury working together on *Moby Dick* in 1954.

Ray Bradbury to John Huston

JUNE 18, 1954

The science fiction writer Ray Bradbury was a big movie fan, and when he decided it was time to try his hand at screenwriting, he reached out to his favorite writer-director: John Huston. In 1953, Huston invited Bradbury to collaborate with him on his adaptation of Herman Melville's *Moby-Dick*, and Bradbury enthusiastically signed on for the assignment. Huston was then living in Ireland, and Bradbury traveled there to work with him for six months on the script, a monumental task that was especially challenging for a first-time screenwriter. By all accounts it was a rocky partnership, made even more tense when Bradbury later tried to claim sole screenwriting credit on the film, much to Huston's surprise. That dispute was resolved, but the relationship was never the same. Bradbury later wrote fictional accounts of his experiences with Huston in the 1984 story *Banshee* and the 1992 novel *Green Shadows, White Whale*. Though Bradbury mentions talking to Montgomery Clift about playing the role of Captain Ahab, the part eventually went to Gregory Peck. After an arduous production, *Moby Dick* was finally released in 1956.

June 18, 1954

Bradbury
10750 Clarkson Road
Los Angeles 64, Calif.

Dear John:

You have probably been cursing me, mentally and aloud,
for some time now. Time gets by and I haven't sent you
the rewritten Father Mapple speech or the scene between
STARBUCK, STUBB, and FLASK. There's no excuse except
complete exhaustion on my part. If you saw the letter
I wrote Lorry from Rome, I think you know already how
I must have felt. I've never been so beat, fagged, and
bushed in my life. If Jesus Christ himself walked
up to me this afternoon and said he'd produce THE MARTIAN
CHRONICLES on a screen two miles wide by one mile high,
I'd scream and run the other way. I don't want to do
another screenplay for two or three years. My decision,
years ago, to do few screenplays, was based on some
vague half-knowledge of how exacting the form could be.
Now that I've gone in one end of MOBY and out the other,
I haven't nothing but awed respect for people like Peter,
and yourself, who can stick to that business year in
and year out without getting stomach boils. My flight
from the script, into Italy, was not unlike Jonah's
flight before the wrath of God.

Well, now we 're home. I'm beginning to touch my
typewriter again. I saw Paul Koehner yesterday and
talked to him about the script, briefly, and I hope
now, before many days have passed, to have the FATHER
MAPPLE speech rewritten and off to you, plus the
STARBUCK-STUBB-FLASK scene. You have probably said
"goddam"to me and done the thing yourself by now, but
maybe my version will be of some help. I hope so.

I got in touch with Clift, in New York, not knowing
that he had already given a final refusal to you on
the film. I hoped I might be able to make a selling
point or two with him. We had a pleasent talk one
afternoon; he seems very nice indeed and he was
explicit and concrete in his reasoning on not taking
the job. I couldn't help but admire him; though I
was disappointed, on your behalf, that the film would
lack his work. I hope you have luck now in finding
a proper Ishmael.

More from me, God willing, in about a week. I hope
you will forgive this long silence. Believe me, I
owe so much to you. I'm sorry I have delayed in paying
some of it back, in the pages you need.

Thanks again, and love,
from,

RAY

August 11, 1954

Mr. Frank Caffey

WARDROBE FOR BRICKPITS EGYPT

There have been discussions here about costuming the
(approx.) 3,500 persons in the Brickpits scenes, and
concern about plans and preparations for wardrobe for
these scenes. We must in no way use or borrow from the
controlled costuming shipped from Studio and additional
being prepared for the Exodus sequences in Cairo.

I suggest natives be dressed in various loincloth drapes,
have stills made and send us a set, airmail, for approval
by Mr. DeMille -- together with samples of rough fabrics,
color available, and cost, keeping cost at absolute minimum.

After approval, fabric yardage should be purchased, dyed and
aged in Cairo to provide 2,150 loincloths for the men, and
800 simple, workable, functional garments for the women and
100 children (50 boys, 50 girls). Dying should be rich,
ruddy colors to contrast with the elephant color of the mud
and the dark skin tones of the slaves. If suitable ties or
tapes are provided attached to each loincloth, no additional
belt need be issed.

Dorothy Jeakins

Dorothy Jeakins

One of the brick pit scenes filmed on location in Egypt in 1954 for *The Ten Commandments*.

Dorothy Jeakins to Frank Caffey

AUGUST 11, 1954

This note from costume designer Dorothy Jeakins to Frank Caffey, one of the production managers on Cecil B. DeMille's 1956 epic *The Ten Commandments*, illustrates the amount of planning and labor that went into dressing the thousands of extras used in DeMille's most extravagant Hollywood spectacles. A highly acclaimed designer who had already won two Oscars, Jeakins was one of five costume designers credited on the monumental production, along with Paramount's prolific Edith Head, longtime DeMille associates John L. Jensen and Ralph Jester, and the artist Arnold Friberg, who worked with the director on the overall look of the film. In August 1954, Jeakins travelled to Egypt for location shooting, where, along with a small army of assistants, she coordinated both the costuming of the featured actors and the dressing of the extras required for the crowd scenes around the Pharoah's city and the massive

Exodus sequence. According to Adele Balkan, an illustrator and designer who was Jeakins's wardrobe assistant in Egypt and worked closely with the local extras hired for the film, DeMille and Jeakins had very different working styles. This is borne out by another letter from Jeakins to Caffey dated January 5, 1955, in which she explained that she could no longer "emotionally cope" with working for DeMille and informed Caffey that she was resigning from the production team. Even though Jeakins was no longer on the payroll when DeMille started shooting the bulk of the film in Hollywood in March 1955, her exquisite design aesthetic and attention to detail are evident throughout *The Ten Commandments*, which is one of the most lavishly costumed films of the 1950s. Not surprisingly, she and the other costume designers were nominated for an Academy Award for their outstanding work on the production.

Sept. 30

Dear George;—
                Yesterday Dale and I saw "A
Star Is Born" and we are still under its spell.
I wept sometimes quietly, sometimes hysterically
for three hours. Later when Dale, who had been
sobbing rhymically, dared to say he thought
Judy's finishing the Jamen number after the
devastating scene in the dressing room with Oliver
was just slightly corny I spat out, "Then
you think courage is corny."
                You know, of course, that this is a
great film and that you have told more
than Norman Maine's or Esther Blodgett's story.
You have said a lot about courage and
aspiration and life after death, if you please.
You also know that both Judy and Mason
are superb and that the script is witty and
mature. But I should like to tell you about
the small things that I felt only I understood.
Your stamp, incidentally, was on every scene.
        1. The way the movie star lovers (before
their marriage) moved across the lot and into
Oliver's office. I've seen Crawford and Franchot
etc. walk this way and Lana etc. and all
the rest of them. But not until you pointed
it out did I realize these lovers move differently.
They are story book sweethearts really.
        2. My favorite line when Mason says to
Carson, "How's the A. P. and the U. P."
        3. That dreadful fan outside the preview
jumping up to get a look. They always jump.
        4. And her being sick by the oil well.
And when she got back in that car she had
been sick, brother. And then everything he said
about preview audiences—
                                        (over)

Katherine Albert to George Cukor

SEPTEMBER 30, 1954

This letter from fan magazine writer and screenwriter Katherine Albert to her friend George Cukor demonstrates just how meaningful stories about Hollywood can be to people who have lived and worked in the movie capital. Albert's emotional reaction to Cukor's remake of *A Star Is Born*, starring Judy Garland and James Mason, shows that the director and his screenwriter, Moss Hart, were devastatingly accurate in capturing the realities of toiling in the Hollywood studio system. Albert and her husband, the writer Dale Eunson, were close friends with actress Joan Crawford, and the reference to "Crawford and Franchot" in the letter refers to the star and her second husband, the actor Franchot Tone, who married when they were both under contract at MGM. Unfortunately, some of the Hollywood scenes that Albert describes ended up on the cutting room floor after Warner Bros. decided to shorten the film by nearly thirty minutes following its New York premiere in October 1954.

Sept. 30

Dear George—

Yesterday Dale and I saw "A Star is Born" and we are still under its spell. I wept sometimes quietly, sometimes hysterically for three hours. Later when Dale, who had been sobbing rhythmically, dared to say he thought Judy's finishing the gamin number after the devastating scene in the dressing room with Oliver was just slightly corny I spat out, "Then you think courage is corny."

You know, of course, that this is a great film and that you have told more than Norman Maine's and Esther Blodgett's story. You have said a lot about courage and aspiration and life after death, if you please. You also know that both Judy and Mason are superb and that the script is witty and natural. But I should like to tell you about the small things that I felt only I understood. Your stamp, incidentally, was on every scene.

1. The way the movie star lovers (before their marriage) moved across the lot and into Oliver's office. I've seen Crawford and Franchot etc. walk this way and Lana etc. and all the rest of them. But not until you pointed it out did I realize these lovers move differently. They are story book sweethearts really.

2. My favorite line when Mason says to Carson, "How's the A.P. and the U.P."

3. That dreadful fan outside the preview jumping up to get a look. They always jump.

4. And her being sick by the oil well. And when she got back in that car she had been sick, brother. And then everything he said about preview audiences.

5. And, of course, the make-up department that looks like the operating theater of the Mayo Clinic. Those wretched people—make-up, publicity and audiences—have no business to have any authority over artists.

6. The great line in the train scene after the brilliant technicians have created snow and wind and steam—the line, "We saw your face" as if it were some kind of obscenity.

7. The scene on the roof—a reunion almost ruined by those brats swarming over his car and the wonderful woman who pointed out, gratuitously, that this is the United States of America and her husband had fought two wars.

So for all these things and everything else I thank you. Dale and I both feel that this is one of the few pictures of enduring stature. We are proud to know you.

Love,
Katherine

Sal Mineo to Claudia Franck

APRIL 17, 1955

In this letter to his acting teacher Claudia Franck, the sixteen-year-old New York actor Sal Mineo describes his experiences making his breakthrough film, *Rebel Without a Cause*. A touchstone for teen audiences in the 1950s, the movie featured indelible performances from Mineo and James Dean, as well as from their costar Natalie Wood. Directed by Nicholas Ray, who seems to have made a great impression on Mineo, *Rebel* was shot at Warner Bros. and, famously, at locations around Los Angeles, including the Griffith Park Observatory. The young actor, who had appeared on Broadway in *The King and I* with Yul Brynner, did not end up playing a role in *The Ten Commandments*. However, despite his misgivings, he did work again with Dean in the epic *Giant*, which was shot in the summer of 1955. Strangely, the three stars of *Rebel* all came to tragic ends: Dean died in a car accident in 1955, Mineo was murdered in 1976, and Wood drowned in 1981.

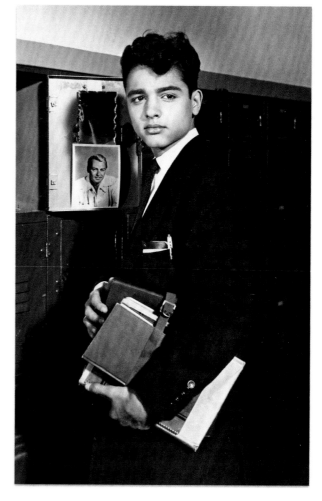

Sal Mineo in *Rebel Without a Cause*, 1955.

April 17, 1955

Dear Miss Franck,

Thank you for your letter. I was very happy to hear from you.

The weather is beautiful and the picture is coming along very nicely. I'm having a nice time doing it, it's very exciting. I worked very late last night at an old mansion. I'm still a bit "crogy" [*sic*] from it. We will be shooting there every night until Friday night. Then we will shoot for about ten nights at the planetarium.

It's fun but it's a lot of work. I'll be very glad when I'm back in New York.

I visited Brynner Friday at Paramount. He's doing the "Ten Commandments." He introduced me to DeMille. DeMille was thinking of a part for me in the picture. He saw the "King & I" and I told him about the pictures I've done and "Rebel Without Cause." Who knows, I may be working in the "Ten Commandments" too.

Well, I hope you're fine and not working to hard. Please send my love to Marie. My jokes are getting pretty bad without Marie.

I miss you and I'm thinking about you when I do my part.

I think of all the things you've taught me and I apply them to the part during rehearsals. I try all different things with my body and hands, and I work the lines different ways, during rehearsals. When it comes time to shoot I don't do a thing but be "Plato." Nick Ray is very pleased with my work. He's a wonderful director. I wouldn't like to work with James Dean again. Have you seen him in "East of Eden"?

I'll say goodbye now and take care.

Love
Sal

April 17, 1955

Dear Miss Franck,
          Thankyou for your
letter I was very happy to hear
from you.
          The weather is beautiful
and the picture is coming along
very nicely, I'm having a
nice time doing it, it's very
exciting. I worked very
late last night at an old
mansion I'm still a bit
"crogy" from it. We will
be shooting there every night
until Friday night. Then we
will shoot for about ten
nights at the planeterium.

Its fun but its a lot of work. I'll be very glad when I'm back in New York.

I visited Brynner Friday at Paramount. He's doing the "Ten Commandments". He introduces me to DeMille. DeMille was thinking of a part for me in the picture. He saw the "King & I" and I told him about the pictures I've done and "Rebel Without Cause". Who Knows, I may be working in the "Ten Commandments" too.

Well I hope you're fine and not working to hard. Please send my love to Marie. My jokes are getting pretty bad without Marie.

I miss you and I'm thinking about you when I do my part.

II

I think of all the things you've taught me and I apply them to the part during rehearsals. I try all differant things with my body and hands, and I work the lines differant ways, during rehearsals. When it comes time to shoot I don't do a thing but be "Plato." Nick Ray is very pleased with my work. He's a wonderful director. I wouldn't like to work with James Dean again. Have you seen him in "East of Eden"?

I'll say goodby now and take care.

Love Sal

THE DORCHESTER

PARK LANE, LONDON
MAYFAIR 8888

June 29 55

Well,you ,my eternal love, have been silent for so long that
my batteries are running dangerously low.

I am still without joy,except work is good ,I sing better and
have fun changing in one minute from the femininest dress into
white tie and tails and shock the daylights out of them.
Otherwise I am lonely . It's a good profession this,but a lonely
one. You are all on your own in every way. I'll be here till
end august ,then New york,then Vegas where I'll be from Oct. 5
for four weeks,then Newyork again.

Have cabled Rice toask if they still plam on döing the short-
stories. I had suggested Orson Welles to direct because the direction,I feel, is all important . Also döne imagination we need in order
not to copy the other readings as far as staging goes.

Orson pruduced his own version of MOBY DICK here and and I have
rarely been so drunk about anything theatrical. Knowing his great
talent I still was surprised at the resources he has and uses to
perfection.   I asked him if he was not interested in our plan and
he said he had not been approached. We could not ask for something
better to do justice to the stories than Orson. You know from my last
letter about the project how deeply I feel that it should be done
right or not at all .

Anyway he is wildly enthusiatic about it and if you still want to
do it I would suggest that you O K to have Rice ask him directly.

42

Orson is also full of hope and bursting with ideas for
another project,if he can obtain your permission.
' The sun also rises ' on the stage. Not a play and not
a Reading . But something he can explain to you better than
I if you allow it. The book as it is ,not only dialogue
but also leaving the descriptive sentences as they are .
I got so excited when he told me his ideas that I said :
" Can I be in it ? " And he said:"if if if   he would let me
do it and you would play the woman   --- " and then the
eloquent Orson was speechless for the first time.
I don't know how I had the courage to say "Can I be in it"
I have shy-ed away from the stage for so long ,always fearing
mediocrety   and exploitation of the 'glamour - bit ' but
this would make me take the jump . Here first - and then
America. I wonder if there is a chance that you say yes .
Please write to me about everything,how you are and Mary
and what you are thinking and if you still love me.

Marlene Dietrich to Ernest Hemingway

JUNE 29, 1955

Marlene Dietrich, one of the great movie stars of the 1930s, had mostly stepped away from film and was a celebrated international cabaret star preparing her latest appearance at London's Café de Paris when she wrote this letter to her longtime close friend, Ernest Hemingway. Though Dietrich had not made a movie in several years, it's clear that she is still excited about acting, especially if there is a possibility of appearing in a staged reading of Hemingway stories or a theatrical adaptation of *The Sun Also Rises* conceived and directed by her old friend Orson Welles. These ideas never came to fruition, but in 1958 Welles did memorably cast Dietrich in the film noir *Touch of Evil*, which marked the first time that Welles and

Dietrich worked together on screen. Dietrich signs this letter "Your Kraut," a nickname that Hemingway sometimes used when addressing her and she often used in letters to him. "Rice," whom Dietrich refers to in the letter, was Hemingway's attorney, Alfred Rice, who handled the writer's legal affairs at this time. The close friendship between Dietrich and Hemingway was known during the writer's lifetime, but details of their intense relationship became more defined when the writer's papers, housed at the John F. Kennedy Presidential Library, were found to contain dozens of intimate letters between the legendary actress and the acclaimed writer, who died in 1961.

Charles Chaplin to
John Howard Lawson

SEPTEMBER 9, 1955

This letter of greeting from Charlie Chaplin to John Howard Lawson, clearly intended to be read at a birthday party doubling as a political rally, shows solidarity with all of those who were blacklisted in Hollywood in the 1950s. A founder of the Screen Writers Guild and a leader in the Hollywood branch of the Communist party in the 1930s, Lawson was the first "unfriendly" witness called to testify at the 1947 House Un-American Activities Committee hearings, and by 1955 he had been blacklisted for nearly eight years. Chaplin, on the other hand, was subpoenaed by HUAC in 1947 but his appearance was postponed three times and he never testified before the committee, though he did send them a telegram telling them that he was not a Communist. Nevertheless, Chaplin continued to be a target of government agents and right-wing groups and was regularly attacked in the press by columnists like Hedda Hopper. Finally, in 1952, shortly after sailing from New York for Europe, Chaplin, a British citizen, was informed that his reentry visa to the US was suspended for political reasons. Though Chaplin had lived in America for nearly forty years, he decided not to fight the order, which would have required him to defend his beliefs to government officials, and instead settled with his family in Switzerland, where he resided until his death. Chaplin did not return to the US until 1972, when he traveled to New York for a tribute at Lincoln Center and to Los Angeles to accept an Honorary Award from the Academy of Motion Picture Arts and Sciences.

CHARLES CHAPLIN

Page ①

9th September, 1955.

[This message, John, on your sixtyfirst
Birthday, is a small token of appreciation to you as
an artist and a man of outstanding courage and
integrity;   a man who has stood resolute against
those who would attempt to control thought and
desecrate the true American spirit.

In these days of trumped-up hysteria,
I think it is important and essential that the artist
and intellectual unite and consolidate against these
political forces that have instigated this deplorable
police system, which attempts to turn the United States
into a nation of informers.

Such morbidity, if allowed to continue, will
grow into a cancer that will not only destroy American
democracy, but will also destroy the soul of the American
people.

Nevertheless, the true American spirit as
exemplified in such men as yourself, Paul Robeson, Dalton
Trumbo and legions of others, exalts my faith that the
eventual outcome will be a victory for those who believe
in true Americanism.

Good health and good luck to you John, and
my salutations to everyone present.]

[=Charles Chaplin
Film artist
Vevey, Switzerland]

Manoir de Ban
Corsier Sur Vevey
Vevey, Suisse

YUL BRYNNER

December 9th 1955

Dear Charlie:

One matter has been worrying me ever since it
was decided to cut the "Puzzlement" number out of
the picture, and I would like to share with you my
experience of cutting that number, and the effect
it has on the character of the King for the balance
of the story.

I was forced to cut it on several occasions in
the stage production, (on losing my voice), and each
time "Puzzlement" was dropped out of the show it had
a tremendously powerful effect upon the character and
his relationship with Mrs. Anna.

Through not having that moment of intimacy with
the King, where his thoughts and feelings are clearly
spoken, the audience seemed to consider him an unnecessarily rough man and could never grasp the inner conflicts that motivate his actions.

I have been worrying about this for the past week
because there is nothing now in the script to give the
audience that insight into the character, and I am becoming increasingly afraid of playing the King as rough
as he should be played. It is also a very disturbing
thing for the admiration and respect that Mrs. Anna
has to develop for this man. In the theatre, with
"Puzzlement" cut, I found that audiences could not understand why she should care for the King, or have any
respect for him whatsoever.

I am just jotting down these thoughts in a hurry,
but I would like very much for you to consider them
carefully and talk to me about it at your earliest convenience.

As always,

Yul Brynner

Mr. Charles Brackett
Twentieth Century Fox Films
Beverly Hills, Calif.

Yul Brynner to Charles Brackett

DECEMBER 9, 1955

The Russian-born Yul Brynner was a stage actor and television director with one movie role under his belt when he was cast as King Mongkut of Siam in Rodgers and Hammerstein's musical *The King and I*, which opened at the St. James Theatre in New York on March 29, 1951. The show ran for 1,246 performances and made Brynner one of the top stars on Broadway. Twentieth Century-Fox bought the rights to the acclaimed musical in 1953, and it was shepherded to the screen by Charles Brackett, the screenwriter who had become a top producer at Fox in the 1950s. In this letter to Brackett, Brynner demonstrates his deep understanding of the complex character that he had come to embody, and how important it was for him to create a bond with the audience during the "A Puzzlement" number. As a wise producer, Brackett took his star's advice and the scene remained in the film. Not surprisingly, Brynner won an Academy Award for his performance. He went on to play many other memorable characters in such films as *The Brothers Karamazov* and *The Magnificent Seven*, but throughout his career he was most closely identified with the role of the charismatic, temperamental, and ultimately tragic King Mongkut, a character he performed on stage more than 4,600 times.

Deborah Kerr to John Huston

JUNE 26, 1956

The story of a Roman Catholic nun and a US Marine who are stranded together on an island in the South Pacific during World War II, *Heaven Knows, Mr. Allison* paired Robert Mitchum with Deborah Kerr, the Scottish actress who was one of Hollywood's most popular leading ladies in the 1950s. In this letter from Kerr to the writer-director John Huston, the actress seems to recognize that *Allison* is different from other roles that she has played and is clearly excited and intrigued by the challenges that it presents. Kerr's mention of having "loved the story and the idea for so long" most likely refers to the fact that this project had been floating around Hollywood since 1952, when Eugene Frenke had purchased the rights to the source material, a novel by Charles Shaw. Before ending up at Twentieth Century-Fox with producer Buddy Adler, the property had changed hands a few times and had been under consideration for several stars, including John Wayne, Kirk Douglas, and Clark Gable. Shot on location in the West Indies, *Heaven Knows, Mr. Allison* was Kerr's first film with Mitchum, who played the tough Marine who falls in love with the Catholic nun he is trying to protect. The two actors became good friends during the making of the film and later appeared together in *The Sundowners* and *The Grass Is Greener.*

Tuesday 26th June

My dear John—
  I cannot begin to tell you how positively <u>sick</u> with excitement I was when Buddy told me there was a possibility of your directing Allison—and when possibility became certainty, I was absolutely overjoyed. I have been in the middle of all the attendant panic there is to visiting one's hometown, and today is the first chance I have had to sit down & write & tell you how thrilled I am. I have loved the story & the <u>idea</u> for <u>so</u> long, & feel it can be a most unusual & compelling movie, as well as an obviously "provocative-relationship" type one! If you know what I mean! The "East is East & West is West" premise is <u>always</u> good & I think in <u>this</u>, one gets a chance to show that East <u>can</u> understand West if you try hard enough! Are we going to be able to beat the censor without removing the guts?!! Please let me know <u>all</u> you think. I am incredibly excited & overawed at the prospect of working with you—and hope & pray I shall not prove inadequate. Forgive me if I have sounded too emotional—but I can only work well when I care <u>profoundly</u> for what I am doing—& I hope you will care too!

In anticipation—
With affection—
Deborah

Tuesday 26th.
June.

My dear John –

I cannot begin to
tell you how positively sick with excitement
I was when Buddy told me there was
a possibility of your directing Allison –
and when possibility became certainty, I
was absolutely overjoyed. I have
been in the middle of all the attendant
panic there is to visiting one's home –
town, and today is the first chance I
have had to sit down & write &
tell you how thrilled I am. I have
loved the story & the idea for so long,
& feel it can be a most unusual &

compelling movie, as well as an obviously 'provocative - relationship' type one! If you know what I mean! The 'East is East & West is West' premise is always good & I think in this, one gets a chance to show that East can understand West if you try hard enough! Are we going to be able to beat the censor without removing the guts?!! Please let me know all you think. I am incredibly excited & overawed at the prospect of working with you - and hope & pray I shall not prove inadequate. Forgive me if I have sounded too emotional - but I can only work well when I care profoundly for what I am doing - & I hope you will care too! In anticipation -

With affection -

Deborah.

JOAN CRAWFORD

30th October 1956

Jane dear,

Loved your long friendly letter; it was so like you, so
warm --- it was like having a chat and a nice visit with
you. I hope by now all the painters and carpenters are
out of your hair and that the house is all clean.

How exciting about your book on Cantor,and his telling
them all about it on Ed Murrow's show. I am so happy for
you.

Thanks for telling me about the "Giant" premiere. And
honey, I've heard many a story about Mr. Grainger. Everyone who likes her could kill him because of his treatment
of her.

I am so glad your Albert did such a fine job at the
Costumers' Ball.

I was presented to the Queen last night — nearly died of
excitement and fear. Found the Queen very charming, also
Princess Margaret. It was one of the most exciting moments
I have ever had. Of course, I was not too happy about being
presented with that group of people representing the Motion
Picture industry, such as Marilyn you-know-who, and Anita
Ekberg. Incidentally, Marilyn and Anita were howled at
because of their tight dresses — they could not walk off
the stage. It was most embarrassing.

Must run to do a scene, darling. Have no idea where I'll
be for Christmas.

Love,

Joan Crawford to Jane Kesner Ardmore

OCTOBER 30, 1956

A prompt and attentive writer of thank-you notes and get-well cards, the actress Joan Crawford must have penned thousands of letters to friends, fans, and acquaintances in her lifetime. Among her frequent correspondents was her close friend Jane Kesner Ardmore, a Hollywood biographer, reporter, and novelist who later collaborated with Crawford on her 1962 autobiography *A Portrait of Joan*. In this note sent from London, where she was making the film *The Story of Esther Costello*, Crawford shows both the thoughtfulness of a friend and the cattiness of a movie diva, especially when it comes to dishing about Marilyn Monroe and Anita Ekberg. The event that threw all of these unlikely players together was the premiere of the film *The Battle of the River Plate*, held in London on October 29, 1956. The other premiere that Crawford refers to, for the George Stevens epic *Giant*, could be one of two events: the New York premiere of the film on October 10, or the Hollywood premiere that was held a week later, on October 17.

Ingrid Bergman to Cary Grant

MARCH 29, 1957

Ingrid Bergman was living in Europe in 1957 when she was nominated for an Academy Award for her work in *Anastasia*, her first American film in eight years. Bergman had left Hollywood in 1949 after she was widely condemned in the media for having an extramarital relationship with Italian director Roberto Rossellini during the making of the film *Stromboli*. Their son, Roberto, mentioned in the letter, was born in 1950, and Rossellini and Bergman married. She and her husband continued to make films together in Italy, and in 1952 they had twin daughters, Isabella and Ingrid. In 1956, Bergman agreed to play the title role in *Anastasia*, the historical drama about a possible surviving Romanov, with the stipulation that the film be shot entirely in Europe. On Oscar night, Bergman's friend Cary Grant accepted her Academy Award for her at the RKO Pantages Theatre in Hollywood, saying, in part, "Dear Ingrid, if you can hear me now or if you see this televised film, I want you to know that each of the other nominees and all of the people with whom you worked on *Anastasia*, and dear Hitch, and Leo McCarey, and every one of us here tonight and in New York send you our congratulations, our love, our admiration, and every affectionate thought. Thank you for Ingrid." The Oscar for *Anastasia* was Bergman's second Academy Award. She had won her first in 1944 for *Gaslight*, and she would win again in 1974 for her supporting performance in *Murder on the Orient Express*.

Paris 29- 3- 1957

My dear Cary, my wonderful friend!

I got the news about the award in the
morning at 6 o'clock. I said on the phone: "I got it?" The
answer was yes --- and I fell asleep again. This seems a
very indifferent way of accepting an Oscar, but I was full
of sleeping pills so that I could go through the night!
A couple of hours later I was awakened and what seems to me
I000 photographers. The whole day I did nothing but answer
questions in all laguages about how I felt. I really felt
a very dull happiness and was only hoping the day would
end. Finallay it was over and I went to my room to take a
bath and to see Tola and celebrate - in peace - the evening. I hear a scream and my 7 year old son rushes into
the bathroom with the radio in his hands, yelling¥ Mama,
they aretalking about you" He came in just as I heared my
name mentioned and the roar of the public in Hollywood. It
was a transmission - on wire- with a French commentator
about the awards. In the back of the commentator I heared
your voice. You said something about " if you can hear me
now" and"wherever you are the the world" and I said: "I
am here, Cary, in the bathroom!" And then you gave me the
good wishes and I could hear all the people cheer. That
was the moment I really received the Oscar and I felt tears
coming to my eyes. Having known about it all day but still
not GETTING it, I GOt it in the bathroom! What a place to
get an Oscar! Nothing could havemade me happier than that
you took it and I thank you for the sweet words you said.
How lucky that I heard them, it was all due to my little
boy!
                    With my love,

                         Ingrid

Burt Lancaster as J. J. Hunsecker and Tony Curtis as Sidney Falco in *Sweet Smell of Success*, 1957.

Clifford Odets to Hedda Hopper

JUNE 6, 1957

In this letter to Hedda Hopper about the film *Sweet Smell of Success*, the playwright and screenwriter Clifford Odets tries to convince the gossip maven that the vicious columnist J. J. Hunsecker, played in the movie by Burt Lancaster, was *not* based on the powerful and fearsome New York legend Walter Winchell. While Odets sounds sincere, his claim is dubious. *Sweet Smell of Success* was based on a 1950 novelette by Ernest Lehman, who had started his career as a press agent in New York and had firsthand knowledge of Winchell and his brutal tactics. Officially, Lehman denied the connection, but the similarities were too numerous to ignore, even for Winchell

himself, who, according to his biographer Neal Gabler, was so worried about the film that he waited across the street from the New York premiere so he could look at the faces of the audience as they left the theater. Though Odets avoided even mentioning Lehman in his letter to Hopper, the two writers shared screenplay credit for the film. Odets had been hired by the producers, Harold Hecht and Burt Lancaster, to finish the script after Lehman left the project, ostensibly due to health problems but mostly because he was suffering from stress and exhaustion.

Hecht-Hill-Lancaster

202 North Canon Drive

Beverly Hills, California

CRestview 4-6921

Cable Address: Halburt

6/6/57

Dear Miss Hopper,

Perhaps you will permit me to comment on a pair of items that have appeared in your column, the last one of yesterday's date.

"The Sweet Smell of Success" is not an original story of mine. It was adapted into a screenplay from a magazine story by other hands. What I did was to rewrite theatrical and human plausibility into an already written movie.

Secondly, no attack on columnists is intended by the film. We will, however, all agree with the words of Lord Acton that "absolute power corrupts absolutely." The film does portray such corruption, but in truth the story could have been about any type of powerful, wealthy man, his sister and his stooges.

Thirdly, the picture very carefully shows that there also exist many incorruptible newspaper men, even when shrewd blackmail attempts are made upon them.

In the fourth place, there is surely no view of or attack upon some one certain columnist in the film, as your column of yesterday implied.

Several times I have heard that a portrait of Walter Winchell was intended in "The Sweet Smell of Success." You have it, Miss Hopper, directly from this equine mouth, that I should not have touched this picture with a ten foot pole if Winchell had been its subject.

The reason for that fact is certain and simple. Winchell and I have been friends for thirty one years. I said 31! In all that time he and I have never quarreled once; and with myself, my writing and its products he has been only kindness itself.

I have been hungry many times in my life, Miss Hopper, but never so hungry that I have found it necessary to feast on roasted friend.

Sincerely yours,

Clifford Odets.

271 Central Park West
New York, N. Y.
Nov. 15, 1957

Mr. George Stevens
20th Century-Fox Studios
Los Angeles, Calif.

Dear George,
    I have thought a long time about this letter and I've finally de-
cided to send it. Herb Brenner has told me that you might be interested
in having me play the part of Mrs. Van Daan in"The Diary of Anne Frank."

    When I saw the play I kept wanting to identify with Edith Frank
and I was going to ask you to test me for that role. My reasons being
that the part seemed blurred-but perhaps that is in the writing and
is a necessary part of the work-but it doesn't feel that way to me.
You see George I have a little girl and and I am watching her grow and
develop and flower, sometimes she loves me...sometimes she is annoyed
with me and often she competes with me, but she is the most miraculous
thing I ever had connected with my life.

    Since talking to Herb I have done a great deal of thinking about
Kerli Van Daan---I guess my areas of identification with her are harder
to acknowledge and therefore maybe more powerful. The basis of her
life being theconstant emphasis and trust in all the wrong values-(to
die because of your furniture). Yet I look at many of the women I know
and it does seem a universal malady and not just a special or Jewish one.
How funny and tragic is a middlaged baby. Her impossible task of helping her boy to manhood under such blighting circumstances, when she
herself is so immature. I wonder how many woman can recognize,her and
thank God that the consequencesoof immaturity are seldom so terrible--
but then again maybe they always are in different ways.

    George a few years ago I went to Israel and I was deeply affected
by the kind of country that my people (who managed to escape the ovens)
are trying to build there. They are still surrouned by those who wish
to annihalate them. I know how your pictures are shown and respected
almost everywhere in the world--and when I heard that you were doing
"The Diary of Anne Frank" I was most relieved and happy. I know that
the humanity and sympathy that will be generated from this film is very
important to the Jewish people. I hope you get the best possible actor
for each role. What I am trying to say-is that I would not wish to be
in the picture unless I was exactly right forthe role I was playing.

    I still look in the mirror and remind myself where you got the
factory girl from. I think that actress is still with me (per haps
more mature). In case you didn't know George I'm in my thirty's and
if I had been lucky I could now easily have a child of 15 or 16

                                 With kindest personal regards,

                                  Shelley Winters

P. S. --Needless to say I would be most happy to play any role
       you saw me in.

opposite

Shelley Winters to George Stevens

NOVEMBER 15, 1957

In 1951, George Stevens had cast Shelley Winters against type as a doomed factory worker in *A Place in the Sun*, and her acclaimed performance had changed the direction of her career. Six years later she came back to Stevens to ask for a part in *The Diary of Anne Frank*, based on the Pulitzer Prize–winning play that had opened on Broadway in 1955. Trained at the New School and the Actors Studio, Winters was a Method actress who carefully considered every facet of the roles that she undertook. In this letter to Stevens, Winters draws on her Jewish background and her life as the mother of a young daughter in order to make a case for how she might play both of the roles under consideration, finally realizing that the more difficult of the two parts, Mrs. Van Daan, would be the more rewarding and challenging. Stevens also brought personal experience to the production. During World War II, his film unit had documented the liberation of the Dachau concentration camp, and ever since he had been haunted by what he had witnessed. That fact makes it even more admirable that Stevens spent several years meticulously producing and directing *Anne Frank*, one of the first Hollywood films about the Holocaust. Winters won an Academy Award for her performance as Mrs. Van Daan, and in 1975, she donated her Oscar statuette to the Anne Frank House in Amsterdam.

following page

Charles Laughton to Billy Wilder

MARCH 28, 1958

Witness for the Prosecution, Billy Wilder's adaptation of Agatha Christie's twisty British courtroom drama, had an impressive roster of stars, including Tyrone Power and Marlene Dietrich, but the film was dominated by stage and screen legend Charles Laughton, who played the ailing barrister who risks his health in order to defend a man accused of murder. In this letter to Wilder, the mild-mannered Laughton seems relieved to have been spared from having to accept an Oscar, especially since he, like many actors, is ambivalent about its value given the number of artists who have never won a statuette. Of course, Laughton could not count himself among that group, since he had been awarded an Oscar for best actor of 1932/1933 for his performance in *The Private Life of Henry VIII*. Laughton and his wife, Elsa Lanchester, who also appeared in *Witness*, were married in 1929 and often worked together. The play that Laughton wanted his agent Taft Schreiber to share with Wilder was *The Party* by Jane Arden, which opened in London in May 1958. Laughton directed and starred in the production along with Lanchester and a young Albert Finney. A consummate professional, Laughton continued to work on stage, screen, and television until his death in 1962.

28th March, 1958.

My dearly beloved Billy,

        I hope you know me well enough to see that
I am telling the truth when I tell you that I am
very glad I was not awarded the Oscar.   Every time
I thought of it, I got into a frightful state of mind.
I do not believe in the integrity of the damn things
when I think that Garbo never had one, Chaplin never
had one, and Hitchcock's never had one.   Have you
had one, my dear fellow ? I don't remember.

        It would have made a nasty mark on me not to
turn down something which I so heartily look down on,
and I had been advised by Loyd Wright that I <u>must</u> not.

        I was terribly shocked when I heard that you
were not even nominated for your script and directing
of "Witness", as I am not one of those fools, and I
know the score of what's what.   I sometimes think that
in some ways it is bad for you that you are not an actor,
and that you do not see ordinary people's faces light up
when they come and tell you that they have seen a film
like that.   It is the only thing that really makes our
so difficult game worth the candle.

        Bless you, my dear Billy, and "Witness", and
the time we had after on holiday; it was one of the most
innocent and best times of my life.   I do hope that it
is going to turn up in the cards that we work together
again soon.   I have lost all relish for jockeying for
position, or making any compromise in working with people
whom I do not admire and like.

        The script of the play is now completed. Taft
Schreiber has a copy. I cannot get another one to send
to you.   The management is close-fisted about money, which
is probably a good thing in the theatre. All I have is a
script for me and a script for Elsa.   I have dropped Taft
a note to give you the script I sent him. I shall be
dithering until I know your opinion.

        Love to Audrey.   Elsa arrived yesterday, thank

God - I was very lonely.   Elsa has just shouted from
the next room that she sends her love.

                        Affectionately,

                        Charle .

Colonel Tom Parker to Hal B. Wallis

DECEMBER 18, 1958

When "Colonel" Tom Parker—a folksy Nashville music promoter and manager who adopted a Southern persona but was really born in the Netherlands—signed on to work with Elvis Presley in 1955, he took on the client of a lifetime. In 1956, Parker negotiated the singer's nonexclusive movie contract with the producer Hal Wallis, who would go on to make a dozen films starring Presley. In this letter to Wallis, Parker gives the producer some tips on getting free publicity, and offers up a rambling but remarkably detailed outline for a semi-biographical Presley movie set in Hawaii that predicts the future popularity of beach movies and Hawaiian music. Presley was interested in pursuing a career as a dramatic actor, but Parker's suggestions show that his manager saw the screen as just another opportunity to cross-promote Elvis to as many markets

as possible. Parker also shows a canny understanding of Presley's appeal to the youth audience and cites the experiences of squeaky-clean Pat Boone to caution Wallis about toning down Presley's dangerous side, the quality that made him so appealing to female fans. Though Parker seems to be going full-speed ahead, at the time this letter was written, Presley's career was on hold. The singer had been drafted in early 1958 and inducted into the army in March, and he was serving out his two-year military commitment in Friedberg, Germany. When he was discharged in 1960, his first film was, not surprisingly, *G.I. Blues*. Elvis starred in more than twenty-five mostly forgettable films in the 1960s, many of them produced by Wallis. Parker continued to manage Presley's career until the singer's death in 1977.

Colonel Tom Parker and Elvis Presley, 1957.

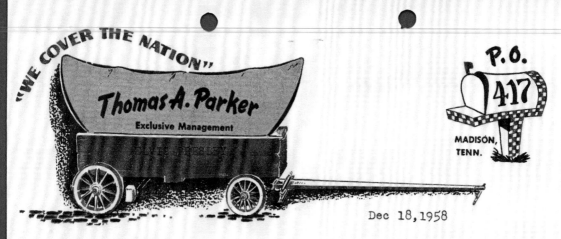

"WE COVER THE NATION"

Thomas A. Parker

Exclusive Management

P.O.
417

MADISON,
TENN.

Dec 18,1958

(Col) Hal Wallis
Hal Wallis Productions
Hollywood California.

Dear Col Hal;

        Thanks for your letter dated December 16,as you can see you
are getting an answer in 2 Days wich is pretty good in these hard times,
of getting out all our Christmas promotion .

Be sure and watch the Eddie Fisher show Dec 23rd for with the exception
that I have been snowed under by the powers in New York there should be
a pretty good Elvis Presley plug on this TV show for us.I at least did
try to do One of my Second best snowjob in trying to get another plug before the Year 1958 ends,the other was on the King Creole LP last Summer.
Since a spot like that cost RCA Victor about $ 21,000 for One minute on
this Coast to Coast network show you know of course that I have to use a
special brand of Snowoil at all times.

I am glad to know that you are interested in my idea of an Hawaiian story
My main reason for this idea comes from the type of music these folks play
and the idea is that since you myself and Joe Hazen did hold out on getting the King Creole material released just like it was done in the picture,an
and it surely has proven that it sold very well and the kids liked the
songs .And of course Elvis was of the same belief that we were.

Now my thoughts are that with Rock & Roll type of music,The Dixie Land Music
we had in King Creole,why it would not be a good idea to try perhaps the
Native Hawaiian beat type songs wich more or less are of the same type(wild.
and also in ballads very soft and soothing. This type of music brought out
into some sort of native Love story with of course some tough elements included in a story and the fine pictorial display that One can get in the Islands
seems to me would lend itself to something to think about,also shooting a
trip going on a large steamer either to the Islands or coming back with a
Love affair included aboard ship by either a Girl from the States or a native
Hawaiian Girl perhaps a stowe-away or something like that,My idea is to work
a story out in someway where Elvis could be running away from all the
with the fans going wild not knowing where Elvis went the Recording Companies
being without record re-leases doing everything possible to find him,and
somehow a gang of some sort of promotors Con Artist that is snowing Elvis
into singing with the natives while he is doing this they would somehow record all this on tape and sneak this into Honolulu and start promoting this
new find selling records like Hotcakes and all the time it would be Elvis
but no One would know this untill they had to bring Elvis to the Islands to

Page 2. Hal Wallis.

do a show,Elvis not knowing that he has been exploited by these people under
another name with these stolen tapes from his singing on the other Island
of course,thinks that when he arives in Honolulu that this big reception at
the Docks is for him ELVIS PRESLEY OR WHATEVER NAME HE HAS BEING A STAR,but
when he goes on the stage and somehow he gets the idea that he has been promoted into something else,I am this far with the story .The idea of course
mv this part of the story is just to give you some idea the way I am thinking
I dont say that this is the right approach however I have several others I
am working on,perhaps with you Joe,Paul Nathan and myself we can come up
with a pretty good setup and we could keep the story and complete Idea in
the WALLIS,HAZEN,PARKER,PRESLEY AND COUSINS FAMILY.Knowing that none of us
work cheap we know we will come out with a good deal and if all of us are
in on it we surely would all be happy with the price.

I also have been thinking of a story regarding Elvis doing a complete turn-
about and being the type he is you could also very well use him in some big
story regarding Gypsies as he surely is that rugged type that could be cast
in this type of story also as a foundling or stolen baby boy by a bunch of
Gypsies traveling in wagons sleeping outdoors and whatever that type of life
calls for with shows,as you know very well Elvis is at his best in a rugged
type of performance with a good love angle involved,this of course also can
apply into the Hawaiian setup,I do know that the kids would not buy a smooth
story on him with nothing else involved other than love and understanding.

Well anyway I am sure you can get my thinking pretty well,I am also enclosing
Todays Front page of the Nashville Tennessean wich gives you some idea that
to paint any artist too good can also kickback if we should believe this
story on Pat, I know that Pat Boone must know what he is talking about if
he say's like in this story that it has hurt is carreer being painted as a
all around good boy,Knowing Pat as I do I feel sure that some of this pub-
blicity he received as being such a good boy did not come from him but by
exploitation departments from some sort.Anyway I thought you would be interested in reading this for yourself.

Hope you have a Merr y Christmas and Happy New Year,also my best to MR.Joe.
and his Family, if the sausage does not arive on time for Christmas you will
have to eat it after Christmas .

                              Sincerely
                              The Colonel .

UNIVERSAL-INTERNATIONAL PICTURES
UNIVERSAL CITY, CALIFORNIA
Inter-Office Communication

To   **KIRK DOUGLAS**   Date **February 25, 1959**

From **EDDIE LEWIS**   Subject

Dear Kirk:

I have taken one more crack at the censors on the "oysters and snails" scene. Unfortunately, their objection to this scene is based upon the one remaining strong hold of their department which is an absolute taboo against portrayal of homosexuality. I believe they are honestly unsure that this is or is not a scene of homosexuality, but I have been unable to overcome their nervousness in this behalf. It is possible (although they will not say for certain) that they would pass the scene if we substituted "artichokes" and "truffles" for "oysters" and "snails". They also question the use of the word "appetite" in the scene. However, they are far from adament on the entire scene, and have suggested that perhaps we should shoot the scene and that then they might be able to give their approval. My feeling on the matter is that I would hate to substitute the words, although in the final analysis I believe I would prefer the scene with artichokes and truffles to no scene at all. However, it is my feeling that with the scene on film, we would be able to take our best crack at these guys with a 50-50 chance that we can get them to approve. It would therefore be my recommendation that we shoot the scene as it is presently written as one of the first Olivier-Curtis scenes, and show it to them as quickly as possible thereafter. I think we should then battle it through as though this is our only alternative. We could then take the position that in our judgement, this is the only way that the scene could play and that there is no possibility of substituting words or modifying the sequence. Then if by any chance we should lose this fight, we would have plenty of time to go back and pick up singles on the Olivier and Curtis scene to make it acceptable to them by the use of substitution. In any event, it seems to me that we would have to compromise less if we had the initial scene on film then we might have to now in script form.

If you agree with this procedure, I will so schedule the shooting.

Eddie

UNIVERSAL-INTERNATIONAL PICTURES
UNIVERSAL CITY, CALIFORNIA
Inter-Office Communication

To __KIRK DOUGLAS__   Date __February 25, 1959__

From __EDWARD LEWIS__   Subject _____

Page 2

P.S. Subsequent to my talks with them, I received a call from
Al Van Schmoos of the Censor's office. He says that upon careful
reflection and discussion with the staff, their strong recommendation is that we submit the scene with replacement words for "oysters
and snails" so that we would have the protection of having the
scene passed. His recommendation was that the proper procedure
would be for us to shoot the scene both ways, but put the "oysters
and snails" version in the first cut of the film for them to screen.
His feeling was that to screen a scene before the completed film
is ready would be an extreme disadvantage to us as they would be
viewing the scene out of context and would be less inclined to pass
it.

Eddie Lewis to Kirk Douglas

FEBRUARY 25, 1959

In this memo from producer Eddie Lewis to Kirk Douglas, the star and producer of *Spartacus*, the inner workings of the Production Code and the complex negotiations that took place in order to bring controversial material to the screen are brought to the forefront. The scene in question involved Crassus (Laurence Olivier), the Roman general, attempting to seduce a slave (Tony Curtis) by suggestively asking him whether he enjoyed eating both snails and oysters, or just one or the other. The Code had undergone several revisions in the late 1950s that made it less stringent and opened up more opportunities for screenwriters to explore previously taboo subjects. But as Lewis points out, homosexuality was still considered out of bounds, and even though the scene as written merely suggested the possibility of a same-sex encounter, the Code officials were nervous about it. In the end, Douglas took Lewis's advice, shooting the scene as scripted and including it in the print that was screened for the Production Code staff. Records from the time indicate that the Code staff did reluctantly approve the scene, but later the studio deleted it, as well as several moments of graphic violence, in order to appease the Legion of Decency. In 1991, when Universal was restoring *Spartacus*, the studio discovered that the footage of the cut scene still existed but that in the intervening years, the soundtrack had been lost. The producers of the restoration arranged for the lines to be rerecorded by Tony Curtis and Anthony Hopkins, standing in for the late Laurence Olivier, and the scene was restored to its proper place in the film.

Claudia McNeil in *A Raisin in the Sun*, 1961.

Claudia McNeil to Daniel Mann

JUNE 1, 1959

Although she only appeared in a handful of films during her
career, the African American stage actress Claudia McNeil's
observations about Hollywood are as clear-eyed as a seasoned
veteran's. Her indelible performances in both the stage and
screen versions of *A Raisin in the Sun*, opposite Sidney Poitier,
made her famous, but it was clearly her humanity and her
humor that endeared her to friends like the director Daniel
Mann, who had worked with her on the 1959 film *The Last
Angry Man*, costarring Paul Muni. The restaurant run by James
Wong Howe that McNeil describes was Ching How, which the
noted cinematographer owned from 1941 to 1950. Mann and
Howe were close friends who collaborated on several films,
including *Come Back, Little Sheba*; *The Rose Tattoo*; and *The Last
Angry Man*.

Barrymore Theatre

June 1, 1959.

Hello Danala:

This letter has been long in coming but I know
I do not have to apologize to you because you
are a friend.

When I received your wonderful wire on opening
night,it was the one thing that lulled the but-
terflies in my stomach, because of the wonderful
things you said. The fact that any one as busy
as you are could take time out to remember my
opening date, is, in itself, a wonderful thing.
When the critics of Hollywood say nasty things
about the people of Hollywood, they never get
around to mentioning that people like you are
there too. I suppose it is because people like
you are rare, and friendship is rare.

You know Danny, many nights when I am making up
to go on stage I think about you and the friendship I feel for you. Outside of Bob Mulligan the
television director, I have never known any one
in this crazy business that I worked with so short
a time, that I learned to love. Working with you
was one of the greatest things that ever happened
to me. It taught me to walk with my shoulders
high and my head straight up. You gave me the
confidence to face broadway with out fear. Sure
working with Muni helped me technically, but what
you gave me was respect as a person, a human
being. You believed in me, you loved me and for
the first time I forgot I was a negro. I began
to feel like a human being. You acted just as
you are , you are not only a great director
Danny, but a wonderful person as well. People

like you do more for humanity than all the laws of
the Supreme Court. However, I must get off the subject of how I feel about you because when I look back
on my days in Hollywood working with you, I fill up
inside and begin to cry. They were happy times, the
first real happiness I have ever known.

Broadway has accepted me and seems to like me, so I
am remaining with the play throughout its run. Then
in June 1950, God spares me, I will make the picture
"Raisin In The Sun". Unfortunately, it will be made
in Chicago and New York, not in Hollywood. Unless you
and your family visit New York, it looks like we won't
see each other again for two years. I hope when the
"Last Angry Man" opens here in New York you will come
if only for a week-end. It would please me very much
to have your approval of the role I am now playing in.
You are my peer and I respect your opinion very much.
Please Danny try and come some time soon.

Did you keep the car you bought for your moral, or did
you decide it wastoo expensive? (smile). The furs
I bought for my moral at the same time, I think I
have worn them three times. They have been in the
closet ever since. Ah Danny, Hollywood was wonderful.
Of course I could never live out there because I would
become lazy and not be able to create, and with this I
would die. It is different with you because ten months
out of the year you are doing a picture and the rest
of the time you are on vacation.

I intend to come to Hollywood in late 1960 for a weeks
vacation, and if I don't see you before then, I will
take advantage of your invitation and come and visit
you and your family for a day. Jimmy Wong Howe sent
me a wire opening night and I don't have his address
so willyou please call him and thank him for me.

have you ever seen a more wonderful guy than Jimmy?
What a technition and what a heart' I love this
guy.

I read in the newspaper a few days ago, about Jimmy
opening a resturant and trying to tell the photographer about the camera he should use, and the
stupid remark the photographer made to Jimmy. It is
funny as hell too, Jimmy being Hollywoods top photographer and the guy thinking he was a cook. Boy,
people will never learn will they.

Take care of yourself and come to New York soon.
When you do you will get a big surprise, because
Sidney Poitier will have left the show and I will
have been elevated to stardom. After we opened,
they offered me co-star billing with Sidney, but
I told Sidney to keep the billing. He is young,
a great actor, and I wanted him to have the memory
of starring all alone in his first broadway production. He is a fine person and I feel he deserves this. I am older and the theatre is my life
and I have waited twenty-six years for this, so a
few more months won't make any difference. Besides,
now that I have achieved stardom I find it wasn't
what I really wanted. I found the peace of mind
that came with it and having achieved this peace
of mind, I am content.

God bless you and take care of you and your family.
Please explain to your wife that when I say I love
you very dearly Danny, it is the love that God intends for one human being to feel for another, to
keep this crazy world in tact. Good-by Ketzala.

                              Sincerely,

                              Claudia

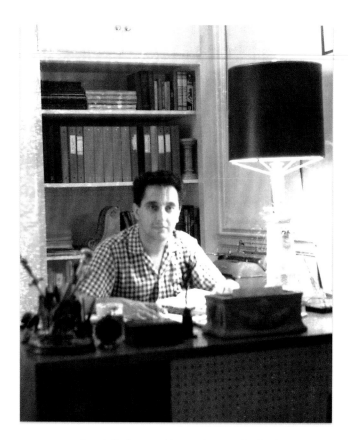

Joseph Stefano working on the script for *Psycho*, circa 1959.

Joseph Stefano to Janet Leigh

MARCH 30, 1960

Joseph Stefano, the screenwriter who adapted the novel
Psycho for director Alfred Hitchcock, takes a moment to
write to Janet Leigh about her performance in the mas-
terful film. Much has been made of the shock of seeing
Leigh's character, Marion Crane, murdered in the shower
just forty-five minutes into the movie, but as Stefano so
eloquently points out, the scene would have had much less
impact if Leigh had not created, in just a few sequences,
such a sympathetic and tragic character. Expertly made
and brilliantly promoted, *Psycho* was one of Hitchcock's
biggest successes, and it is still perhaps the film most
identified with his unique brand of suspense and horror.
Janet Leigh was nominated for a supporting-actress Oscar
for her memorable performance.

JOSEPH STEFANO

1543 MARMONT AVENUE

HOLLYWOOD 46, CALIFORNIA

—

OLDFIELD 6-1673

MARCH 30ᵗʰ, 1960

DEAR JANET:

YESTERDAY I SAW THE COMPLETED, SCORED AND TITLED
VERSION OF "PSYCHO." IT IS AN IMPRESSIVE PICTURE
IN MANY RESPECTS, A STRANGE AND RATHER HAUNTING
PICTURE. I THINK IT WILL BE A FINE SUCCESS. AND
I THINK, TOO, THAT YOUR PERFORMANCE IN IT IS ONE
OF THE MOST EXPERT SCREEN PERFORMANCES I'VE EVER
SEEN. WHAT YOU HAVE DONE IS SO MUCH MORE THAN
MERE ACTING. YOU'VE CREATED A PERSON, A LIVE
AND TOUCHING AND EXTREMELY MOVING PERSON, AND
I BELIEVE IT IS YOUR INTERPRETATION OF MARION
CRANE THAT GIVES THE PICTURE A DIMENSION WHICH
EXTENDS IT SOMEWHAT OUTSIDE THE BOUNDS OF THE
USUAL MOTION PICTURE. I KNEW WHEN I SAW A FEW
OF THE RUSHES THAT YOU WERE BUILDING SOMETHING
HIGH AND SHINING; THE COMPLETED PICTURE PROVES
IT. BECAUSE OF THE GIRL YOU CREATED, THE MURDER
OF THAT GIRL BECOMES A THING LESS OF HORROR AND
MORE OF TRAGEDY. I ALMOST WANTED TO SIGH "NO,
STOP IT," WHEN YOU WERE BEING SLAIN. I WAS SO
BROUGHT INTO YOUR WORLD OF MARION CRANE THAT I
WANTED HER TO GO BACK AND RETURN THE MONEY AND
CORRECT AND RECTIFY HER MISTAKE. MY WIFE TOLD
ME THAT IN THE MIDST OF HER HORROR REACTION TO
THE MURDER IN THE SHOWER, SHE BEGAN TO CRY. SHE
WAS CRYING FOR A GIRL YOU MADE REAL TO HER. YOU
ARE TO BE CONGRATULATED AND, ESPECIALLY BY AN
AUTHOR, LOVED FOR YOUR WORK. THANK YOU, DEAR,
FOR BEING ONE OF THE PRIME REASONS WHY I AM
PROUD OF "PSYCHO."

SINCERELY,

[signature]

January 23, 1961

CARY GRANT

Dear Eva Marie and Jeffrey —

If I weren't such a travelling man you would have been
thanked long ago for that fascinating teleidoscope.
What a happy idea for a Christmas present. Thank you
very much. I've looked through it at my thumb, Betsy's
eye, the moon and an old pair of argyle plaid socks.....
and all of them, even Betsy's eye, which needed no such
embellishment, seemed much more colorful and attractive.
Perhaps it's the way all things should be seen. Have
you one that could turn in upon one's own faults and
negligences? It might teach me that they are not, even
in kaleidscope, appreciated by friends who should be
thanked for thoughtful gifts at the time they are
received.

                    Gratefully and affectionately,

                              Cary.

I don't see you enough...and I should...because,
coincidentally, Leonard Kaufman also recently gave me
a teleidoscope and I want to report how it appears to
look at my thumbs with one at each eye. Try that some
time.

                    Love,

                              C.

opposite

Cary Grant to Eva Marie Saint & Jeffrey Hayden

JANUARY 23, 1961

This disarming thank-you note from Cary Grant to his friend and *North by Northwest* costar Eva Marie Saint and her husband Jeffrey Hayden captures the offbeat charm and self-deprecating humor of one of Hollywood's most iconic leading men. At the time this letter was written, Grant was married to the actress and writer Betsy Drake, who had costarred with him in *Every Girl Should Be Married* and *Room for One More*. Grant and Drake divorced in 1962, and he later wed the actress Dyan Cannon, with whom he had a daughter, Jennifer, born in 1966. Leonard Kaufman, whom Grant mentions in the letter, was a prominent Hollywood publicist who represented Grant and many other stars. Grant retired from acting in 1966 but continued to be active in the industry. In the 1980s, the charming star toured the country in *A Conversation with Cary Grant*, a one-man show featuring film clips and stories from his life and career.

following spread

Charles K. Feldman to Angie Dickinson & Jean Negulesco

APRIL 21, 1961

The actress Angie Dickinson and the director Jean Negulesco were on location in Italy shooting the film *Jessica* when they received this heartfelt letter from the agent and producer Charles K. Feldman, who represented Dickinson through his Famous Artists agency. A close, longtime friend of the Academy Award–winning star Gary Cooper and his family, including Cooper's wife, Rocky, and daughter, Maria, Feldman captures the shock and sorrow felt throughout the industry when Cooper, one of the most popular actors in the film community, was diagnosed with terminal cancer at the age of fifty-nine. Feldman wrote this letter to his friends four days after the emotional Honorary Award presentation by James Stewart, and just three weeks before Cooper died on May 13, 1961.

April 21, 1961

Again dictating
over the telephone
on account of be-
cause.

Dear Angie and Jean:

   I suppose by this time all of you have
heard about the gravity of Gary Cooper's condition.
Yes, dear Angie, you were very, very right -- your instinct
was correct -- when you asked me around the Holidays, "Is
Coop all right? Is anything wrong with him?" I answered
in the negative. Yes, I went to the doctor's office with
Rocky and Maria about six o'clock last New Year's Eve,
and I received the shattering news.

   It was to be a secret in which only his
wife and his daughter shared. I was not to divulge it
to anyone. All these months I have been keeping this
secret. Up to that time, the family and I had told
Coop that the X rays were wrong and that he was in the
pink of condition, and that there was no further recur-
rence of the malignancy.

   To go back, that is why I got so stinking
drunk New Year's Eve, and that is why I toasted Coop at
every turn.

   Yes, you were right again when we went
to the testimonial dinner for Coop at the Friars. It was
more an eulogy for him, than a festive occasion. Actually
I almost cried several times at this dinner. It was one
of the worst evenings I ever spent -- knowing the score.

   About four weeks ago, when he returned
from Florida, Coop was out washing the car, swimming, etc.
Because the doctors feared that pneumonia might set in,
the family and the doctor told him for the first time.
I must say that I have never known anyone to be as brave
as the "Marshal".

   He has made his peace -- never brings
the subject up, gets up two or three times during the
day, watches television, and then back to bed where they
ease his pain with various strong drugs. I have seen
him practically every day. We talk as if there is no
tomorrow.

Actually during the Academy Awards, the
other night, I had dinner with Coop, Rocky and Maria and
we listened to the Awards. I knew that Jimmy Stewart was
going to accept the Honorary Award for Gary, which the Academy bestowed on him. You can imagine how I felt when
Stewart got up and made his acceptance speech on behalf
of Gary. What kept me from breaking down, I don't know.

Gary watched all the proceedings -- thought
they were very good -- and immediately went off to bed.
Never once did he show any sign of breaking up, or concern,
or anything else. I assume you read Stewart's speech, which
triggered all the publicity which has come out -- at least
in the States -- regarding the Marshal's grave condition.
At best, I think it is a matter of a couple of months --
maybe only a few weeks. As you know, I love Coop very,
very much and this is as big a blow to me as it is to his
family and those very, very close to him. Enough of this.

I received a long letter from Jean telling
me how wonderfully cooperative, how truly effective and how
good (as an actress) you are in the film -- also how wonderful the cast, the crew and everyone is, and how blissful
the days and nights all of you are spending in Taormina
are. I was very happy to receive this good news. I do
hope this picture will do, careerwise, for you everything
you have always desired -- and I know it will.

There isn't very much to tell you, dear
Angie and Jean, except that I did want you, Angie, to know
that your hunch was right about Coop, and that I was very
happy to hear that you were not seriously hurt. I also
want you to know, dear Jean, that I was very happy to
hear from you that the picture is coming along in great shape.

Please show this letter to Jean, as it
is really written to both of you, but because you had the
premonition about Cooper, I have addressed it to you,
Angie. Another reason is because I adore you much more
than I love Jean.

                              Kisses, kisses,

Miss Angie Dickinson
c/o International Film Service
Via Piemonte 117
Rome, Italy

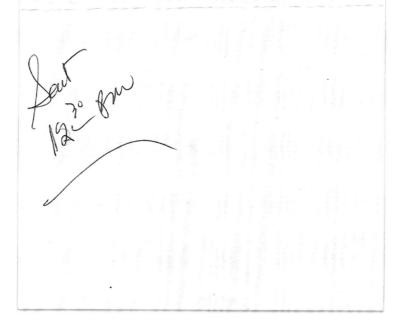

8/23/61

L/T

Harry Saltzman - Warwicfilm - London

Blumofe reports New York did not care
for Connery feels we can do better

CUBBY

Albert "Cubby" Broccoli to Harry Saltzman

AUGUST 23, 1961

With just a few Telexed words to his partner Harry Saltzman, the producer Albert "Cubby" Broccoli sums up the progress on casting the leading role in *Dr. No*, the first film based on the popular James Bond novels by Ian Fleming. Though they were produced in England, the films were bankrolled by United Artists, and clearly UA was keeping an eye on its investment. Luckily for Bond fans everywhere, Robert Blumofe, UA's head of production, changed his mind about Sean Connery and approved his casting, though no doubt he would have preferred Cary Grant, who was also at one time under consideration for the part. One of the most durable franchises in movie history, the Bond films are still produced by Broccoli and Saltzman's company, Eon Productions.

Mr. Alan Pakula
Studio

Dear Alan:

I arrived here in Monroeville this afternoon after a very interesting and beautiful drive from Montgomery. Although this is my first visit to Alabama, I have worked in the south a number of times. During my drive I was very much impressed by the lack of traffic, the beautiful countryside, and the character of the negro shacks that dot the terrain.

Harper Lee was there to meet me, and she is a most charming person. She insisted I call her Nell--feel like I've known her for years. Little wonder she was able to write such a warm and successful novel.

Monroeville is a beautiful little town of about 2,500 inhabitants. It's small in size, but large in southern character. I'm so happy you made it possible for me to research the area before designing TO KILL A MOCKINGBIRD.

Most of the houses are of wood, one story, and set up on brick piles. Almost every house has a porch and a swing hanging from the porch rafters. Believe me, it's a much more relaxed life than we live in Hollywood.

So far I have seen all the types of buildings we need for our residential street, but they are scattered throughout the town so it would have been impossible for us to shoot the picture here in Monroeville. Therefore, I feel that the freeway houses we purchased for our southern street, with sufficient remodeling, will better suit our purposes. I have also photographed a wonderful Boo Radley home, which we can duplicate on our street.

Henry Bumstead to Alan J. Pakula

NOVEMBER 1961

Art directors see the world differently, a fact that is beautifully illustrated in this letter from Henry "Bummy" Bumstead to Alan J. Pakula, the producer of *To Kill a Mockingbird*. Though the period film was shot entirely on studio streets and stages in Hollywood, Bumstead was given the opportunity to make a research trip to Monroeville, Alabama, the home of author Harper Lee and the inspiration for the novel's fictional town of Maycomb. Bumstead's eye for detail, and his delight at being shown around Monroeville by Lee, come through in every line of his letter, as does his deep understanding that the town itself will be an important character in the final film. Not surprisingly, Bumstead, supervising art director Alexander Golitzen, and set decorator Oliver Emert won Academy Awards for their outstanding work. This retyped copy of the letter from Bumstead's personal papers is misdated; his research trip most likely took place in November 1961, not November 1962.

I also visited the old courthouse square and the interior of the courtroom Nell wrote about. I can't tell you how thrilled I am by the architecture and the little touches which will add to our sets. Old pot bellied stoves still heat the courtroom and beside each one stands a tub filled with coal. Nell says we should have a block of ice on the exterior of the courthouse steps when we shoot this sequence. It seems the people chip off a piece of ice to take into the courtroom with them to munch on to try and keep cool. It reminded me of my "youth" when I used to follow the ice wagon to get the ice chips.

Nell is really amused at my picture taking, and also my taking measurements so that I can duplicate the things I see. She says she didn't know we worked so hard. This morning she greeted me with "I lost five pounds yesterday following you around taking pictures of door knobs, houses, wagons, collards, etc.--can we take time for lunch today?"

The way people look at me around town they must think I'm a Hollywood producer rather than just an art director. Nell warned me about this--that they knew someone from Hollywood was in town, but they didn't know who I was or what I did.

Yesterday afternoon the news was around town that that man from Hollywood was taking pictures in Mrs. Skinner's collard patch. They couldn't understand it because the opinion is that there are much better collard patches around town than Mrs. Skinner's. It seems that after giving me permission to photograph her collards, she rushed to the phone to give out the news. I must admit that when I confessed that I'd never seen a collard, both Mrs. Skinner and her colored help looked at me with raised eyebrows.

Nell says the exterior of Mrs. Dubose should have paint that is peeling. Also, the interior should have dark woodwork, Victorian furniture, and be grim. Her house would be wired for electricity, but she would still be using oil lamps--to save money, so Nell says. Boo Radley's should look like it had never been painted--almost haunted.

Other items which will be useful----the streets should be dirt, and there are no lamp posts as we know them today. The lamps hung from the telephone poles. Also, in 1932 they were still using wooden stoves for their cooking and heating.

The almond trees that line some of the streets are beautiful, but I feel we can get the same character by using white oaks.

There are no mailboxes on the houses--seems people go to town to the main post office to pick up their mail.

We photographed some negro shacks, which will be of great help when we come to do the exterior of Tom Robinson's shack. Many of the shacks are located in areas covered with pine trees so we could do this sequence on the Upper Lake section of the lot where we have pine trees.

We also photographed some back porches, which will come in handy when we do the back of Boo Radley's.

All in all, I certainly feel this trip will be of tremendous help in the designing of the picture. Again, my thanks to you.

Warmest regards.

Sincerely,

Henry Bumstead

Harper Lee and Henry Bumstead, 1961.

Jerry Wald to Fred Zinnemann

NOVEMBER 17, 1961

A hard-working showman who charmed his way through Hollywood, Jerry Wald spent years as a screenwriter and producer at Warner Bros. before moving on to producing stints at RKO and Columbia, where he became the vice president in charge of production under the mercurial Harry Cohn in 1952. When Wald arrived at the studio, pre-production was already underway on *From Here to Eternity*, which Cohn had assigned to producer Buddy Adler, screenwriter Daniel Taradash, and director Fred Zinnemann, who all went on to earn Academy Awards for their work on the film. In this 1961 letter, Wald addresses claims about his role in the production of *From Here to Eternity* that were made in a recent article in the journal *Films in Review*. By the time Wald wrote this response, Zinnemann had already fired off a scathing letter to the magazine contradicting the author's assertions and denying that Wald had made any significant contributions the film. In his reply, Wald artfully walks a line between agreeing with Zinnemann's objections to the article and suggesting that perhaps the director does not recall, or know, everything that went on behind the scenes. Wald's colorful account of his role at the studio and his involvement in the production provides fascinating insights into Cohn's working methods and the wheeling and dealing that went on in Hollywood's executive offices. Despite its apparent sincerity, it's doubtful that Wald's explanation was given much credence by Zinnemann, who continued to insist that Wald was taking credit where it wasn't due. Unfortunately, they were not able to continue their debate on the subject. Jerry Wald died in July 1962 at the age of fifty.

jerry **W** *ald productions*

November 17, 1961

Dear Fred:

Like yourself, I was astonished at the in-
accurate job of reporting by Mr. Nolan in the story
regarding FROM HERE TO ETERNITY. First, I never met the
gentleman; second, I have no idea where he got his
facts and third, since you were around, you know how
jealously Harry Cohn guarded his relationship with
Buddy, Danny and yourself on that film. If anything,
I was hung up in a closet to remain silently until Cohn
wanted to use me. While it has nothing to do with
your letter, it might amuse you to know that in addition
to jealously guarding the FROM HERE TO ETERNITY domain,
for some four months prior to my arrival at Columbia
Studios Harry Cohn met with me every Saturday and Sunday,
had me send him copious notes (what he did with them
I never knew, but I do have copies).

When I arrived at the Columbua Studios he carefully
shepherded me around on various points of FROM HERE TO
ETERNITY and kept me in hiding for several months. It was
Buddy Adler who first caught on to the fact that I had sent
Harry notes on the story during a meeting in which Harry read
some of them. Buddy then came to see me and indignantly de-
manded to know why I had not sent him copies. I explained
that Harry had requested that no one connected with
FROM HERE TO ETERNITY was ever to see any of my ideas - good
or bad - except himself. Buddy and I then agreed to exchange
any notes either of us wrote so that he would be prepared for
any criticism Cohn might toss at him.

I, too, was amazed that the writer of the article
in question went so far afield as to claim that he did not know
that you c ould not play chromatic jazz on army bugles. In
fact at this writing I don't know what the hell that is.

For your own personal information, Frank Sinatra
was not responsible for securing the role of 'Maggio' for himself. Ava Gardner was. I was present at Harry Cohn's home
when Ava came to see Harry and said she wanted Frank to play
the role and that if Harry would grant her this favor she would
try to break loose from one of her Metro commitments and make
a picture for him. There were no guarantees on Ava's part,
merely a promise. Harry was flattered and told Ava infront of
me about the Eli Wallach test. He kept trying to pin her down

twentieth century fox studios · beverly hills, california · crestview 6-2211 · cable address: jerwald

to a definite commitment, but Ava was evasive. Harry knew
perfectly well at that time that Eli Wallach was not going
to do the part because he had a commitment with Kazan and
'Camino Real.' I sat silently by watching this extraordinary
game of ping pong between Cohn and Ava, which resulted in
Harry promising that he would have a long talk with Buddy
and yourself and try to persuade you gentlemen to use Sinatra.

May I also remind you about the time we met in
Cohn's office and discussed the role which was eventually
played by Deborah Kerr. Perhaps you have forgotten that
Adler and yourself had made a deal with Joan Crawford
to play the role and despite the fact that Joan is a good
friend I protested vigorously that she was wrong for the
role. It was on that occasion that I jokingly said, "Let's
miscast somebody who is right for the part." Bert Allenberg
and I met secretly three nights conspiring between ourselves
on how to convince Cohn that Deborah Kerr should play the role,
then how to persuade Miss Kerr to give up her very lucrative
contract with MGM. But this is all behind us and this letter
is sent, not for publication, but to merely point out that
the reason I quit Columbia was because of Harry Cohn's maniacal
attitude toward everyone in the studio. If I had an idea
for casting, a script change or story buy, it always had to
be told to Cohn and no one else. Eventually Cohn would
convince everyone that it was his patience, perseverance and
persistence which was responsible for all films made by
Columbia and that no one contributed anything at all, including
writers, producers and directors, as well as the low man on
the totem pole -- me. It was a frustrating and irritating
four years in my life.

It might also interest you to know, ~~that~~ as a point
of historical information, that under my deal with Columbia
I had the right to 50% of the net profits of any two pictures
per year. Having worked for months prior to my arrival
at Columbia on FROM HERE TO ETERNITY with Harry Cohn, I told
him one night that I planned to collect, as part of my first
film profits, 25% of the net profits from FROM HERE TO ETERNITY.
Cohn almost blew his stack. Milton Pickman, who was my
assistant at the time, and Ben Kahane, were called in by Cohn
and told in as gentle a fit of rage as only Cohn could muster,
that I could not do this. Kahane said I had the right to do
so under my contract. This was strictly a rib on my part
because the script had been completed prior to my arrival at
the studio by Adler, Taradash and yourself and I was a guy
on the sidelines -- but it is important for you to know that
Cohn recognized that my position was clear and that despite
the fact that he had given Danny and you a piece of the picture,
If I so elected I could have taken 25% of the net profits.
I refrained from doing so on my own election and not because
Cohn intimidated me. But we had a lot of fun with Harry
exploding like a Chinese firecracker for a week before we

finally told him it was just a rib. Anyway, your letter
regarding Mr. Nolan's inaccuracies only took up a page and
a half. I could take up the entire magazine. I am sure over
the years you have been subjected to these so-called biographers
who fail to take the time to investigate the basic facts.
How the hell you stop these unsolicited biographies is something I don't understand. Unfortunately most of the time they
are written in slapdash fashion without the people written
about ever being given any opportunity to correct the copy.

I have made it a policy for more than twenty-five
years to just ignore detractors, shin-kickers and people
who prefer to tear down to building up. I have learned that
the only way to go forward in this business is to distinguish
the possible from the impossible. It is my firm belief that
it is impossible to change that which has already been
published. Nobody reads denials. However, in this case I
agree with most of the points in your letter.

One last point: sometime you should ascertain
how Burt Lancaster got into the picture. It would make 'Once
in a Lifetime' sound like a serious drama. It does not involve
Cohn, Adler or anyone else at the studio. Pickman and myself
convinced Hal Wallis to loan Burt to Columbia but the details
of the negotiations have never been printed, nor do I ever
intend that they should be...but when you feel in the mood I'd
like to have lunch with Pickman and yourself and present you
with the unvarnished truth.

Please forgive this lengthy dissertation but I wanted
to get some of the facts straightened out.

Warmest regards,

Sincerely,

JERRY WALD

Mr. Fred Zinneman
1766 Westridge Road
Los Angeles

January 23, 1962

Dear Jerry:

Do you remember some years ago when I wrote you
and Dino a joint letter (this doesn't mean I wrote it in a
joint) pleading with you not to go your separate ways, for
it would only mean disaster for both of you? Since then you
have made $18,000,000 (net) and Dino, I imagine, ~~thexxame~~ has
made about the same. Therefore I will abstain from giving
you any advice .

However I do want to thank you for your complimentary
letter. The big surprise ~~in~~ of my performance Sunday night was
that it created so much surprise, despite the fact that good
dramatic performances have been delivered by Cantor, Benny,
Wynn, Berle and, of course, you.

One member of elderly Hillcrest stopped me the other day,
shook a quivering finger in my face, and in a voice choked
with emotion said, "That's the first time you've ever been any
good!"

I think that dramatic acting, except for the greats,

is a big racket, and from here in I will grab almost any part

that doesn't require laughter. I only wish I had discovered

this twenty years ago.

I hope your suit with Paramount turns out more

successfully than the one I'm wearing.

I would like to wind this up with a Latin phrase

like "Pro hac vice" but, unfortunately, I don't know what the

hell it means.

Regards,

GROUCHO

Groucho Marx to Jerry Lewis

JANUARY 23, 1962

In 1962, comedy legend Groucho Marx, who had become a fixture on television with his show *You Bet Your Life*, took on a serious role in "The Hold Out," an episode of the anthology series *General Electric Theater*. In the half-hour program, Groucho plays the loving but concerned father of a seventeen-year-old daughter who is determined to marry her college boyfriend over her parents' objections. In this letter to Jerry Lewis, Groucho humorously deflects praise for his work by joking that dramatic acting is a racket that isn't as hard as it looks, and points out that he is just one of many comics who has recently taken on a serious role. Lewis, whose split from partner Dean Martin had been big news in the industry in 1956, was also expanding his horizons at this time. In 1959 he had starred in a dramatic television remake of *The Jazz Singer*, and in 1960 he had

directed his first film, *The Bellboy*, though he was currently embroiled in a well-publicized lawsuit with the studio about his next screen role. Hillcrest Country Club, the site of Groucho's encounter with an elderly fan, is a club and golf course in Los Angeles that was frequented by Jewish members of the movie colony. It was founded in 1920 in response to the fact that the other private clubs in Los Angeles did not accept Jews, and from the 1930s on was an important gathering place for Hollywood's powerful Jewish elite. In addition to studio heads and other bigwigs, the club was a regular hangout for comics like Groucho, George Burns, Jack Benny, Georgie Jessel, Milton Berle, and many other famous stars who regularly lunched in the dining room.

STUART R. HEISLER
134 SOUTH PALM DRIVE
BEVERLY HILLS, CALIFORNIA

February 7, 1962

Mr. Boris Leven
527 Hanley Place
Los Angeles 49
California.

Dear Boris:

Last night Randy and I went to the screening of
your picture, WEST SIDE STORY, at the Director's
Guild theatre.

The picture is great. JUST SIMPLY GREAT. IN FACT,
THE GREATEST AND MOST PROFESSIONAL JOB OF MAKING
A MOTION PICTURE FROM EVERY ANGLE THAT HAS BEEN
DONE IN AT LEAST THE LAST TEN YEARS. ALSO IT IS
THE FIRST PICTURE IN GOD KNOWS HOW LONG THAT HAS
THE FEELING OF "NEWNESS" IN PRESENTATION. Every-
body concerned deserves the highest praise that
is possible to put into words.

Your part in making this picture was sheer genius.
It was easy to see your contributions went far
beyond the usual work of an Art Director. Congratulations is a weak word to use when such brilliance
has been executed in so magnificent taste and style,
but because I can't think of a better word, it will
have to suffice. MY SINCEREST CONGRATULATIONS. If
you never make another picture as long as you live
you will have made your mark...and you will be remembered as long as there is any such thing as a
picture business.

If you don't get an "Oscar" for this, every member
of the Art Director's Guild should be " tarred and
feathered" and run out of the business.

AND IF YOUR WIFE ISN'T THE PROUDEST WOMAN IN HOLLY-
WOOD, SHE SHOULD BE RUN OUT OF TOWN!

Randy and I are both very happy for you and Vera.

Warmest regards,

Stu

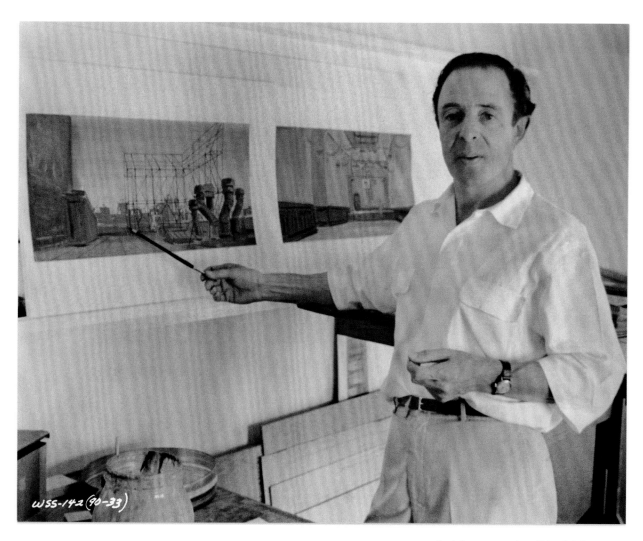

Boris Leven at work on *West Side Story*, 1961.

Stuart Heisler to Boris Leven

FEBRUARY 7, 1962

This letter from the director Stuart Heisler to production designer Boris Leven captures the excitement generated in Hollywood by the release of *West Side Story*. Working with producer Walter Mirisch and director Robert Wise, for whom he would also design *The Sound of Music*, *Star!*, and *The Sand Pebbles*, Leven's vision for *West Side Story* combined actual deserted locations on the west side of Manhattan, where Lincoln Center would soon be constructed, with stylized sets built at the Goldwyn Studios in Los Angeles. As Heisler predicted, Leven and the set decorator

on the production, Victor Gangelin, did win the Oscar for color art direction for their work on the film, which earned a total of ten Academy Awards, including best picture. Late in his career, Leven would design several films for Martin Scorsese, including *New York, New York*, another musical that created a stylized version of the Big Apple. An interesting figure in his own right, Heisler started as a prop man and editor during the silent days and later directed such films at *The Glass Key* and *Smash-Up: The Story of a Woman*.

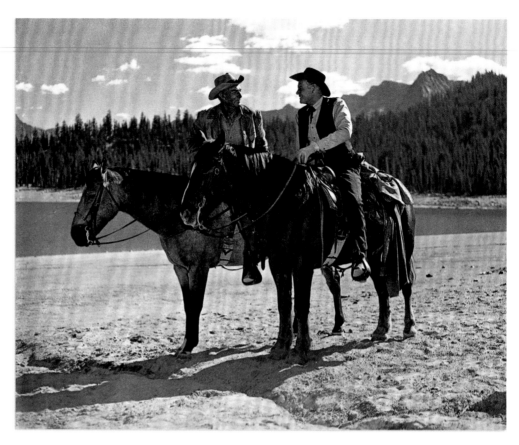

Joel McCrea to Sam Peckinpah

SPRING 1962

In 1961, the veteran actors Joel McCrea and Randolph Scott teamed up to star in *Ride the High Country*, the second feature film helmed by Sam Peckinpah, a television director whose work on shows like *The Rifleman* and *The Westerner* had established him as a promising new talent. The story of the principled Steve Judd and the cynical Gil Westrum, two old friends and aging former lawmen who take on the job of escorting a shipment of gold, the beautifully made film explores many of the themes that Peckinpah would later probe in groundbreaking revisionist Westerns like *The Wild Bunch* and *Pat Garrett and Billy the*

Kid. Like Peckinpah, McCrea was a native Californian, and both men were Westerners at heart. When he wasn't working, McCrea spent most of his time at his ranches in California and Nevada, and he appeared almost exclusively in Western films during the last twenty years of his career. A surprise critical and popular success when it was released in 1962, *Ride the High Country*, as McCrea noted, announced the arrival of a "man who can write, direct and knows the West." Twenty-two years later, when Peckinpah died at the age of fifty-nine, those words could also have been a fitting epitaph.

Dear Sam:

Thank you so much for the album—I really enjoy it. Many Nevada towns covered in it I go thru on my way to our ranch.

It was a pleasure to do a picture with a man who can write, direct and knows the West. I saw the picture at the Studio and think everyone connected with it did a good job. I hope the public like it as well as I do—If so, we have a "hit."

I'll expect to hear big things about you in the years ahead—

My best to you and your family.

As Ever
Joel
"Steve Judd"

Dear Sam:

Thank you so much for the Album — I really enjoy it — Many Nevada towns covered in it — I go thru on my way to our ranch —

It was a pleasure to do a picture with a man who can write direct and knows the West — I saw the picture at the Studio and think everyone connected with it did a good job — I hope the public like it as well as I do — If so, we have a "hit" —

I expect to hear big things about you in the years ahead —

My best to you and your family

As Ever
"Steve Judd"

Joel —

James Wong Howe to Sanora Babb

MAY 16, 1962

Cinematographer James Wong Howe wrote this letter to his wife, the writer Sanora Babb, shortly after arriving in Texas to shoot Martin Ritt's latest film, *Hud*, starring Paul Newman and Melvyn Douglas. Born in China but raised in Pasco, Washington, Howe was one of the most respected and innovative cameramen in Hollywood, with a career that spanned nearly sixty years, from the silent days to the 1970s. Howe's command of cinema imagery was legendary, and this letter, with its references to the Texas landscape, skies, and wind, shows how attuned he was to his environment. It's also a testament to the unpredictability of remote location shooting, where weather conditions can dictate creative decisions and snakes can be a workplace hazard. Jimmie was devoted to Sanora and wrote to her frequently when they were apart. They first met in the 1930s and were married in Paris in 1937, but their union was not recognized in California until 1948, when the state's miscegenation laws were overturned. Dorothy, whom Howe mentions toward the end of the letter, was Sanora's sister, who frequently lived with the couple. Chico was Jimmie and Sanora's beloved dog. *Hud*, for which Howe won his second Academy Award, was the first of four films that he photographed for Martin Ritt in the 1960s. Howe died in 1976 at the age of 76. Sanora Babb died in 2005 at the age of 98.

Wed. Nite May 16

Darling—

I miss you very, very much, as usual. Also, I miss little Chico—I do hope you both are well and happy. I'm happy because I have a job, but unhappy to be away from you & home.

We all had a very long and tiresome flight. Was delayed in L. A. for over two hours. The flight was little rough at places, otherwise O.K. Just O.K.

Getting up at seven a.m. each morning. Driving out to location at eight. The wind is blowing & blowing every day and every minute of the day. Rained, hailed, and lightning to-day. We had to stop work at noon. Came into town and I did shopping for a pair of cowboy boots— need them here to work in, because of snakes.

The people here are just wonderful and friendly. We all are very happy with their warmth & friendliness.

Claude, the small town, reminds me of Pasco, Washington. I will take pictures and send them later. I only wish you could be here with me.

Martin Ritt, director, & Paul Newman are very fine people in all ways. I am sure I will enjoy working with them. Rest of the company personnel are very nice— I expect and look forward to a pleasant assignment— (over)

Hope to get a fine movie. The country here is very beautiful in its own way. Lots of space & the skies are very interesting so far.

It was so nice talking to you darling. I'm happy that Melissa is visiting with you. Too bad it had to be as it is. I know she must feel very bad. You two can do something to cheer each other up, by reading or talking & visiting.

Hope you get Dorothy in to stay with you for awhile and take her to Oceanside. It may be what she needs to help her.

I love you my darling—
I will write again soon.

All my love to my wonderful wife.
J.

James Wong Howe and Sanora Babb at home in the 1960s.

"Luxury for Less"

1001 N.E. 8TH STREET • AMARILLO, TEXAS • PHONE DRAKE 6-5681

Wed. Nite - May. 16 -

Darling -

I miss you very, very much, as usual. Also, I miss little Chico - I do hope you both are well and happy.

I'm happy because I have a job, but unhappy to be away from you + home.

We all had a very long and tiresome flight. Was delayed in L.A. for over two hours. The flight was little rough at places, otherwise O.K. just O.K.

Getting up at seven A.M. each morning - Driving out to location at eight. The wind is blowing + blowing every day and every minute of the day - Rained, hailed

and lightning to-day. We had to stop work at noon. Came into town and I did shopping for a pair of cowboy boots. Need them here to work in, because of snakes.

The people here are just wonderful and friendly. We all are very happy with their warmth & friendliness.

Claude, the small town reminds me of Pasco, Washington. I will take pictures and send them later. Only wish you could be here with me.

Martin Ritt, director & Paul Newman are very fine people in always. I am sure I will enjoy working with them. Rest of the company personal are very nice. I expect and look forward to a pleasant assignment — (over)

Hope to get a fine movie. The country here is very beautiful in it own way. Lots of Space & the skies are very interesting so far.

It was so nice talking with you darling. I am happy that Melisa is visiting with you. Too bad, it had to be as it is. I know, she must feel very bad. You two can do something to cheer each other up, by Reading or talking & visiting —

Hope you get Dorthy in to stay with you for awhile and take her to Oceanside. It may be what she needs to help her.

I love you my darling —
I will write again soon.
All my love to my
Wonderful Wife —

J.

June 5 1962

Dear Joe:

    Realizing how scarce your time is outside of writing
and directing to meet and discuss musical problems, I am
leaving a few notes with you before departing on Saturday.
The experience of witnessing the shooting and looking at the
assembled film footage several times has given me a very
good idea of the immense task ahead of me and the opportunity
to work out many ideas. in advance to final cutting.

    I wont attempt to make any detailed observations
because it is premature in view of the editing that has to be
done. But I would like to suggest that I start working out
temporary, and in some cases permanent tracks for all the scenes
where musical instruments are evident and visual; an abundance
of "source" music which we can assume is coming from other
rooms in the palace of Cleo., music in the streets(market place);
celebration of victory, Tarsus, processional, taverns, dances,
entertainment etc. I have a rough continuity from Dorothy Spencer
and whenever I need dupes she can send them to L/A. where I can
work out more accurate timings, synchronization and recording.
Naturally, I shall use a small combination of musicians for
this purpose (if only to pace the film) until the final cut
is ready and can then expand the orchestra to fit the dramatic
needs of the scenes. I also feel some music can be used
temporarily for those personal scenes between Caesar and Cleo---
Antony and Cleo..

    The relationship between Caesar and Cleo vs. that of
Antony and Cleo poses and interesting and intriging uingmusical
problem. This again is premature thinking but my feeling about
the first afx half of the film should be objective and sort of
depersonalized in musical terms...chiefly designed to add color,
flavor, locale, subliminal sounding music. As far as music for
Cleo and Caesar is concerned, I feel the emphasis should not
be placed on the usual romantic ,sweet, lush..but rather a
musical comment delving beneath the surface of these two characters,
reflecting Caesar's primary motivation..his dedication to Rome
(and thereby stated in a quasi-martial fashionxxx with soft
muted brass and percussion;Cleo in terms of her opportunism
despite the "love" that has developed and come to fruition
in severl sensuous scenes.

    Of course, the Cleo-Antony relationship is another
story with deeper hues of color, brooding, moody and dramatic
sweep. Here, without getting sacharine and overpowering, the
music should perhaps be delicate, gentle and at times reach
great emotional levels to add another dimension to the
frustration and erupting moods of these two lovers.

I hesitate to make any observations as far as the over-all
film is concerned because I think it unfair until all the
essential scenes which will "open" up the film and provide
a proper balance and contrast between the many dialogue
scenes (taking it out of the four walls) and the outdoors
with people and activity and action are placed in their true
perspective...Again I say I am tremendously impressed with
the exquisite beauty of the film (sets, costumes, camerawork,
lighting etc) your fresh welcome literary style in this kind of
period epic and the excellent performances.

I look forward to meeting with you when your hectic
schedule relaxes so we can discuss further the musical
approach to the film.

Thank you and Mr. Wanger for this opportunity
and my sincere hopes for a great achievement (of course,
success wont hurt either)!!!

as ever,

Alex

P/S/ As a result of the many screenings, I have loads of
notes and musical ideas which will enable me to get a jump
on the score...because it never fails when it comes to the
music.   the usual rush rush rush for release...

Alex North to Joseph L. Mankiewicz

JUNE 5, 1962

Few films in the history of Hollywood have garnered the amount of publicity directed at *Cleopatra*, the massive Twentieth Century-Fox production that preoccupied the film industry for years before its release in 1963. Amid all the hype, it's easy to forget that the elaborate four-hour film was the result of years of work by hundreds of dedicated artists and craftspeople. One of those important contributors was the composer Alex North, whose earlier scores had included *A Streetcar Named Desire* and *Spartacus*. North was hired in August 1961 and almost a year later was still working out the complex score for the film, which included extensive underscoring as well as a great deal of source music that needed to be carefully researched and then recorded on authentic period instruments. This letter from North to the director Joseph L. Mankiewicz provides a look at the intricate thought process of the film composer, who often labors under extreme time pressure but whose work can have a monumental impact on a film's structure, characters, and narrative. Despite its epic proportions, *Cleopatra* met with a tepid reception when it was released in 1963, and its filmmakers were later unfairly blamed for nearly bankrupting the studio. However, North's score for the film was greatly admired, and it earned him an Academy Award nomination. A popular soundtrack album featuring selected themes was released in 1963.

Rex Harrison to Arthur P. Jacobs

SEPTEMBER 8, 1962

A seasoned actor who first appeared on British screens
in 1930, Rex Harrison was at the peak of his career when
he wrote this very self-aware and calculating letter to the
Hollywood publicist Arthur P. Jacobs in September 1962.
Not only was Harrison one of the stars of *Cleopatra*, alongside Elizabeth Taylor and Richard Burton, but he would
soon be invited to re-create his Tony-winning role as Henry
Higgins in the screen version of *My Fair Lady*, a performance
that would earn him an Academy Award. It's interesting
that in addition to capitalizing on the publicity surround-
ing *Cleopatra* and campaigning for the role in *My Fair Lady*,
Harrison suggests to Jacobs that he broaden his image by
working with some of the cutting-edge "new wave" figures
in British film and theater, like Karel Reisz and Lindsay
Anderson. Harrison's wife, who had appeared in films by
both directors, was the actress Rachel Roberts, whom he
married in 1962. The "period of great personal unhappiness" that Harrison mentions in the letter refers to the death
of his third wife, the actress Kay Kendall. They were married
in 1957, and she died in 1959 of leukemia. Jacobs had been
a studio publicist before setting up his own publicity firm in
1956. Soon after signing Harrison as a client, Jacobs moved
into producing. They must have forged a good relationship,
however: Harrison later starred in *Doctor Dolittle*, the ill-fated
1967 musical produced by Jacobs and released by Twentieth
Century-Fox.

8th September, 1962.

Dear Mr. Jacobs,

I received your cable today and am
delighted that you are starting immediately
on the campaign. Let me take the three
headings from your letter to Aaron Frosch
briefly and one at a time :

"Cleopatra":

There is little to add to what you
say. To my mind, Caesar is the most interesting part in the picture or at least,
let us say, in the script of the picture.
What the end product will be one doesn't
know! Joe Mankowitz in writing Caesar
has done so in such a full and rounded way
that he too was obviously fascinated by
the man. He certainly explored Caesar's
personality and its reactions in a subtle
and thorough way, which made it an absorb-
ing part to play. His humour, his weak-
nesses, particularly in health - for the
first time, Caesar is depicted as suffering
from epilepsy, or as Shakespeare says, the
"falling sickness", which he overcame with
fantastic strength - his kindness, his
arrogance and power, and finally almost as

a fanatical autocrat for what he thinks
is right for Rome. He was also a great
one for the ladies. Shortly before we
finished the first half of the film, Joe
very seriously said to me that he would
like to make a large bet- and he added
that he was always right in these matters
- that I must win the Academy Award for
the performance. Joe has promised me to
fight tooth and nail to keep Caesar intact
in the final cut, for his own sake as a
picture maker and writer, so let us hope
he succeeds. Anyway, no possible harm
can be done in letting the American public
know that I am one of the three stars
with a great part that I loved playing.

"Fair Lady":
       What you said about that was very
interesting re the lines you wanted to
work on (simply can't be done without
Rex Harrison etc.). Interesting, because
recently all my fanmail has been to that
effect after Cary Grant's nice quote in
the English "Sunday Express" in an interview with Roderick Mann, which you might
use : Question: "We understand that you
have been asked to play Professor Higgins?"

Cary's reply was (if you use this, you'd
better check the wording with the "Sunday
Express") "I have not been offered the
part; and if I had been, I certainly would
not do it because nobody could follow Rex
Harrison."   As far as I myself am concerned, I would like to get an offer, though
I have my reservations about the picture.
The show has been such a legend, and where-
ever I go it's Professor Higgins, that one
has some doubts as to whether the film will
match the stage production and the record.
However, no harm in getting an offer, and
I think your suggestion of referring to my
brilliant friend Robert Preston a very good
one.   Incidentally, re Robert Preston, I
now recall a very good quote in "Time" -
again, check if you are going to use it -
when the "Music Man" opened, giving me a
very good notice saying that Robert Preston
had done again what Rex Harrison was the
first to do, which was in fact the beginning
of a new musical technique - the technique
taken up later by many other big names, e.g.
Olivier and Scofield.

<u>"Institutional Image"</u>:

I particularly approve of the new
and not old-fashioned thinking you refer
to. The so-called "new stuff" does, indeed,
fascinate me. After "Fair Lady" and a
period of great personal unhappiness, I
came to life again in the "avant-garde"
theatre in London - The Royal Court Theatre
in Sloane Square (where all Bernard Shaw's
plays were originally produced). I played
for the first time in England in an old
and only recently unearthed play of Anton
Chekov, written when he was only 21
and called "Platonov". Platonov was a
Russian school-master rake, and the play
was a great success for the season I
played it, and I won the Best Actor of
the Year Award with Alec Guinness, who got
it for "Ross". I also met Rachel, who I
have now married. She was my leading lady
and for her performance got the American
Award - The Clarence Derwent Award for the
best supporting actress of the year.

Through Kenneth Tynan, I have met
a lot of the young writers and directors -
the "new wave" group - resulting in my
going last year, just before "Cleopatra",
to the Edinburgh Festival, and later again
to The Royal Court Theatre, in a new play

by a brilliantly funny writer called Nigel
Dennis. It was a satire and was not a great
success because it was too modern and too
new, making fun of everything - the British
"Establishment", Socialism, the Church, the
Press - especially the Press, which didn't
help! It should be pointed out that these
adventures are of my own choosing, because
in the theatre I can do pretty well what I
like.

Karel Reisz, who directed Rachel in
"Saturday Night and Sunday Morning", is a
great friend and he and I very much want to
work together. Karel won everything in
sight, as you probably know, for "Saturday
Night and Sunday Morning", and Rachel got
the British Film Academy Award for her performance in it. Rachel was doing a new film
for Karel Reisz and another brilliant young
director, Lindsay Anderson, when I was in
Rome doing Caesar, and in my few and far
between breaks I flew over and watched them
making it - very fascinating.

One final point, I saw in your letter
to Aaron Frosch you said you tried to contact
me in Rome for Public Relations purposes.
First; I never got to know of this attempt,

and secondly, the Press badgered Rachel
and I, who weren't married then, to such
an extent that, for obvious personal
reasons, too much publicity was not
possible. But now is different. I liked
the tone of your letter very much, so when
do we start and how? I do not like doing
photographic lay-outs but I have got a
lovely villa in Portofino. In fact, I
built it twelve years ago and it has never
been photographed! If you advise, I would
submit to having it photographed if it was
done at the very top level and not thrown
away on just anybody, because my life has
been very private - at least, as far as my
home is concerned. I have also a very
beautiful cabin-cruiser in the port,
which might also make useful lay-out. I
will also give interviews, providing they
are carefully sorted out and we know in
advance the angle of the interviewer etc.
etc.

        To sum up, I believe I do need re-
presentation at a top level in America
and Europe and am very glad to be in your
hands.

I feel that certainly as far as
"Cleopatra" and "Fair Lady" are concerned, there is no time to waste and
speed is of the essence.

Regards,

Rex Harrison

Villa San Genesio,
Portofino,
Ligure,
Italy.

RH/EJ

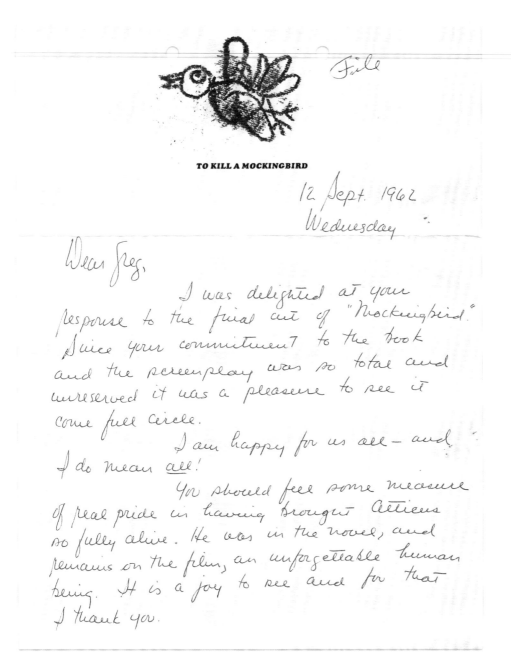

TO KILL A MOCKINGBIRD

12 Sept. 1962
Wednesday

Dear Greg,

I was delighted at your response to the final cut of "Mockingbird". Since your commitment to the book and the screenplay was so total and unreserved it was a pleasure to see it come full circle.

I am happy for us all — and I do mean all!

You should feel some measure of real pride in having brought Atticus so fully alive. He was in the novel, and remains on the film, an unforgettable human being. It is a joy to see and for that I thank you.

Robert Mulligan to Gregory Peck

SEPTEMBER 12, 1962

This letter to Gregory Peck from Robert Mulligan, the director of *To Kill a Mockingbird*, captures the dedication of the filmmakers and actors who shepherded Harper Lee's bestselling novel to the screen. Mulligan and his producing partner, Alan J. Pakula, had gotten their starts in television, and they brought a straightforward simplicity to the adaptation, which was made in black and white and featured nuanced, understated performances by Peck and the other actors in the film, many of whom were unknowns. Made at the height of the civil rights era, *To Kill a Mockingbird* has inspired generations of moviegoers with its message of courage in the face of injustice and its unflinching look at the South's legacy of racism. Atticus Finch became Peck's signature role, and he was awarded the best-actor Academy Award for his performance in the film, which also won Oscars for its screenplay by Horton Foote and its art direction by Henry Bumstead, Alexander Golitzen, and Oliver Emert.

I have just returned from a brief vacation with my family. My first in years. It was marvelous. During the next several weeks the scoring and dubbing will be completed and we expect to preview on or about Oct. 19. I'm certain we will see each other long before then. I hope so.

Elmer Bernstein will be playing some of the score for me next week. Alan and I both feel he will do a marvelous job. As I told you, we are now more than ready to see the next stages of the film completed — but to perfection, in this best of all possible worlds.

Please give my very best to Veronique. Enjoy your holiday.

Warmest regards,

Bob.

---

12 Sept. 1962
Wednesday

Dear Greg,

I was delighted at your response to the final cut of "Mockingbird." Since your commitment to the book and the screenplay was so total and unreserved it was a pleasure to see it come full circle.

I am happy for us all—and I do mean <u>all!</u>

You should feel some measure of real pride in having brought Atticus so fully alive. He was in the novel, and remains in the film, an unforgettable human being. It is a joy to see and for that I thank you.

I have just returned from a brief vacation with my family. My first in years. It was marvelous. During the next several weeks the scoring and dubbing will be completed and we expect to preview on or about Oct. 19. I'm certain we will see each other long before then. I hope so.

Elmer Bernstein will be playing some of the score for me next week. Alan and I both feel he will do a marvelous job. As I told you, we are now more than ready to see the next stages of the film completed—but to perfection, in this best of all possible worlds.

Please give my very best to Veronique.
Enjoy your holiday.

Warmest regards,
Bob.

Audrey Hepburn to George Cukor

APRIL 6, 1963

When Jack Warner paid $5.5 million for the screen rights to *My Fair Lady*, many fans thought that he would naturally use the Broadway cast on screen, but the veteran studio head had other plans. Famously, he offered the role of Eliza Doolittle not to newcomer Julie Andrews, who had originated the part on stage, but to Audrey Hepburn, then one of Hollywood's top leading ladies. Though Warner undoubtedly cast Hepburn because she was a box-office draw, in many ways she was an inspired choice. Trained as a dancer in her youth, she had starred opposite Fred Astaire in the musical *Funny Face*, and she was widely considered one of the most versatile actresses in Hollywood, comfortable in comedy as well as drama. In this charming letter to the film's director, George Cukor, Hepburn communicates the excitement she feels about playing Eliza and shows just how seriously she was taking what she clearly saw as a once-in-a-lifetime opportunity. She also shows that she was a pro all the way, deferring to designer Cecil Beaton when appropriate, but also feeling confident enough to suggest that Cukor consider hiring choreographer Eugene Loring and asking for her personal shoemaker to create Eliza's footwear. In the end, Hepburn delivered a luminous performance, though her work was overshadowed by the fact that the studio chose to dub her singing voice. Overlooked by the Academy, she nevertheless was on hand at the Oscars to graciously present Rex Harrison with his best-actor award for *My Fair Lady*—and to congratulate Julie Andrews, who won the best-actress statuette for her film debut in *Mary Poppins*.

6 April '63

Dearest George

Well! Your sweet letter and the <u>SCRIPT</u> arrived. As I was just off for a few days in Madrid with Mel, I took it with me and read it one afternoon, resting in bed. There are not words! It's <u>MARVELLOUS</u>, I am beyond myself with happiness and excitement! It is <u>all</u> so good and so solid, warm funny and enchanting. I just pray every day to be as good as the role, or is that too much to ask for? All the wonder of the musical and the play are there, it's just smashing! What a moment it was when it came in the mail, and there it was for <u>me</u>!!!

It goes without saying that I long to see and work with you, at last at last, what a summer to look forward to! Am really in quite a "state" with the joy of it all.

Have thought much about your search for a "musical number setter." Think again about Gene Loring. The reason I dare to even make the suggestion is that I know him and you. You would <u>like</u> him. He is totally without the kind of "ego" that would make him insist on "his way" if you know what I mean. He is a gentle soft-spoken, very talented man and does have humour. I don't know whether you saw the sequence in the nightclub in "Funny Face." It was humorous and fun. You might want to see it? Paramount has it. That of course was a "way out" bit of choreography to match the scene—but I do think he can do any kind of style required, and you would find him wonderfully easy to work with. Just a thought.

Then do you think Cecil could send me the designs for any shoes that I will be wearing in the picture, except of course the clodhoppers I am bound to be wearing in the first part. I tell you why. One is an awful lot on one's feet when working—and since my days in the ballet I have had "trouble with me feet" unless properly "shoed." The last few years I have taken to having my shoes for movies made by my own private bootmaker in Paris and have tripped through many a picture without a moment's bother. It does make all the difference. Perhaps the Wimpole Street, Ball, and Ascot shoes could be made here—he makes them quickly, no fitting as he has my last. If Cecil does not like them when he sees them we will immediately discard them. Cecil might want to enclose a sample of material if the ball slippers have to match the dress—they dye any colour one wants.

Sorry to bother you with this, but I just say if ye feet are comfy......It may be all too complicated for Cecil at this time, in that case, no mind.

All all my love and a kiss for Cecil
Audrey

6 april '63

Dearest George
          Well! your
sweet letter and the SCRIPT
arrived. As I was just
off for a few days in
Madrid with Mel. I took
it with me and read
it one afternoon, resting
in bed. There are no
words! It's MARVELLOUS,
I am beyond myself
with happiness and
excitement! It is all so

good and so solid, warm
funny and enchanting,
I just pray every day to
be as good as the role.
or is that too much to ask
for? all the wonders of
the musical and the play
are there, it's just
smashing! What a moment
it was when it came in
the mail, and there it
was for me !??
It goes without saying
that I long to see and
work with you, at last
at last, what a summer

to look forward to!
I am really in quite
a 'state' with the joy
of it all.
Have thought much about
your search for a 'musical
number setter'. Think again
about Gene Loring. The
reason I dare to even make
the suggestion is that I
know him and you. You
would like him. He is
totally without the kind
of 'ego' that would make
him insist on 'his way',
if you know what I mean.
he is a gentle softspoken

very talented man
[seal] and does dance numbers.
I don't know whether you
saw the sequence in the
night club in 'Funny Face'.
it was humorous and fun.
you might want to see it?
Paramount has it. That of
course was a 'way out'
bit of choreography to
match the scene - But I
do think he can do
any kind of style required,
and you would find him
wonderfully easy to work with.
Yust a thought.
Then do you think Cecil

could send me the designs
for any shoes I will
be wearing in the picture,
except of course the
clod hoppers I am bound
to be wearing in the first
part. I tell you why.
One is an awful lot
on ones feet when
working - and since my
days in the Ballet I have
had 'trouble with me feet"
unless properly 'shoed'.
The last few years I have
taken to having my shoes
for movies made by my

own private boot-
maker in Paris and
have tripped through
many a picture without
a moments bother, it
does make all the difference.
Perhaps the Wimpole street,
Ball, and Ascot shoes
could be made here - he
makes them quickly, no
fitting as he has my last.
If Cecil does not like them
when he sees them we will
emmediately discard them.
Cecil might want to enclose
a sample of material t
the ball slippers have to match

the dress. they dye any
colour one wants.
Sorry to bother you with
this, but I just say
if ye feet are comfy ....
it may be all to complicated
for Cecil at this time, in
that case, no mind.

    All all my love
and a kiss for Cecil
        Audrey

SIDNEY LUMET

Aug. 4, 1963

Sweet Kate,

I didn't get in touch
during Spence's illness
because, one: you'll
handle it better than
anyone; two: the
last thing you'd
need is coping with
concerned friends.
But my thoughts
were with you and
the standing offer
is forever: if you

Sidney Lumet to Katharine Hepburn

AUGUST 4, 1963

In 1962, Sidney Lumet had directed Katharine Hepburn in the acclaimed film adaptation of Eugene O'Neill's *Long Day's Journey into Night*, and clearly they had forged a close friendship when working together on the production. Like so many Lumet films, *Long Day's Journey* was shot in New York, primarily at the Chelsea Studios. Now, the following year, Lumet was writing to Hepburn in Los Angeles, where she was taking time off from acting to care for her longtime companion Spencer Tracy. Lumet's letter illustrates the support system of friends who surrounded Hepburn, and it also sheds light on the filmmaker's current projects, which included *Fail Safe*, a political thriller, which he did direct, and *The Heart Is a Lonely Hunter*, a film based on the Carson McCullers novel, which he did not end up directing. The producer that he refers to as Eli is most likely Ely Landau, who coproduced *Long Day's Journey*.

August 4, 1963

Sweet Kate,

I didn't get in touch during Spence's illness because, one: you'll handle it better than anyone; two: the last thing you'd need is coping with con-cerned friends. But my thoughts were with you and the standing offer is forever: if you need anything, just yell. Cross country or what, I'll be there.

"Fail-Safe" is good, I think. My God, I'd forgot-ten how much help a good <u>story</u> is. About to start "Heart is a Lonely Hunter" for Eli. He's building an empire and I think will own everything one day.

All's well, except I feel too tired to fall in love again, and I hate not being in love. Are you well?

I've moved and am having a ball furnishing it. Write the new number down:
68 Charles St.
N.Y. 14 N.Y.
Tel.: WA98320

Love, love to you and be well.
Sidney

September 23, 1963.

Mr. Samuel Goldwyn
Samuel Goldwyn Studio
Santa Monica at Formosa
Hollywood, California

Dear Mr. Goldwyn:

One of the chief disappointments in my re-visit
to Hollywood this past summer for the article I am
writing for Life on the Changing Face of Hollywood,
was my failure to talk with you. When I phoned your
office you were in Europe and when I returned to Hollywood last week for a last minute roundup, you had not
yet returned from New York.

Since you have been a leader of the Hollywood
community from its very inception until the present
time, I wanted to ask you what you thought of the future
of Hollywood and American film-making. As I made the
rounds last July and August it seemed to me that Hollywood was so changed from the industry I knew thirty
years ago as to be almost unrecognizable. Though Hollywood was still taking two out of every three dollars in
the world market, it seemed to have lost its creative
leadership. Time Magazine, for instance, was able to
publish a long cover story on "Cinema as an International
Art" with hardly a mention of Hollywood film-makers. I
felt that perhaps a new Hollywood was in the making with
the flags of the major studios hanging limp, with carpet-
baggers seemingly popping out of the woodwork to package
important productions, with a few established directors
enjoying more freedom than ever before; it seemed to me
a period of confusion, uncertainty, a groping toward
goals and programs not clearly understood.

This may sound as if I am answering the
questions rather than asking them, but I am really
curious as to your reaction to my observations. As a
producer I have long admired for succeeding in being
his own man in a company town, you are in an ideal
position to tell me where you think the Hollywood of
the Sixties is headed? Downward, onward, upward? Will
it be able to compete with the revolutionary filmmakers of Italy, France, England, even India, who

Mr. Samuel Goldwyn
Hollywood, Calif.   -2-   September 23, 1963.

seem to be capturing more and more the imagination of
a new generation of film-goers? Does the super-studio
conception of Wasserman-MCA-Revue-U.I. bode positively
or negatively for the future? Is the star system out
of hand? Will young, enthusiastic, gifted film-makers
like the Perrys of "David and Lisa" find genuine encouragement in Hollywood, or will they be either ignored or
absorbed into the old system? These are some of the challenging questions I am asking myself as I outline my
article and your thoughts on these subjects will be
greatly welcome and appreciated.

     Unfortunately, while the questions are long,
my deadline is almost upon me and so although I realize
it may be an imposition, I would appreciate your writing
me at your earliest convenience.

     I do not know when I shall be back in Holywood
again, but when I am, entirely aside from professional
interests, I shall take the liberty of calling on you
as I have always enjoyed our visits.

     With warm best wishes,

                                        As always,

                                        Budd Schulberg.

BWS/sb

Budd Schulberg to Samuel Goldwyn

SEPTEMBER 23, 1963

The son of studio executive B. P. Schulberg and the agent Adeline Jaffe Schulberg, writer Budd Schulberg was raised in Hollywood and was always fascinated by what made the movie business work. In 1941, Schulberg made a name for himself in his hometown when, at the age of twenty-seven, he published *What Makes Sammy Run?*, a satirical novel that skewered the film industry and introduced the world to Sammy Glick, the scheming studio hack who cheats his way to the top. Though it was fiction, Schulberg's appraisal of the business made him somewhat of an expert on Hollywood, and for the rest of his career, he not only wrote for the movies but also frequently wrote about them. When Schulberg contacted Sam Goldwyn in 1963, he was working on a wide-ranging article for *Life* magazine about the current state of the movie industry, and it's clear from his letter that he had not only done his homework but also had a very good sense of where the industry was headed. The in-depth article, "How Are Things in Panicsville?," was published in the December 1963 issue of *Life*.

Jay Presson Allen
to Alfred Hitchcock

FEBRUARY 23, 1964

Jay Presson Allen was a New York–based novelist and playwright who had never written a feature film script when she
was hired by Alfred Hitchcock to write the screenplay for
Marnie, based on the novel by Winston Graham. Working
on the script initially with Joseph Stefano and later with
Evan Hunter, who had written the screenplay for *The Birds*,
Hitchcock wanted to go in a new direction and hired Allen
after reading her as-yet-unproduced stage adaptation
of the book *The Prime of Miss Jean Brodie*. The formidable
director and the vibrant younger writer hit it off, and she
spent several months in Los Angeles working closely with
Hitchcock on the script and spending time with both
Hitchcock and his wife, Alma, at their home in Bel-Air.
This letter from Allen to Hitchcock, written from New York
when the film was in production in Los Angeles, provides a
sense of the close friendship that Allen had formed with the
Hitchcocks during their time together. The "writers' union"
that Allen refers to is the Writers Guild of America, which
arbitrates screenwriting credits when there is a dispute.
Evan Hunter, who had parted ways with Hitchcock over
the script, had asked the Guild to award him co-screen-
writing credit on *Marnie*, and it sounds like the Hitchcocks
were more than happy to report that Hunter's appeal had
been rejected and Allen had been given sole credit. Allen
later worked on the script for *Mary Rose*, an adaptation of
a ghost story by J. M. Barrie that Hitchcock had wanted to
do for years but was never able to complete. She continued
to write for the stage, and also found great success as the
screenwriter for film adaptations of her plays *The Prime of
Miss Jean Brodie* and *40 Carats*, as well as for *Cabaret*, *Funny
Lady*, and *Prince of the City*. Allen's second husband, whom
she mentions in the letter, was the theater and film producer Lewis Allen.

Milord,

I got official notification on Saturday from that
writers' union out there about the billing. I
thought it was so sweet of you to call me, however,
when the first word came through. I was nowhere
near as concerned about it as you and Alma were...
but then I wasn't having to make the gesture of thanking
some miss nobody for her contribution to my picture,
was I? I do love you, you pathologically greedy-compulsively
generous old thing!

Funny doings. /Evan Hunter hates Lewie...has for years. *to LEWIE?*
Naturally, he/now hates me as well. So guess who sent
his new play (Lewis mumbled grudgingly...no compulsive
generousity there ....that it was pretty good. Slick
and very commercial) to Lewie? The old black-hearted
Hunter himself, that's who. I figured either some agent
did it without consulting the author, or else Hunter did
it himself so as to make Lewie sit up and beg and then
he could sorry, old chap...some secretary's mix-up...it's
already sold. We'll never know. Lewie sent the script
back with no comment. But he's been pretty tight-lipped
for a couple of days.

My beautiful Rose blouse came and it is every bit as
delicious as I had remembered. My big problem is when
am I going to be able to sit down to dinner or spend an
evening at home with someone in to gaze at my finery? I
am farmed out over here working my hump off and that seems
to be all of my foreseeable future. I wrote a long letter
to Alma about this problem...will you remind her to solve
it?

You are a lousey correspondant and never even send a mildly
dirty postcard flying my way. You know I am consummed with
curiousity about the flick and the folks involved. I am
3000 miles away, damn it!

Please check on short, short story that appeared in Sunday
the 23rd issue of This Week...we get it in the Sunday
Herald Tribune. The story is by John D. MacDonald and
is called Blurred View. It would make a good TVer.

All my love,

Jay

From Saul Chaplin, on
location with the
shooting of "The Sound
of Music". Ernest Lehman

HOTEL ÖSTERREICHISCHER HOF
SALZBURG

Thursday, May 21, 1964.

Dear Ernie-baby:

I know this letter has been a long time a-comin' but there's
a very good reason for its not having been written before:
there just hasn't been any time. My life these days is as
follows: I get up between 6 and 6:15 every morning and return at about six thirty or seven at night. I get cleaned
up and about the time when dinner is over, at about 10:30
or 11, it's time for bed. If there is any recreation time
I don't exactly feel like writing letters. As a result, I'm
sure I'm leaving a trail of enemies on both continents - from
London to Los Angeles.

Now about the picture. The film, to date, looks absolutely
marvelous and we're all very pleased. We have shot up to now
The Wedding, The Mother Abbess's Office, The Mirabell Gardens,
Winkler's Terrace, The Horse Fountain, The Chapel (faces of
nuns praying), Rocky Riding School (Night and day sequences),
Nonnberg Abbey (Night and day sequences), and various other
places that I can't off-hand remember. The cast is uniformly
excellent. The most temperamental member of the company turns
out to be Ted McCord but since the results he's getting are so
good we can live with it. This week we have finally been faced
with the dreaded problem of location shooting: we've run out
of cover-set and it's been raining since Tuesday. (Monday was
a non-shooting day since it was a holiday - Whit Monday.) This
morning it cleared up for a few hours so we scurried out of the
cars in which we had been waiting for just such a break and shot
the Horse Fountain. However, this afternoon - more rain - hence
this letter. As it turns out we have been shooting mostly numbers. Bob used yesterday (during the rain) as a rehearsal day.
He rehearsed the scene in the car coming to the Trapp Villa and
the one that follows it on the Trapp Villa Terrace. I was only
there for part of it and it seemed to be going well. Incidentally,
building the exterior next to Leopoldskron turned out to be a
break since we can shoot towards Leopoldskron and have the full
scope of our lawn plus theirs.

The cast is divided between the Oyster House (my name for the
above Hof) and the Bristol. Pamela Danova rules over the bar
at the Bristol where she's had a piano installed and almost
every night Chris Plummer gets crocked and plays the piano end-
lessly. I haven't heard him yet because I think he's appre-
hensive about playing when I'm within earshot. I've been
told he plays magnificently. We seem to be in two factions but
we're not warring - as a matter of fact, everyone is getting on
so well, it's scary. The kids are getting along fine except that
every once in a while one of them becomes a pain because of needless complaining but even that happens very seldom. We have a
man assigned to looking after the kids and their mothers which
is one of the wiser decisions we made. Richard Haydn has turned
out to be fabulously witty and Gil Stuart (he plays Franz) has
turned out to be the wolf of all time. We have found a fabulous
"Maria's Mountain" and are now in the process of trying to work
it out because it happens to be in Bavaria. We also found a-
nother one in Bavaria for the end of the picture. All other

locations, with a few exceptions (the kids in the trees, the turn-off from the road fo Vienna to the Trapp Villa) have been found and secured. I neglected to mention that on Sundays we look for locations.

Beyond all of this there's nothing more I can tell you. There are endless strange and funny things that have happened but those'll have to wait until I next see you. I can only tell you we're all working very hard — the results are excellent and if we got several sunny weeks we'd finish somewhere near on time. I think we must be about 6 or 7 days behind now. I haven't checked recently. What's infinitely more important is that we're getting what we came after.

I'm a little happy not to be suffering through the early part of this season with the Dodgers. We get the papers here late as you know and it sure looks disastrous. You always have your Yankees, however, so it can't be too bad. How is VIRGINIA WOLF coming? What color have you decided for your offices? Is there such a place as Los Angeles? It doesn't seem so at the moment. There's just Salzburg, The Sound Of Music and location hunting. That's not completely true — I've been to a few marvelous concerts and we went to Vienna for Whit Sunday and Monday and had a marvelous time.

I just looked out of the window and the sun is blazing away. The only problem is that it's now 6:30 and we wrapped up at 5:30.

Bob said that if I wrote to send his best which is what I'm doing. Give my love to Jackie, Roger and Allan. Please write.

Saul Chaplin
to Ernest Lehman

MAY 21, 1964

Saul Chaplin was a songwriter, composer, and music director who started out on Tin Pan Alley and ended up working on a string of successful MGM musicals during the 1950s, winning three Oscars along the way. In this fascinating letter to Ernest Lehman, the screenwriter of *The Sound of Music*, Chaplin, an associate producer on the film, paints a detailed portrait of the company's overseas shoot in Salzburg and other nearby locations, including a rundown of the uncooperative weather. In addition to cast members Christopher Plummer, Richard Haydn, and Gil Stuart, Chaplin mentions Pamela Danova, who was the dialogue coach on the film, and Ted McCord, the cinematographer. After eleven weeks in Austria, the company returned to Los Angeles in July to shoot the rest of the interiors on the Twentieth Century-Fox lot. This was the second film collaboration for Chaplin, Lehman, and the director Robert Wise. Three years earlier they had all worked together on the critically acclaimed screen adaptation of *West Side Story*.

WARNER BROS. PICTURES. INC
BURBANK, CALIFORNIA

INTER-OFFICE COMMUNICATION

TO MR. __J.L.Warner__   DATE __October 16, 1964__

FROM MR __Ernest Lehman__   SUBJECT __"WHO'S AFRAID OF VIRGINIA WOOLF?"__

Dear Jack:

First let me say I hope you are enjoying your stay in New York.

This communique is about our "leading man." I have given it nights and days, weeks and months of deepest thought, and have come to the conclusion that, if we can get his representatives to be reasonably accommodating, the best man for the role, from both the artistic and box-office standpoint, is Richard Burton.

Elizabeth Taylor told me, at our last meeting, that she wanted very much to have Richard play the role. I told her, and Richard, that I had certain reservations: (a) we probably couldn't afford him; (b) he might be too "strong" for the role; (c) a Taylor and Burton picture might appear to be "gimmicky," and this film is too important to be that.

She disagreed with me on all counts, said the picture needs a great actor, which he is, a man who suggests great intellectual depth, which he has, an actor who can belt out the great dialogue like no one else can.

Richard said he wanted to re-read the script to convince himself that he was eminently right for the role, but that he would be, of course, available to play it if we wanted him.

My impression, at the time, was that he was itching to have the role, but a bit too proud to make a pitch to me, particularly in view of my reservations.

I have considered every possible actor for the role, and the few who are even close to being possibilities are either wrong for the part, or have been turned down by Miss Taylor, or are, even though not right for the part, just as costly as Burton.

VERBAL MESSAGES CAUSE MISUNDERSTANDING AND DELAYS
(PLEASE PUT THEM IN WRITING)

Ernest Lehman to Jack L. Warner

OCTOBER 16, 1964

Ernest Lehman, the versatile screenwriter of *North by Northwest*, *West Side Story*, and *The Sound of Music*, took on one of his most challenging assignments when he tackled Edward Albee's black comedy *Who's Afraid of Virginia Woolf?* The writer as well as the producer of the film, Lehman oversaw every aspect of the production, including the casting and the hiring of director Mike Nichols, though as this memo shows, other directors, including John Frankenheimer, were under

WARNER BROS. PICTURES. INC.
BURBANK. CALIFORNIA

INTER-OFFICE COMMUNICATION

TO MR. J.L. Warner   DATE October 16, 1964

FROM MR. Ernest Lehman   SUBJECT "WHO'S AFRAID OF VIRGINIA WOOLF?"

#2

    I came to the conclusion that we'd be lucky to have him. It would not only give us a fine, world-renown actor and recently born movie star, but it would give us an important steadying influence on Miss Taylor during the making of the picture (she would not have to be wondering, and worrying, where he is).

    I also came to the conclusion that the Taylor-Burton combination, tearing each other to bits in this savage, humorous, sad and terrifying picture would not be gimmicky -- it could be a giant plus at the box-office.

    Today I spoke to Hugh French (there he is again) in London. He told me Richard has decided he definitely would like to be in the picture. Hugh also said categorically (though we'll have to get it in writing): "Elizabeth and Richard together agree to do the picture with John Frankenheimer directing."

    There it is, Jack. My feeling is (and Walter concurs with me) that we should try to make a deal with Burton as soon as possible, if it is one you can live with. And then immediately close with Frankenheimer if he is still available.

    If we are not going to be able to make a deal with Burton, the sooner we know it, the better. Because we will then have to get Miss Taylor's approval of someone else -- and if that's going to be a problem, the sooner we know that the better.

    I don't mean to sound at all negative about the prospect of Elizabeth Taylor and Richard Burton in "Who's Afraid of Virginia Woolf?" Actually, it's pretty damned exciting.

          As ever,

EL/b   Ernest Lehman

VERBAL MESSAGES CAUSE MISUNDERSTANDING AND DELAYS
(PLEASE PUT THEM IN WRITING)

consideration before Nichols was offered the job. In this communication to studio head Jack Warner, who had paid half a million dollars for the property, Lehman makes a pitch for casting Richard Burton in the leading role, arguing not only that he is the best actor for the part but also that the charged relationship between Burton and his wife Elizabeth Taylor would add even more drama to the scenes they had together. Though it was a difficult production, with frayed nerves all around, the completed film was widely acclaimed and nominated for thirteen Academy Awards, winning five, including the best-actress Oscar for Taylor. Walter, whom Lehman mentions in the letter, is most likely Walter McEwen, a Warner Bros. executive who worked closely with studio head Jack Warner. Hugh French was a former actor turned talent agent who represented both Taylor and Burton in the 1960s, as well as many other well-known Hollywood stars.

December 2, 1964

My dear Katharine:

I've been meaning to write you for a long time, but when this photograph came in yesterday, I thought, "What the hell!" You might like to see how beautiful you look -- even without makeup and a dirty face. Both you and Bogie were so wonderful in the picture.

I don't know why we can't be friends. Perhaps you do. But I'd like to be able to call you up once in a while and say hello and perhaps reminisce a bit, and promise not to put a word of it in the column. I have always admired you and think it's a crime that you're not acting. We have no one fit to kiss your feet. You have a gaiety, a gallantry, a gentlemanly way of expressing yourself that no other dame in this town had -- not even Garbo. As I grow older, I've mellowed and think of days gone by instead of the trash they're putting out in the name of motion pictures today. You were a big part of that era, and I miss you.

Yours,

Hollywood 83686
Cr 6 9428

Hedda

Hedda Hopper to Katharine Hepburn & Hepburn's Reply

DECEMBER 2, 1964,
& DECEMBER 7, 1964

In December 1964, the aging gossip columnist Hedda Hopper, in a nostalgic mood, wrote an admiring letter to Katharine Hepburn, and sent it along with a photograph of Hepburn with Humphrey Bogart in *The African Queen*. Hopper's comment that "it's a crime that you're not acting," refers to the fact that Hepburn was taking a break from her career in order to care for her longtime companion, Spencer Tracy, who was in failing health. In her reply, Hepburn reminisces about working with Bogart, recalls how pleased he was to win the Academy Award, and graciously accepts Hopper's praise, while being careful not to suggest that she endorses Hopper's destructive choice of profession or her right-wing beliefs. The fiercely private Hepburn was always wary of gossip columnists, but Hopper had been particularly hard on the actress in the 1940s, when they were on opposite sides of the political spectrum. Hopper, who claims to have "mellowed," seems to want to forget those times, but Hepburn's sly reference to the conservative statesman John Foster Dulles suggests that the actress has not forgotten—or forgiven—Hopper's behavior. Hopper died in 1966, so was not around to witness the impressive revitalization of Hepburn's career, which started with her return to the screen opposite Tracy in the 1967 film *Guess Who's Coming to Dinner*. Hepburn won a best-actress Oscar for that role and went on to win two more Oscars, for *The Lion in Winter* and *On Golden Pond*.

XII - 7 - 1964

Dear Hedda

That's a wonderful picture of old Bogey
and me --- Wasn't it great that he won that fool
thing - he was the one person I knew who said-"I
should win it - I'm going to try and win it"- he
and Bett planned the party before the outcome
was in any way certain - not afraid of being a
fool - Also he loved being an actor - thought he
was a damned good one and was as proud of his
profession as a wonderful furniture maker or
silversmith-- like Constance - In Africa - every
week or so he'd come to me - " You happy? Got
everything you need ? - Room comfortable ? " He
really was a gent - a well mannered gentle fellow -

You and I are friends Hedda - Time has
seen to that - You have survived - I have survived
and so there is a natural admiration - not of your
politics not of your profession but of you - and your
stride and your looks and capacity to get on with it -
your character - on your own terms - and that I
think - is what you admire in me - - - As my father

said about Dulles " I disagree with almost everything
he says - but by gum the old boy has guts "
Your letter was very flattering - too
much - but I enjoyed reading it -

Dear Billy & I. A. L.

August 20, 1965.

I didn't want to come to your office to tell you about my reaction to your "FORTUNE COOKIE" because I was afraid I might interrupt the song of the Muses, to which both of you are probably just tuned in. So I jot down a few lines.

Since you familiarized me a few weeks ago with the basic idea of your new picture, it was a pretty sure thing that I would like it anyway. As you know, I took to the idea right away. But your 84 yellow pages surpassed my expectations. I was amused, thrilled, truly enthusiastic. All this s i n e i n v i d i a.

Tuesday, at lunch at the Brown Derby, Billy commented on his state of confusion about today's market, which is easily understandable considering the ludicrous box office successes of "KNACK" and "PUSSYCAT". But there is absolutely nothing confusing in the conception and construction of your first 84 pages. They are clear, disciplined, scintillating. Puritan that I am, my applause for your achievement is much the heartier since there are no double entendres or unnecessary risqué situations.

Walter Matthau to Billy Wilder & I. A. L. Diamond

AUGUST 20, 1965

The first film to team Walter Matthau with Jack Lemmon, *The Fortune Cookie* was also Matthau's first collaboration with writer-director Billy Wilder and his writing partner I. A. L. "Izzy" Diamond, who had been working together since the late 1950s. In this letter from Matthau to Wilder and Diamond, the actor shows great enthusiasm for the team's latest script and remarkable insight into their work

You really got (just like in "THE APARTMENT") a slashing satire
on paper, and not one that will close on Saturday, as George S.
Kaufman put it. Your ambition and good taste have resulted
beyond any doubt in a rare comedy like in the good old days, a
comedy with depth of characterization, not just funny situations
or conflicts. In spite of the hilarity of action and dialog,
you really got some beautiful delineation of the three characters:
Harry, Willie, and the colored football player. All three have
identification. Seldom have you achieved such fully developed
characters. They will play by themselves, and thank God
Mr. Lemmon is not lecherous for once and is permitted to play
a human being right out of 1966. My highest praise goes to the
topicality of the story. We now live in the sad age of greed,
with twenty-four hour strife for fringe benefits, insurance,
severance pay, deductions, tax evasions, and you got them all in
with charm and devastating humor.

Since I don't know the balance of the script - contentwise
and pagewise - it seems to me that the sequence called the Snake
Pit, pages 69-71, is overwritten, what we called contract talk
at M.G.M. Maybe some of the lines could stand trimming, although
this could also be done in the cutting room. All in all ...
my wholehearted congratulations! To speak with Willie Gingrich,
"Carry on, brothers!"

love
Walter

P.S. I'll mail the script under
separate cover.

as both comedy and social commentary. *The Fortune Cookie* was something of a career turning point for Matthau, who had been an accomplished character actor on stage and in film and television for fifteen years but had rarely played leading roles on screen. After his acclaimed performance as the scheming Willie Gingrich in *The Fortune Cookie*, which earned him a supporting-actor Oscar, Matthau moved permanently into playing leading roles, often opposite Lemmon. *The Knack . . . and How to Get It* was a British youth-oriented comedy directed by Richard Lester, and *What's New Pussycat?* was a sex farce that is notable as the first feature film written by Woody Allen. Both were popular in the summer of 1965, but apparently not at the Brown Derby, where old Hollywood still went to lunch.

December 10, 1966

Dear Mr. Goldwyn,

I would like to take this opportunity to express my deep
gratitude not only for the start you gave to me, but for the
continuing interest in my film career. I don't think you can
ever know how inspiring it is to know that one of the very
corner-stones of the world film industry is aware of you, and
hopes for your success. This is something I will be proud of
for the rest of my life.

I have found the pathway very difficult; many compromises
are asked of me, and I have had great disappointments in the
films that were made of my writing. In a number of cases, my
scripts were re-written during shooting and the results were
most disheartening. Nonetheless, I look at this business of
film making with the most excitement, awe and seriousness, and
will keep working toward my goal, which is to make a film that
has warmth and humanity, two characteristics which I feel are
lacking in most of today's films.

In "You're a Big Boy Now", which I understand you will see
on Sunday, and which I hope you will enjoy, I attempted to make
a contemporary film, told in the venacular of today's youth,
but which is basically innocent, and expresses some of the love
that I feel for people in general, and innocent young people
in specific.

Looking at the film, I know I made many mistakes, and there
are things that I would do differently if given the chance...but
done is done, and I look forward to the opportunity of making
a second film, one in which I can apply all the things I learned
from the first.

Thank you most sincerely once again; not only do I hope you
like this film, but more important, that you see an improvement
in the films I will make in the future.

Respectfully,

Francis Coppola

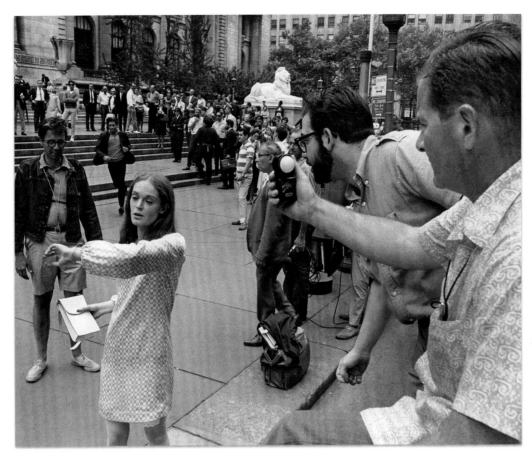

Francis Ford Coppola directing Elizabeth Hartman in *You're a Big Boy Now*, 1966.

Francis Ford Coppola to Samuel Goldwyn

DECEMBER 10, 1966

Francis Ford Coppola was a young writer-director just starting his career when he wrote this letter to Sam Goldwyn, then approaching the end of his tenure as one of Hollywood's most important independent producers. In May 1962, when he was a graduate student studying film-making at UCLA, Coppola had won the Samuel Goldwyn Foundation Creative Writing Award for an original screenplay called *Pilma, Pilma*. Goldwyn had established the prestigious award in 1955 in order to encourage and develop young writers, and he had been on hand to personally present the $2,000 award to Coppola. Four years

later, Coppola had worked as an assistant on several films for Roger Corman, made a couple of low-budget movies, written two screenplays for studio films, and already started working on *Patton*, a script that would finally come to the screen in 1970. *You're a Big Boy Now*, however, was Coppola's first opportunity to write and direct a film for a major studio, and it marked the arrival of a new voice in an industry that was in transition. Sam Goldwyn died in 1974, the same year that Coppola released *The Godfather Part II*, the film that would win him three Academy Awards, for directing, writing, and best picture.

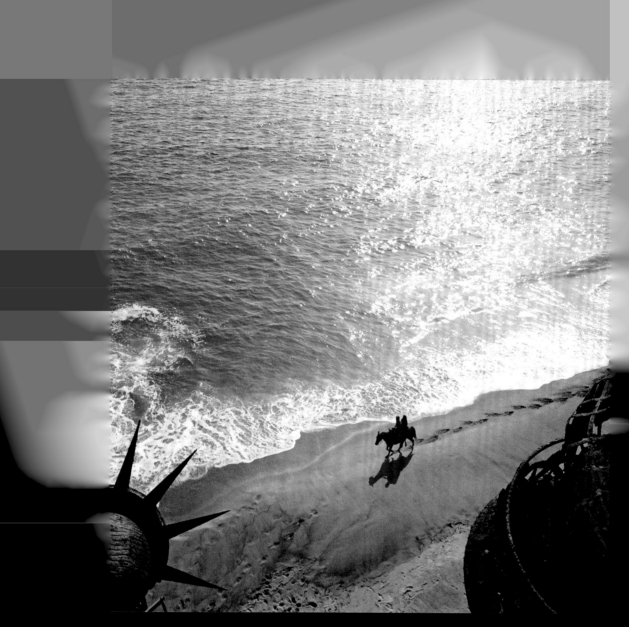

The escaping hero and his female companion approaching the ruins
of the Statue of Liberty at the end of *Planet of the Apes*, 1968

...el Wilson to Arthur P. Jacobs

..., 1967

...: to the screen by producer Arthur P. Jacobs,
...*the Apes* was one of the surprise hits of 1968.
...ad acquired the rights to the novel by Pierre
...n 1964 but spent several years trying to convince
... to finance the unusual project, which finally
...at Twentieth Century-Fox. In this letter to Jacobs,
...enwriter Michael Wilson, who was working
...th the novel and several script drafts by the
... fiction auteur Rod Serling, convincingly argues

famous shocking ending that Serling had devised
have even more punch if the leading character is f...
to live with his realization that Earth's civilizatio...
destroyed itself. Wilson, who shared an Academy ...
for writing *A Place in the Sun* in 1951, was one of th...
accomplished screenwriters who was forced unde...
during the blacklist. His uncredited work in the 1...
included *Friendly Persuasion* and *The Bridge on the R...
Kwai, which was also based on a novel by Pierre B...

MICHAEL   WILSON

March 15, 1967

Mr. Arthur Jacobs
Apjac Productions
20th Century Fox Studios
10201 West Pico Blvd.
Los Angeles, California.

Dear Arthur:

In a few days I will have completed the revised screenplay
of PLANET OF THE APES -- except for the final sequence, the
substance of which is the only remaining bone of contention.

In past conferences you have stated that Thomas should
die at the end of the picture, and both Mort and Frank have
more recently supported this view.

I have given considerable thought to this finale, and have
tried to accommodate to your position. However, I have come to
believe more firmly than ever that to kill off Thomas would be
a grave mistake.

It is possible that your preference for the so-called
tragic ending is a holdover from a previous and altogether
different script. Rod Serling's screenplay is a science fiction melodrama, solemn and earnest in tone, and in his treatment of the material Thomas's death does indeed, as you suggest,
add stature to the whole piece.

My screenplay, on the other hand, while on one plane a
tale of suspense and terror, is basically a satire. My treatment of the material, I think you will agree, is often light
and playful and outrageous. A measure of mordant wit and
sardonic comment is made possible by the changed characterization of Thomas, from whose point of view the entire picture
is seen. In the classic sense of the term, my screenplay is
a comedy -- just as Gulliver's Travels, A Connecticut Yankee
and Animal Farm are comedies.

This being so, the question of Thomas's fate is not a
matter of personal preference or taste. His death would not
add stature to the story I have told; it would simply be inappropriate. It would be inconsistent with the satiric mode of
the picture.

The final revelation of our film -- that we are on Earth,
and that man in his folly has blown up his civilization -- is
both satiric and tragic. This catastrophe cannot be topped by
having Thomas die. His death becomes anti-climactic, merely a
morbid aftermath.

It's not that I'm bucking for a "happy" or "uplift" ending. If Thomas lives, he faces a grim struggle for survival as the only evolved human on Earth -- scarcely a happy prospect. But such an ending is consistent with the satiric theme of the picture. I think it both amusing and just that Thomas, who in the beginning of our story was a misanthrope and cynic, is fated to carry the terrible burden of a second Adam. It befalls the man who was contemptuous of humanity to rehumanize the species. Whether he will succeed or fail no one knows, and we leave it to the audience to speculate on the odds for and against survival. I find such a finale intriguing and satisfying, and I believe audiences will react as I do.

You may argue that pregnant Nova fulfills this function, that she carries within her the hope and possibility of recreating civilized man. It just ain't so. This mute girl will never teach her child to speak. Without his father, Thomas's son will remain as backward as all the other brutes in the jungle -- and humankind is doomed.

Let me remind you once again that the entire story is told from Thomas's point of view. We see what he sees of the apes' civilization, and nothing more. In effect, therefore, the last surviving civilized man on Earth is telling his own story. If we kill him off at the end, we kill off our narrator -- and I find this singularly fortuitous and illogical.

At any rate, I ask you to reconsider your position on the ending in the light of the above observations. I can write the so-called tragic ending but, to be candid, it will be written without conviction of its merit.

Sincerely,

Michael Wilson

cc: Mort Abrahams
    Franklin Schaeffner

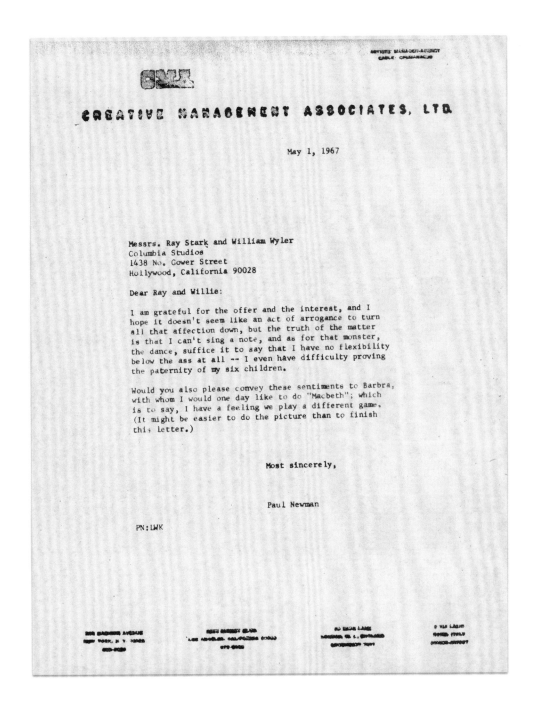

Paul Newman to William Wyler & Ray Stark

MAY 1, 1967

Paul Newman makes his feelings about appearing in a movie musical perfectly clear in this amusing letter to producer Ray Stark and director William Wyler, who were in the process of bringing *Funny Girl* to the screen. The casting of Barbra Streisand, who had triumphed in the title role on Broadway, was of course a given, but since it was her film debut, Stark wanted a big male star to play opposite her. After considering many possibilities, Stark and Wyler finally offered the part of Nick Arnstein to Egyptian actor Omar Sharif, who had recently played the leading role in David Lean's *Dr. Zhivago*. Newman and Streisand never appeared in a film together, but they did join forces, along with Sidney Poitier, in 1969 to launch an actor-centered production company called First Artists. They were later joined in the venture by Steve McQueen and Dustin Hoffman.

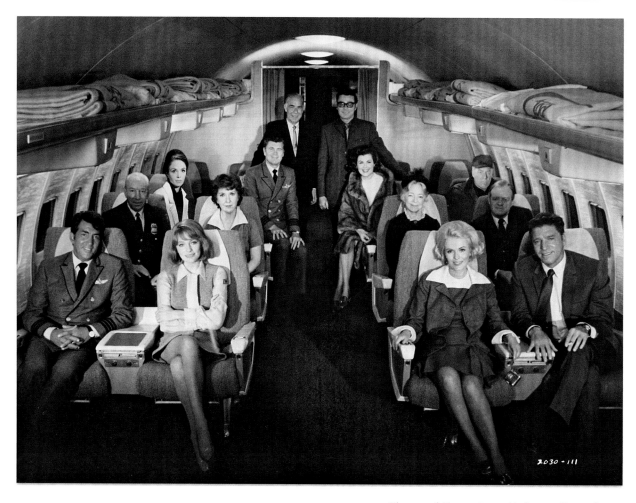

The cast of *Airport*, along with director George Seaton
(standing at left) and producer Ross Hunter, 1970.

Milton Pickman to George Seaton

NOVEMBER 22, 1968

In a letter that points to the transition from old to new Hollywood, talent agent and industry insider Milton Pickman writes to director George Seaton proposing his client, movie star Rita Hayworth, for a role in the upcoming film adaptation of *Airport*, which was released in 1970. A glossy melodrama produced by Ross Hunter, *Airport* was a bona fide smash that set the stage for Universal's dominance of the box office in the 1970s. Though it starred Hollywood veterans Burt Lancaster and Dean Martin, in typical Hollywood style the leading female roles were played by the much younger Jean Seberg and Jacqueline Bisset. The juicy character part that Pickman had his eye on for Hayworth was given to Maureen Stapleton, who

earned an Academy Award nomination for her work. Unfortunately, Hayworth never had a chance. In his reply to Pickman's letter, Seaton made it clear that he thought that Hayworth was wrong for the part, and he also mentioned that when her name came up during a casting conference "it received all the enthusiasm of Wallace for President," a reference to the recent election bid of George Wallace, the racist governor of Alabama. Hunter and Seaton did include one aging actress in the ensemble. They cast stage and screen veteran Helen Hayes as Mrs. Ada Quonsett, a plucky stowaway on the doomed flight. Hayes went on to win an Oscar for the supporting role.

THE PICKMAN COMPANY, INC.

ARTISTS' MANAGER-AGENCY

SUITE 812

9000 SUNSET BOULEVARD

HOLLYWOOD, CALIFORNIA 90069

(213) 273-8273

Nov. 22, 1968

My Dear George,

As Jerry's young, good looking, rich
Brother, I would like to feel I can take
a small liberty with you as to this rather
large reminder about your casting of the
INEZ role in AIRPORT.

Incidentally, as Ross related to you
when you happened to be in his office as
we talked on the phone, I believe you did
a magnificent job adapting this book - the
Lancaster role is enormous - the Dean Martin
character will give him and his career a
mighty acting boost and new dimenson.

While carefully avoiding the use of the
usual agent's jargon, I also believe you've
got a great, big potential on your hands.
All you've got to do now is make the picture.

And I believe too, and my own self-respect
wouldn't permit me to do so unless I believed
this, that the especially striking role of
INEZ is admirably suited for my client, RITA
HAYWORTH.

In her youngish forties, she is INEZ,
and if you would sit and visit with her in
any casual fashion, you'd get the same feeling
that Rita is exactly the INEZ you wrote in the
script - unless one wants to continue thinking
of her as the pin-up girl of World War II and
her memorable starring days at Columbia.

I've told Ross and I vigorously note for
you, Rita is in fine form, looks great, has a
far greater acting range than is generally attributed
to her in addition to a kind of legendary name
known throughout the world.

I believe she is your INEZ because she really
is and I feel I can tell you this more effectively
in this letter than taking your time to do so in
your office.

Need I say more?

All best,

Mr. George Seaton

Paul Jarrico to Waldo Salt

DECEMBER 26, 1969

Though the Hollywood blacklist began to crumble in 1960, when Dalton Trumbo received screen credit on both *Spartacus* and *Exodus*, it took several more years before many of the screenwriters who had been blacklisted by the industry in the 1950s were able to get their careers back on track. Writing to Waldo Salt, who was receiving great notices for his extraordinary screenplay for *Midnight Cowboy*, outspoken formerly blacklisted writer and activist Paul Jarrico celebrates the accomplishments of many of the writers and directors whose names were once again showing up on screens—including Trumbo, Jules Dassin, Carl Foreman, Michael Wilson, Sidney Buchman, and Abraham Polonsky. Unlike his compatriots, Jarrico did not have another big-screen success after he was forced from the industry. Instead, when he returned to California in 1977 after living in Europe for nearly twenty years, he dedicated himself to teaching and lecturing, often about the blacklist, and also worked tirelessly with the Writers Guild of America to restore screenwriting credits to blacklisted writers.

26 Dec. '69

Dear Waldo,

It would be hard to tell you without writing a book (which I may do still, called MEMOIRS OF A LUCKY JEW COMMUNIST BASTARD) just how much pleasure your hitting it big again has given me. How well I remember our conversation on the train from Washington to New York after our appearance in which we were telling each other all the things we planned to do (Sandhog, and a notion that became Salt of the Earth ((that well-known science fiction film about your journey to Mars))) and you suddenly stopped short in consternation and said, "But Jesus! What if we're not blacklisted!"

Seriously, Waldo, I've taken a lot of satisfaction in Trumbo's comeback, and Dassin's and Foreman's and Wilson's and Sidney Buchman's and a number of others—and most recently in Polonsky's. (Not the film, the reviews.) One difference in your case—I've finally understood it, trying to analyse my extreme pleasure—is that I loved the film. It is not enough to come back!—The journey must have GONE somewhere!

P.S. I hear you married Gladys. Splendid. Give her my warmest. Come to London and see us, both of you. Mine is called Yvette. Did you meet her? She's very busy helping Czech intellectuals. As for me, I've a number of balls in the air, one of which is sure to fall on my head.

—Paul

26 Dec. '69

Dear Waldo,

It would be hard to tell you without writing a book (which I may do still, called MEMOIRS OF A LUCKY JEW COMMUNIST BASTARD) just how much pleasure your hitting it big again has given me. How well I remember our conversation on the train from Washington to New York after our appearance in which we ▮▮▮▮ were telling each other all the things we planned to do (Sandhog, and a notion that became SALT of the Earth ((that well-known science fiction film about your journey to Mars))) and you suddenly stopped short in consternation and said "But Jesus! What if we're not blacklisted!"

Seriously, Waldo, I've taken a lot of satisfaction in ▮▮▮ Trumbo's comeback, and Dassin's and Foreman's and Wilson's and Sidney Buchman's and a number of others — and most recently in Polonsky's. reviews.) (Not the film, the ▮▮▮ One difference in your case — I've finally understood it, trying to analyse my extreme pleasure — vs that I loved the film. IT IS NOT ENOUGH TO COME BACK! — THE JOURNEY MUST HAVE GONE SOMEWHERE!

P.S. I hear you married Gladys. Splendid. Give her my warmest. Come to London and see us, both of you. Mine is called Yvette. Did you meet her? She's very busy helping Czech intellectuals. As for me, I've numbered the 3½ one bullshit, which is sure to fall on my head.
— Paul

Hal Ashby (right) directing Beau Bridges in *The Landlord*, 1970.

Hal Ashby to Norman Jewison

JANUARY 8, 1970

Hal Ashby and director Norman Jewison were close friends and collaborators who first worked together on *The Cincinnati Kid* in 1964. Trained as an editor, Ashby worked as an assistant cutter on films directed by George Stevens and William Wyler before meeting up with Jewison, with whom he did four films, including the Oscar-winning *In the Heat of the Night*. In 1969, Ashby directed his first film, *The Landlord*, produced by Jewison and the Mirisch Company. In this letter written during the production, Ashby pours out his heart to Jewison about the fact that he may not be able to work with Neil Young, whom he had chosen to do the music for the

film. The letter captures Ashby's committed resistance to Hollywood commerce and his extreme quest for artistic control of his work, as well as his rejection of the Hollywood status quo. Though the Ashby captured on these pages seems to be questioning whether he wants to continue working in the industry, he stayed the course and went on to make some of the most iconic films of the 1970s, including *Harold and Maude*, *Shampoo*, and *Coming Home*. Neil Young did step away from *The Landlord* for the reasons spelled out in the letter. He was replaced by Al Kooper, one of the founders of the band Blood, Sweat and Tears.

THURSDAY - 1/8/70

MY BEAUTIFUL NORMAN,

AS OF THIS MOMENT, THE NEIL YOUNG THING IS FUCKED, AND I HAVE SPENT
STILL ANOTHER SLEEPLESS NIGHT FILLED WITH FRUSTRATION, ANGER, AND
PAIN. NOW, AT 4 A.M., I'M GOING TO ATTEMPT TO EXPLAIN WHAT IT IS
THAT HAS HUNG UP THE DEAL, AND WHAT MY OVERALL FEELINGS ARE ABOUT
THE WHOLE THING, BY PUTTING SOME WORDS ONTO PAPER, INSTEAD OF SUB-
JECTING YOU, AND ANYONE ELSE WHO'S AROUND, TO SOME KIND OF RANTING,
MANIACAL, DISPLAY OF A CRUSHED SOUL, RIGHT HERE IN THE OFFICE.

AS TO THE DEAL: IT'S THE PUBLISHING RIGHTS THAT HAVE HUNG IT UP.
IT SEEMS AHMAD SOMEBODY, FROM SOME RECORD COMPANY, OWNS 75% OF THE
RIGHTS, WHILE NEIL OWNS 25%, OF EVERYTHING NEIL WRITES, AND TO MAKE
THE DEAL WITH U.A., NEIL WOULD HAVE TO GIVE UP HIS 25% IN TOTO, THEN
AHMAD WOULD BE A BIG MAN AND GIVE UP AN EQUAL AMOUNT, LEAVING EACH
AND ALL HAPPY. FIFTY FOR AHMAD; FIFTY FOR U.A.; ZERO FOR NEIL...
UNFORTUNATELY, ELLIOT WANTS TO RETAIN A FULL 12½% FOR NEIL, SO AHMAD
SAYS "OK, I'LL GIVE UP 12½%, TOO." OBVIOUSLY, THIS STILL LEAVES U.A.
25% SHORT OF THE REQUIRED 50% THEY NEED TO MAKE A DEAL, AND THAT IS
WHERE IT'S AT RIGHT NOW.

TO BE HONEST, I DON'T KNOW ~~KROMANXXHXNK~~ ANYTHING ABOUT PUBLISHING
RIGHTS, AND PERCENTAGES, AND WHAT HAVE YOU, BUT I WOULD ASSUME, BY
THE WAY EVERYONE IS ACTING, THERE'S SOME MONEY IN IT SOMEWHERE, AND
EVERYBODY WANTS A PIECE, INCLUDING THE ARTIST WHO CREATES THE WHOLE
FUCKING THING IN THE FIRST PLACE. NOW, I DO UNDERSTAND U.A.'S POSITION,
AND I AM AWARE OF THE VERY FACT THAT I WAS AWARE OF U.A.'S POSITION
FROM IN FRONT, SO I'M NOT REALLY SUGGESTING THEY BE THE ONES TO BEND.
IN FACT, AT THIS POINT, I'M NOT SUGGESTING THAT ANYONE GIVE ONE WAY OR
THE OTHER, AS I DO UNDERSTAND WHERE IT'S AT FOR U.A. MUSIC, AND I JUST
CAN'T, IN ALL, OR ANY, CONSCIENCE, ASK FOR NEIL TO GIVE UP ALL OF HIS
(SMALL FROM IN FRONT) PERCENTAGE. MY HEART IS TOO MUCH WITH THE ARTIST,
AND CREATIVE PERSON, AND IT JUST REALLY ISN'T WITH THE MONEY PEOPLE.

I GUESS I SHOULDN'T SAY THAT, AS I WILL, IF I CAN GET A NUMBER AND AM
ABLE TO REACH NEIL, ASK HIM TO GIVE AWAY EVERYTHING TO HELP ME AND OUR
FILM OUT, AS WE HAVE ALL WORKED TOO HARD FOR IT TO END UP FUCKED THIS
WAY. SO I WILL ASK, IF I CAN REACH HIM, BUT IT WILL BE KILLING ME IN-
SIDE, AND I'M SO VERY VERY TIRED OF THAT FEELING... OH, NORMAN, IF I
COULD JUST FIND THE WORDS TO TELL YOU WHAT'S GOING ON INSIDE ME. IT
JUST ALL HURTS SO FUCKING MUCH THAT I CAN'T EVEN STOP THE TEARS FROM
COMING, WHILE I SIT HERE TRYING TO WRITE THIS DAMNED NOTE. I GUESS I
HAVE SPENT TOO MANY HOURS THESE PAST FEW WEEKS, SITTING ALONE IN THIS
OFFICE, TRYING TO COPE WITH THE PAIN IN MY LIFE, AND I FEEL LIKE I'M
LOSING , WHILE IT'S GAINING. IT'S A WEIRD THING ~~XX~~ TO SIT ALONE IN THE
WEE HOURS, AND HEAR THOSE ~~XNKKNXKKXAKKX~~ MOANS COME UP OUT ~~KKMX~~ OF MY
ACHING SOUL. IT HURTS! IT HURTS! OH, CHRIST, IT HURTS!

THE
ON TOP OF THIS, I BECOME SO TOTALLY AWARE OF INABILITY TO GIVE ANY-
THING, LET ALONE THE FILM, THE POWERS OF CONCENTRATION WHICH I HAVE
ALWAYS BEEN ABLE TO GIVE BEFORE, AND AN OVERWHELMING GUILT FALLS ON
ME , AND I BECOME EVEN MORE INCAPACITATED, UNTIL I FEEL AS IF I WILL
REALLY JUST BLOW APART INTO NOTHING. I DON'T WANT TO LET ANYONE DOWN.
LEAST OF ALL YOU, MY DEAR DEAR LOVING AND LOVED, NORMAN. I JUST WANT
TO SURVIVE, AND TO KEEP TRYING_IN WHAT EVER WAY I CAN, TO KEEP MAKE OUR
FILM AS GOOD A ONE AS POSSIBLE. PLEASE KNOW IN YOUR HEART THAT I WILL
CONTINUE TO TRY, NO MATTER HOW FUCKED I AM, IF FOR NO OTHER REASON THAN
MY LOVE FOR YOU, AND TO TRY, IN SOME SMALL WAY, TO LET YOU (AND THE WORLD)
KNOW HOW THANKFUL I AM JUST TO HAVE BEEN LUCKY ENOUGH TO EVEN KNOWXXXX
MEET YOU IN THIS TRIP CALLED LIFE, LET ALONE HAVE ALL OF THOSE GOOD AND
BEAUTIFUL THINGS YOU GIVE, AND DO, SO FREELY... IN SHORT, XXXMXXXKXEN
BEING LOVED BY YOU HAS BEEN A VERY GROOVY TRIP FOR ME. I CAN'T EVEN
IMAGINE WHAT MY LIFE WOULD HAVE BEEN WITHOUT IT.

WITH ALL OF THIS, I'LL NOW TRY XMXXEXX TO GET TO WHERE MY HEART IS, AND
TRY TO EXPLAIN MY INTENTIONS FROM THIS POINT ON. AS STATED, IF I CAN
REACH NEIL, I'LL ASK HIM, AS MY FRIEND, TO GIVE, AND GIVE, AND LET THEM
ALL TAKE. IF I AM UNABLE TO REACH HIM, OR HE IS UNABLE TO GIVE, FOR WHAT
EVER REASONS, ALL I WOULD BE ASKING, THEN WE WILL MOVE IMMEDIATELY TO
GET SOMEONE ELSE (I'VE ATTACHED A LIST OF SOME POSSIBLES, ALONG WITH A
FEW COMMENTS), BUT FROM THIS POINT ON, I WILL NEVER AGAIN LET MYSELF BE
PUT IN A POSITION WHERE SOMEONE, OR SOME THING, CAN DICTATE WHO I MUST
USE IN THE CREATING OF MY FILM, AND ESPECIALLY IN AN AREA AS IMPORTANT AS
THE MUSIC. I KNOW THEY AREN'T TELLING ME WHO I MUST USE, BUT THEY SURE
AS HELL ARE TELLING ME WHO I CAN'T USE, AND IT ALL HAS TO DO WITH MONEY.
IT DOESN'T HAVE ONE DAMN THING TO DO WITH CREATIVITY. SO I SAY FUCK U.A.,
AND FUCK ANYBODY ELSE WHO FEELS THEY HAVE TO PUT THE POSSIBILITY OF SOME
REMOTE PROFIT IN THE WAY OF MY DOING WHAT I FEEL IS THE BEST THING FOR MY
FILM. TOO MUCH OF MY LIFE, MY HEART, MY BLOOD, MY PAIN, MY TEARS, HAVE
BEEN GIVEN, AND ARE NOW GONE, FOR ME TO EVER EVER AGAIN BE IN THIS AWFUL
POSITION. LET ME STATE IT VERY CLEARLY: I WILL NEVER AGAIN BE FUCKED BY
THOSE WHO FIND MONEY MORE IMPORTANT THAN MY LIFE. IT HURTS TOO MUCH, AND
I DON'T EVEN WANT TO TRY TO FIND THE STRENGTH TO WITHSTAND THAT KIND OF
PAIN. IT WOULD BE A FALSE AND FOOLISH STRENGTH, WHICH WOULD IN THE END,
I'M SURE, BREAK MY HEART.

PLEASE BEAR WITH ME A MOMENT WHILE I TRY TO EXPLAIN SOMETHING ELSE THAT
HAS BEEN NIBBLING AWAY AT ME SINCE I WAS ABOUT HALF WAY THROUGH THE SHOOT-
ING,_IN THE HOPE XX IT WILL HELP EXPLAIN MY STRONG FEELINGS ABOUT ALL OF
THIS. IT ISN'T ACTUALLY RELATED, BUT IT IS... SOMETIME, AFTER I XXX WAS
INTO THE SHOOTING, AND THE INITIAL TERROR AND FEARS HAD GONE THEIR OWN
NATURAL WAYS JUST XXXXWXXXXXX BECAUSE OF THE FACT THAT I FINALLY KNEW I
COULD DO IT,_I STARTED TO HAVE A LOVE AFFAIR WITH MY FILM AND IT REALLY
BLEW MY MIND. IT WAS A BEAUTIFUL AND GROOVY FEELING. THEN THE OTHER SAD
REALIZATION THAT THEY WOULD ONE DAY TAKE MY FILM AWAY, AND START WITH THAT

XXXXXXXX BULLSHIT OF RELEASE PRINTS AND EXHIBITORS, AND JUST NOT CARING
A FUCK ABOUT OUR FILM, EXCEPT IN RELATION TO HOW MUCH MONEY THEY MIGHT
BE ABLE TO MAKE. IN SHORT, THEY DON'T CARE, AND IT STARTED TO EAT AWAY,
BUT I FOUGHT THE PANIC AND HURT WITH THE KNOWLEDGE OF KNOWING WHERE THEY
ARE, AND WHY THEY WERE THERE, AND WITHOUT THEIR MONEY I WOULDN'T HAVE A
FILM TO LOVE. IT'S A REALITY I HAVE LEARNED TO LIVE WITH, AND ONE I WILL
CONTINUE TO FIGHT, IN HOPES THEY TOO WILL ONE DAY FEEL A LITTLE LOVE, AND
MAYBE CARE A LITTLE, TOO. I DON'T KNOW IF I'LL EVER BE ABLE TO BRING ANY
SUCH THING ABOUT, BUT I AM PREPARED TO KEEP TRYING, AND HOPING. I ONLY
MENTION THIS BECAUSE IT WAS A STRONG FEELING, BUT I WAS ABLE TO COPE WITH
IT AS SUCH. IT WAS ONE OF THOSE COMPROMISES I WOULD MAKE, BUT I KNEW IT
THEN, SOMEWHERE INSIDE, MY TOLERANCE LEVEL ON COMPROMISE WAS A LOW ONE,
WHEN IT CAME TO MY CREATIVE FUNCTIONS IN THIS LIFE, AND I BEGAN TO PRE-
PARE MYSELF FOR MANY BATTLES IN THIS AREA, ALONG WITH THE POSSIBILITY OF
NOT BEING ALLOWED TO FUNCTION AS A FILM MAKER AT ALL, IF MY DREAMS AND
IDEALS GOT IN THE WAY OF THEIR MAKING MONEY. IT'S A PRICE XXM I DON'T
WANT TO PAY, BUT I WILL IF IT COMES TO IT.

AND THAT BRINGS US BACK TO THE NOW, AND OUR PROBLEM WITH ME FROM THIS
POINT ON. I KNOW MY FEELINGS IN THIS FUCK UP EVERYTHING IN REGARDS TO
THE BIG CONTRACT WITH MIRI-UA, AS THE ONLY WAY I'LL EVER BE ABLE TO MAKE
A FILM AS I FEEL IT, WITH THAT KIND OF FREEDOM, WILL BE TO FIND PRIVATE
MONEY, AND THE CONTRACT OBLIGATES US TO A FIRST REFUSAL, ETC., FROM U.A.,
AND I HAVE NO INTENTION OF MAKING ANY FILMS FOR UA... I DON'T REALLY
KNOW WHAT TO SUGGEST, BUT I GUESS THE ONLY THING TO DO WOULD BE TO SIGN
SOMETHING LETTING SIMKOE-MIRISCH XXXXXXX OFF THE HOOK AS FAR AS PAYING ME
A WEEKLY THING, AND TO INCLUDE SOME KIND OF THING WHERE, IN THE EVENT I
DID MANAGE TO FIND SOMEONE WHO WOULD LET ME MAKE A FILM AS I SEE IT, THEY
(SIMKOE-MIRISCH) WOULD RECEIVE ALL MONIES OVER AND ABOVE XXX AN INITIAL
$35,000 I MIGHT RECEIVE FOR DIRECTING SAID FILM. THIS WOULD ALSO INCLUDE
A PERCENTAGE DEAL, I.E., SOMEONE PAID ME 35 PLUS 25%, XXXXXX THEN SIMKOE-
MIRISCH COULD HAVE THE 25%. XX WHATEVER, IT WOULDN'T MATTER JUST AS LONG
AS I COULD MANAGE TO KEEP SOME FOOD IN MY TUMMY AND SOME KIND OF ROOF OVER
MY HEAD, IT COULD BE FOR EVERYTHING OVER A MUCH LOWER FIGURE THAN THE 35,
I'M SURE, AND THEY COULD HAVE THE AGREEMENT AS SUCH FOR 7, 10, OR AS MANY
FILMS AS THEY FELT WOULD BE FAIR TO PAY THEM BACK FOR THE CHANCE GIVEN ME
IN THE FIRST PLACE. AS I REALLY AND TRULY DO NOT GIVE ONE FUCK ABOUT HOW
MUCH MONEY I MAKE, OR BUILDING ESTATES, OR WHAT HAVE YOU, I'M SURE SOME-
THING COULD BE WORKED OUT THAT WOULD SATISFY THEIR MONEY DRIVES, IF, AS
I SAID BEFORE, SOME PRIVATE INVESTOR SAW FIT TO LET ME HAVE THE FREEDOM I
SO DESPERATELY NEED TO MAKE FILMS AS I XXXXX FEEL IT. IF I DON'T FIND ANY
ONE WHO WOULD MAKE SUCH A GAMBLE, THEN IT REALLY WOULDN'T MATTER TO ANY
OTHER SOUL EXCEPT ME, AND I WILL DEAL WITH THAT AS REQUIRED BY NECESSITY.

I HOPE YOU UNDERSTAND WHY I MUST DO THIS, AND I HOPE MORE THAN ANYTHING
THAT YOU KNOW HOW MUCH I LOVE YOU.

1/8/70

SOME POSSIBLES FOR A COMPOSER TO SUCCEED NEIL YOUNG

GALT MCDERMATT: WE TALKED ABOUT HIM. HE DID "HAIR".
    (spelled wrong)

AL KOOPER: YOUNG WRITER. SUPER GOOD. DID A LOT OF THE
                THINGS FOR "BLOOD SWEAT & TEARS". I PLAYED
                AN ALBUM OF HIS FOR YOU ONCE, AND WILL DO SO
                AGAIN, AS IT REALLY SHOWS MANY SIDES TO HIM.

QUINCY: IF IT GOT TO THE NITTY, I WOULD ASK HIM AS FRIEND
            TO BYPASS HIS NOT DOING ANY PICTURES FOR AWHILE,
            AND TO PLEASE HELP.

STEVE WINWOOD: YOUNG ENGLISH CHAP. VERY VERY TALENTED.
                BEST KNOWN FOR HIS GROUP "TRAFFIC". MIKE
                STEWART IS VERY HIGH ON HIM. I HAVE SOME
                THINGS YOU COULD LISTEN TO.

THE FOLLOWING ARE SOME I'M VERY VERY HIGH ON, BUT WOULD WORRY
ABOUT ANY ONE OF THEM BEING ABLE TO DO WHAT I WANT IN SO SHORT
A TIME, UNLESS WE WERE ABLE TO MAKE A DEAL WITH ONE OF THEM BY
MONDAY....

DELANEY & BONNIE: PLAYED SOME FOR YOU THE OTHER DAY. I REALLY
                DIG THEM MUCH MUCH.

JOE COCKER: WHAT CAN I SAY. HE IS SOMETHING ELSE.

CREEDENCE CLEARWATER: JIM FOGGERTY IS THE MAN HERE, AND I
                COULDN'T SAY ENOUGH GOOD ABOUT HIM.
                HE IS VERY GROOVY INDEED.

THE BAND: ANOTHER SUPER GROUP OF SUPER GOOD MUSICIANS. THEY
                USED TO BACK BOB DYLAN.

LED ZEPPELIN: DON'T KNOW TOO MUCH ABOUT THEM, EXCEPT I SURE
                DIG WHAT THEY DO.

SHIT, IT ALL MAKES ME SO ANGRY. NEIL WAS CUTTING HIS TIME SHORT IN
LONDON (SOMETHING I KNOW HIS WIFE WOULD REALLY BE UPSET ABOUT AS SHE
WAS REALLY LOOKING FORWARD TO THE TRIP), SO HE COULD COME BACK MONDAY
AND PLAY ME WHAT HE HAD ALREADY WRITTEN.

following spread

Norman Jewison to Hal Ashby

MARCH 3, 1971

One of the most versatile directors of the 1960s and 1970s, Norman Jewison took on a major challenge when he decided to direct *Fiddler on the Roof*, the adaptation of the smash Broadway musical based on the stories of Sholem Aleichem. By choosing to shoot the film's exteriors almost entirely on location in a small village in Yugoslavia, Jewison created an authentic atmosphere for the film but also ran into many logistical problems for the cast and crew, including the age-old issue of uncooperative weather. In this letter to his friend Hal Ashby, Jewison takes the opportunity to share some of his war stories and also to let Ashby know how his directorial debut, *The Landlord*, which Jewison produced, was faring in England.

Norman Jewison (right) and Topol during production of *Fiddler on the Roof*, 1971.

A Norman Jewison Film

Fiddler on the Roof

as from :-

> Pinewood Studios,
> Iver Heath,
> Bucks. England.

Hal Ashby, Esq.,   3rd March, 1971
C/o 'Harold & Maude' Production,
Paramount Pictures Corp.,
202 North Canon Drive,
Beverly Hills,
California 90210,
U.S.A.

Dear Hal:

I often think of you and wish we could talk. I finished shooting
in Yugoslavia two weeks ago. After all the delays in forcing the
extension of time and the return to Yugoslavia, I still missed
the fucking snow. It had melted five days before we returned and
we got nothing but bright sunshine so I had to scramble around
and wait for clouds and so on trying to get as bleak a feeling as
possible. I must say I'm glad it is over. After seven continuing
months I was beginning to feel my age. It really has been a brute
of a film to shoot.

The cast has been wonderful and all of the technicians devoted
and involved. There is such a different atmosphere about film
making in Europe - it somehow always feels much more personal
and removed from the influences of Producers, Distributors,
Exhibitors, Banks and the rest of the bullshit.

I have just spent two weeks in Switzerland skiing out all my
hostilities and fatigue and depression and feel almost whole again.
Had great snow and spent a lot of time by myself at the top of the
mountain and a little bit of time at the bottom too.

Because Rupert Allan is leaving for the States tomorrow I am
taking advantage of the fact and sending you the opening reviews
on 'Landlord' in London. We managed to get a marvellous break
on B.B.C. television's 'Film Night' and I did as many quick interviews
as I could on behalf of the film before leaving for Yugoslavia.
Business has not been great but the reaction has been sensational.
We will complete our fourth week at the Prince Charles and then
hope to move over to another small house in the West End and
continue running exclusively. I am meeting with David Picker

cont/....

THE MIRISCH PRODUCTION COMPANY · 1041 No. FORMOSA, HOLLYWOOD, CALIF. 90046   released thru United Artists
Entertainment from
Transamerica Corporation

tomorrow to see if we can't get United Artists to buy more
space and utilise to greater advantage some of the excellent
reviews. Pat tells me the picture has grossed about
$1,200,000 so far. I will try and stay on top of the European
openings and make sure you receive all the reviews.

I hope everything is continuing to go well on 'Harold and Maude'
and that you are pleased with what you are getting. Pat and
I have tried to reach you a few times but there never seems
to be an answer. I hope this letter reaches you, I am going to
send it C/o Paramount in case you have completed shooting or
changed your address.

Give my warmest regards to Chuck and all of us here - Pat,
Larry, Bobby, Jerry, Dixie, Kevin, Michael, Jennifer, and of
course myself - send you our love and warmest thoughts.

Always,

me —   *I miss you!*

Norman

Sydney Pollack and Robert Redford, 1975.

Sydney Pollack to Robert Redford

DECEMBER 4, 1971

Based on a semi-autobiographical treatment and screenplay by playwright Arthur Laurents, *The Way We Were* was the third collaboration between director Sydney Pollack and actor Robert Redford, and as this letter shows, Pollack was very enthusiastic about the project. Their second film, *Jeremiah Johnson*, also discussed here, was a western survival story, and clearly a glossy period romance costarring Barbra Streisand promised to be a major change in direction for the director and his leading man. Though in his letter Pollack points out that the film is really a love story with a political background, the director also shows a keen interest in the challenge of recreating the era of the Hollywood blacklist and its key players, an approach that certainly must have appealed to the politically engaged Redford. In fact, *The Way We Were* was one of the first feature films to

tackle the blacklist and the devastating effect it had on the Hollywood community in the 1940s, though that part of the film takes a back seat to the romance between Katie and Hubbell, the starcrossed lovers portrayed by Streisand and Redford. Despite Pollack's enthusiasm, *The Way We Were* was far from an easy production. Laurents had a falling-out with Pollack and Redford, and various other writers were brought in to work on the script, including Alvin Sargent, Paddy Chayefsky, David Rayfiel, and Dalton Trumbo. Pollack's salute to "God, Country and Sundance" references the fact that Redford had started his Sundance Institute in Utah in 1969, and at this stage was largely funding it himself. No doubt Redford's profits from *The Way We Were* did help: the film was a huge box-office hit when it was released in 1973.

                                                    Sat 4 Dec

Redford;

Jesus, don't read this now. I have visions of you three
days behind schedule, not sleeping, arguing with Warners,
fighting the rain and in a generally very receptive and
happy mood to get a letter about a whole new project.

Anyway ..a couple of thoughts before you finish reading.
Laurents is really a playwright and not a novelist. Try
if you can to disregard the mistakes he makes as a novelist.
There are many. What he's got, I think, is a really
wonderful story of two very good people, played against an
interesting canvas and in a fun and romantic period.

Katie is pretty much self-explanitory. She's a flawed
heroine. She's excessive and difficult, but she's a good
lady, always on the right side and deeply committed. Hubbell
is NOT a cop-out or a weak guy, rather he is the most
sophisticated character in the novel. He is a man who sees
too deep and too much (to borrow from Fitzgerald.) Hubbell
sees all sides of the argument and therefore cannot take the
extreme positions Katie does. He HAS considered all these
questions. His not taking part in the same way Katie does
isn't from lack of understanding or consideration but
rather from too much understanding and consideration. He
KNOWS more than she. But he is drawn to her passion..her
ability to "knock herself out' over something or someone
she cares about. Hubbell's arguments with her are always
intelligent and pragmatic. These two people love each other
deeply and yet do not end up together. And it's NOT because
of any political or social issue. It's less definate but
much more true and heartbreaking than that.

The political and social areas should only be background,
with their story always the foreground, but as background
it is fascinating and really never been dealt with. The
whole McCarthy thing can be a great asset if it's handled
un-pretentiously and un-preachy. (we both have pretty good
barometers about that so I'm not worried) But it should
be exciting to deal with.

Contrary to your feeling that any film that deals with
Hollywood is automatically taboo, I feel very positive
about dealing with the Hollywood section. The problem
in the novel, and it's a big problem, is that Laurents
has treated that whole section in an exaggerated and
"campy" way. The people are not real and so it tends to
fall into the very trap you are concerned with. But this
needn't be so. Every one of these characters is based on
I a real person! And while I'm not about to do any exposé

Hubbell & Katie's (handwritten)

on Hollywood, please keep the following people in mind
when you read. If you can visualize the real people or
obviously here, really real actors playing the real people,
as who they are based on, it will change things.

HUBBELL is composed of three people. Three buddies who
have **XXX** been together for all their lives and live in
Switzerland now.

Peter Viertel -----The Athlete
Robert Parrish-----The Look
Budd Schulberg-----The Brains.

Bissinger ----**XXXXXXX** is John Huston...literally
Vicki Bissinger.....is Huston's first wife.
Now get this!....Rhea Edwards, (the agent who squeals on
her husbands clients) Is....Meta Rosenberg.
Monty Fielding.....is Abe Burrows.
Paula Reisner....is Sacha Viertel (Peters Mother) and Greta
Garbo's lover.

Now look, all this means is that one can begin to see the
possibilty of making the whole Hollywood section very
real and even understated because Hollywood by itself is
theatrical. The mistake that is always made when poor
scripts deal with Hollywood is that they forget that the
truth is already theatrical out here and they try to MAKE
it MORE theatrical and it degenerates into camp. Or it
becomes bitchy. When it is treated well (as in Sunset
Boulevard) or All About Eve (even tho that is really
theatre) it's damned exciting.

I don't have to say anything about the period. You love it
as much as I. And the forties is really virgin territory.
You've also seen Streisand as much as I so I don't have to
say much about her. She's unbelievably good in the right
thing...and it's been a long time since you've had any help
outside of BUTCH. There is something about the combination
of you two that has immediate sparks.

We've both talked about doing a love story, and although this
was certainly not what I had in mind when I thought about
finding a love story, I knew by the time I was half way
through it that this was the one. Because it is OFF. It is
not conventional. Not the expected kind of story of romance.
The people are not black and white, they are COMPLICATED.
They have flaws and rough edges and that makes it, for
me, much more interesting.

Anyway I'm just making a plea for you to read when you are
able to really concentrate. And to give it some serious
thought. I've never really felt so good about a project at
this state. There is time to get it right. Seventy percent
of it is there already. The story and the scenes are almost
all there. The people I've got so far are exciting. Steve
Grimes is set as Art Director, Harry Stradling Jr as Camera
Man. Fritz Steinkamp, (did Horses, for me) is the editor.

And I think of the fun of casting J.J., Bissinger, Paula, Frankie, Pony, Skipper and the rest and of shooting at Cornell, and in New York and here at the beach.

If I knew you less well and we weren't friends I wouldn't sell so hard. I'd probably play it very cool...but I'm too excited about this possibility not to push. Please don't rush through it and please don't read it while your mind is on too many other problems. It's important. For me, it's that very rare combination of GOOD and Commercial.

No new developements on Jeremiah Johnson. As I write here on Saturday, Opal Fisher and Companyare looking at the film. I'm keeping my fingers crossed because I can't stand to think about loosing that material. I'll let you know the outcome.

Since I spoke to you last night I have thought a lot about the possibility of a middle-summer release for the picture. Selfishly, I would rather have it go out then than wait until next Thanksgiving, but truthfully, if it does well at all I think it will hurt The Candidate. It's a difficult problem. I gave you all the facts on the phone so there is nothing more to add. We score next week, and The new version of the Violence Montage is XX in. I'm anxious to show it to you. Ithink it works well and takes the curse off of that one unnecessary and extra bit of violence, and still provides the needed rhythym change between Del Gue's farewell and the Qualen scene.

Go back to work. If it means anything Rayfiel is crazy about THE WAY WE WERE and can't picture anyone but you doing it. He speaks the truth. And just to show you how dirty I can play when I want something, I will drop in the fact that you can get your salary on it. "For God, Country and Sundance! "

Call if you have any thoughts;

Charlton Heston to William Wyler

FEBRUARY 24, 1972

Charlton Heston had been a supporter of the American Film Institute since its founding in 1967 and was eager to endorse its programs, like the seminars with notable filmmakers that the institute was recording regularly in the 1970s. In this letter to his old friend William Wyler, Heston makes a pitch for participating in the program, and he also takes the opportunity to comment on how *Ben-Hur*, the epic film that they worked on together in 1959, was faring on the small screen. A few years earlier, the director George Stevens had taken NBC to court to stop them from editing his film, *A Place in the Sun*, when it showed on television, and even argued against commercial breaks. His case was not successful, and viewers became accustomed to seeing films cut to fit inadequate time slots and small screens.

(Left to right) Charlton Heston, Stephen Boyd, and William Wyler during production of *Ben-Hur*, 1959.

February 24, 1972

Dear Willy:

    I'm sorry we had a schedule conflict on your seminar at the AFI. As I said, I'm sure you'll find it an interesting evening when you can fit it in. I'll be back in Los Angeles for a few days on March 10th and may call you then. Failing that, I'll be back the end of April and we'll try and plan the seminar at that time.

    I enclose a copy of a transcript taken from the tape of a seminar I did at the AFI last year. It'll give you an idea of the way they go. Besides, I go on about you at some length. I can't think why. What's the last part you gave me?

    Hey, speaking of that, have you seen the current cut they are running on BEN HUR, on TV? I turned it on for a few minutes the other night, and almost cut my wrists. They go right from Judah's return to the house, to the release of the mother and Tirzah, to them in the garden, to Judah quarrelling in the kitchen with Esther, to Hugh G. laying his bets with the Romans, to the race about to begin. No meeting with the horses, no harnessing scene... they didn't even introduce the cutting wheel on Messala's chariot!! And when I remember they didn't want to let you cut eighteen minutes from it! Ah well, the hell with it.

    See you soon, I hope.

        As ever,

        Chuck

Dear Marty –   Jan. 9, 1973

    I know you're back East for promos
at the moment, but I want to write
you on "Sounder" while the images are
fresh and alive in my mind.

    When I was seven, I saw "Potemkin"
— and, at 34, I recounted the things
that had lingered over a quarter of a
century in my mind, just before going
to see it a second time. The number
and the accuracy amazed me.

    The images of Sounder I'll remember
till the day I go. I think it's the best
thing you've ever done, and will stand
as a classic to be studied, some day.

    Sensitive, sparse, loving, finding the

beauty hidden in even the meanest circumstances, tender, unhurried, unsparing but devoid of malice — my God, Marty it's a remarkable work of art. I felt I'd lived the experience.

I remember your saying to me, in the U-I lunchroom, "See it — I think you'll like it."

You bet your ass I did — and thanks a million for the suggestion.

Sincerely,
Ross

Ross Martin to Martin Ritt

JANUARY 9, 1973

This letter from the actor Ross Martin to the director Martin Ritt is remarkably insightful. Before becoming an actor, Martin attended New York City College and earned a law degree from George Washington University. Starting out on the stage, Martin moved into film and TV, and also did radio and voiceover work; he was perhaps best known for playing Artemus Gordon on the CBS series *The Wild, Wild West*. As he shows in this letter, however, he was also, like many people in Hollywood, passionate about the history of cinema and a perceptive writer who was able to articulate what makes watching a film like *Sounder* such a profound experience. As Martin predicted in his letter, *Sounder* is considered a landmark for its depiction of the African American experience and is one of the seminal films of the 1970s. It was just one of the many socially conscious films directed during this time by Ritt, an iconoclastic filmmaker who was attracted to stories about underdogs and lost causes.

Tom Hanks to George Roy Hill & Hill's Reply

APRIL 1974 & APRIL 26, 1974

Tom Hanks was a seventeen-year-old high school student and George Roy Hill an Academy Award–winning director, but that didn't stop the young aspiring actor from writing to Hill about his future ambitions. Born and raised in northern California, Hanks was living in Alameda and attending Skyline High School in Oakland when he wrote to Hill, whose niece and nephews were among his classmates. The young Hanks's charming scenarios for becoming a star, and his references to Hollywood icons like Humphrey Bogart, Clark Gable, and Lana Turner, reveal him to be smart, funny, and imaginative, and shed light on his bright future as one of Hollywood's most versatile actors. At the time this letter was written, Hill was among the most commercially successful directors working in Hollywood. His latest film, *The Sting*, a 1930s caper movie starring Robert Redford and Paul Newman, was one of the biggest hits of the year, and had just won seven Academy Awards, including best director and best picture. Clearly, Hill was charmed by Hanks's disarming letter, and he seems to have enjoyed crafting his entertaining reply. It would be a few years, but both Hanks and Hill were right—this young performer was destined to be a star.

Dear Mr. Hill,

Seeing that I am very close, dear, good, and long-lasting friends with your nephews Kit and Timothy, and your niece Kate, and that I have seen your fantastically entertaining and award-winning film "The Sting," starring Paul Newman and Robert Redford and enjoyed it very much, it is all together fitting and proper that you should "discover" me.

Now, right away I know what you are thinking ("who is this kid?"), and I can understand your apprehensions. I am a nobody. No one outside of Skyline High School has heard of me, but I figure it I change my name to Clark Gable, or Humphrey Bogart, some people will recognize me. My looks are not stunning. I am not built like a Greek God, and I can't even grow a mustache, but I figure if people will pay to see certain films ("The Exorcist," for one) they will pay to see me.

Let's work out the details of my discovery. We can do it the way Lana Turner was discovered, me sitting on a soda shop stool, you walk in and notice me, and – BANGO – I'm a star. Or perhaps we could meet on a bus somewhere and we casually strike up a conversation and become good friends, I come to you weeks later asking for a job. During the last few weeks you have actually been working on a script for me and – Bango! – I am a star. Or maybe we can do it this way. I stumble into your office one day and beg for a job. To get rid of me, you give me a stand-in part in your next film. While shooting the film, the star breaks his leg in the dressing room and, because you are behind schedule already, you arbitrarily place me in his part and – BANGO – I am a star.

All of these plans are fine with me, or we could do it any way you would like, it makes no difference to me! But let's get one thing straight, Mr. Hill, I do not want to be some big time, Hollywood superstar with girls crawling all over me, just a hometown, American boy who has hit the big-time, owns a Porsche, and calls Robert Redford "Bob".

I hope you have read through all of this, and have enjoyed it.

Respectfully submitted,

Your Pal Forever,

Thomas J. Hanks
2394 Webster St.
Alameda, Calif.
94501

P.S.

Congratulations on your Academy Award for Best Director. I was rooting for you all night. We would be very honored to have you present at our Evening of One Act Plays on May 3rd. I will be appearing in one of them and so will your niece, Kate.

Your Good Old Buddy,
Thomas J. Hanks

Dear Mr. Hill,

Seeing that I am very close, dear, good, and long-lasting friends with your nephews Kit and Timothy, and your niece Kate, and that I have seen your fantastically entertaining and award-winning film "The Sting", starring Paul Newman and Robert Redford, and enjoyed it very much, it is all together fitting and proper that you should "discover" me.

Now, right away I know what you are thinking ("who is this kid?"), and I can understand your apprehensions. I am a nobody. No one outside of Skyline High School has heard of me, but I figure if I change my name to Clark Gable, or Humphrey Bogart, some people will recognize me. My looks are not stunning. I am not built like a Greek God, and I can't even grow a mustache, but I figure if people will pay to see certain films ("The exorcist" for one) they will pay to see me.

Lets work out the details of my discovery. We can do it the way Lana Turner was discovered, me sitting on a soda shop stool, you walk in and notice me, and - BANGO - I'm a star. Or perhaps we could meet on a bus somewhere and we casually strike up a conversation and become good friends (I come to you weeks later asking for a job. During the last few weeks you have actually been working on a script for me and - Bango! - I am a star. Or maybe we can do it this way. I stumble into your office one day and beg for a job. To get rid of me, you give me a stand-in part in your next film. While shooting the film, the star breaks his leg in his dressing room and, because you are behind schedule already, you arbitrarily place me in his part and "BANGO" - I am a star.

All of these plans are fine with me, or we could do it any way you would like, it makes no difference to me! But lets get one thing straight, Mr. Hill, I do not want to be some bigtime, Hollywood superstar with girls crawling all over me, just a hometown, American boy who has hit-th big-time, owns a Porsche, and calls Robert Redford "Bob".

I hope you have read through all of this, and have enjoyed it.

Respectfully submitted,

Your Pal Forever,

Thomas J. Banks
2394 Webster st
Alameda, Calif.
94501

P.S.
congradulations on your Academy award for Best Director. I was rooting for you all night. We would be very honored to have you present at our Evening of One Act Plays on May 3rd. I will be appearing in one of them and so will your niece, Kate.

Your Good Old Buddy,

Thomas J. Hanks

April 26, 1974

Dear Thomas:

    Or how about this Scenario? -

    I am driving wildly down Broadway Terrace
trying to escape from my insane nieces and
nephews when I hit a boy commuting to Skyline
High on his pogo stick. Before he slips into
unconsciousness I tell him of my good fortune
in finding someone for my next movie who has
not stunning looks, is not built like a Greek
God, can't grow a mustache and is willing to
change his name to Humphrey Bogart. The whole
part is to be played in a cast up to the neck
and BANGO - you are a star!

                  Your pal,

                  GEORGE ROY HILL

GRH:adm

Ellen Burstyn to Paul Clemens

In this letter from Ellen Burstyn to Paul Clemens, the teenage son of actress Eleanor Parker, Burstyn offers her thoughts on her work in *The Exorcist*, as well as insights into the craft of acting. One of the most successful films of the 1970s, *The Exorcist* shocked viewers with its terrifying images, but as Burstyn points out, it was more than a horror film and presented some true acting challenges. Burstyn's interpretation of the film not only emphasizes the spiritual side of the story, but also reminds us that the film is, at its core, about a mother fighting to save her daughter from the forces of evil. *The Exorcist* broke box-office records and was also a critical success, earning both Burstyn and Linda Blair Academy Award nominations. The following year, Burstyn won the Oscar for her role in another story of a single mother, *Alice Doesn't Live Here Anymore*. Paul Clemens went on to become an actor himself. Ray Bradbury, whom Burstyn mentions, was Paul's mentor and a lifelong friend.

Sept. 4, 1974

Dear Paul Clemens

Thank you so much for your kind and perceptive letter. It really is so moving to me when someone sees the movie and understands that it is not just a horror film and then takes the time to communicate their feelings.

The film begins before the title with a call to prayer in Arabic (or maybe it's right after the title but I know it's before you see anything else). Whatever else the film is, it is also a call to prayer. That is: a call to all of us to pay attention to the forces of good in this world and in ourselves—and to dedicate ourselves, as Chris does, to fighting evil with whatever means are necessary to overcome it.

I don't mean that that is Blatty's statement or Friedkin's or what the movie intends. It is my statement and what I was doing in the movie. It may also be theirs, but I do not speak for them, naturally.

I love your mother's work. Her film "Caged" was one of the first films I ever saw where I understood the transformation of character that is possible for an actress in a film.

Between your mother and Ray Bradbury you have some very good examples around you and must be receiving the best guidance. It certainly seems so from what I was able to feel of you from your letter.

Acting has been the most rewarding study for me because I've learned about my fellow human beings and of course myself, which is the beginning of wisdom. From every culture and civilization we are exhorted by the sages to "Know Thyself."

As we study our characters we begin to understand our own character and indeed to build one. Stanislavski even called his book that—"Building a Character."

A doctor once said—"I consider acting a healing art." So do I. Good luck in it. You have selected to study an art that can only enrich your life.

With gratitude
Ellen Burstyn

P.S. Academy Awards are nice but that ain't what it's about.

334   ELLEN BURSTYN TO PAUL CLEMENS   1974

WARNER BROS.

Warner Bros. Inc.
4000 Warner Boulevard
Burbank, California 91522
213 843 6000
Cable Address: Warbros

Sept 4, 1974

Dear Paul Clemens

Thank you so much for your kind and perceptive letter. It really is so moving to me when someone sees the movie and understands that it is not just a horror film and then takes the time to communicate their feelings.

The film begins before the title with a call to prayer in Arabic (or maybe its right after the title but I know its before you see anything else). Whatever else the film is, it is also a call to prayer. That is : a call to all of us to pay attention to the forces of good in this world and in ourselves — and to dedicate ourselves, as Chris does, to fighting evil with whatever means are necessary to overcome it.

I don't mean that that is Blatty's statement or Friedkins or what the movie intends. It is my statement and what I was doing in the movie. It may also be theirs, but I do not speak for them, naturally.

A Warner Communications Company

Warner Bros. Inc.
4000 Warner Boulevard
Burbank, California 91522
213 843 6000
Cable Address: Warbros

I love your mothers work. The film "Caged" was one of the first films I ever saw where I understood the transformation of character that is possible for an actress in a film.

Between your mother and Ray Bradbury you have some very good examples around you and must be receiving the best guidance. It certainly seems so from what I was able to feel of you from your letter.

Acting has been the most rewarding study for me because I've learned about my fellow human beings and of course myself, which is the beginning of wisdom. From every culture and civilization we are exhorted by the sages to: "Know Thyself."

As we study our characters we begin to understand our own character and indeed to build one. Stanislavski even called

A Warner Communications Company

WARNER BROS.

Warner Bros. Inc.
4000 Warner Boulevard
Burbank, California 91522
213 843 6000
Cable Address: Warbros

his book that – "Building a Character."

A doctor once said – "I consider acting a healing art." So do I. Good Luck in it. You have selected to study an art that can only enrich your life.

With gratitude

Ellen Burstyn

P.S. Academy Awards are nice but that ain't what it's about.

A Warner Communications Company

Elliott Kastner to Jack Nicholson

JULY 13, 1976

Elliott Kastner was a prolific and passionate producer who moved in and out of mainstream Hollywood. Starting out as an agent, Kastner had an innate ability to convince major stars to appear in non-studio movies, but he was not always successful at raising the funds to make those films a reality and sometimes had to roll the dice. *The Missouri Breaks* was a project that Kastner had been working on for years, so it was a coup when he managed to sign both Marlon Brando and Jack Nicholson, but Kastner had to pay a steep price for that kind of star power. In his contract, Nicholson was paid a salary of $1.25 million and guaranteed 10 percent of

the gross receipts after $12.5 million, but a week before the film was going to open in May 1976, Kastner offered to pay Nicholson $1 million in exchange for 5 percent of his gross participation. Nicholson took the deal, but in June filed suit against Kastner when the $1 million payment never materialized. That's the state of affairs that Kastner is addressing in this letter to Nicholson, which was drafted in July 1976 but perhaps not sent. Beyond the details of this particular case, this letter reveals the tightrope that independent producers walked in Hollywood, and how easy it was to make a wrong step.

DRAFT

Mr. Jack Nicholson

Dear Jack,

It's very difficult for me to write to you concerning the

mistake I made in connection with the purchase of half of your gross

participation in "MISSOURI BREAKS". When I made this deal, I was

taken by the picture and, of course, waxed the enthusiasm that any other

producer would have evidenced in the making of a picture of its

magnitude. My business judgment was completely eroded by my creative

pride in the film. I must say that I was so proud of the picture that

I was a bit distressed by your lack of enthusiasm and guess made a bad

business deal based on emotion rather than sound judgment.

I have turned over to your attorneys a statement of my net

worth. As you can see, I have not much to show from the years that

I have spent in the motion picture industry. The only thing that I

can point to with some pride is the fact that I have been able to

have my name associated with what I consider to be many good motion

pictures. Also, I still take pride in the fact that I was able to put together a complicated picture like "MISSOURI BREAKS" starring

Marlon Brando and yourself. Other than receiving a producer's fee

for this film (which I shared with others), I doubt if I will see

any monies beyond those which I have already been paid.

Like other producers, the balance of my assets is filled

with big hopes and expectations - none of which are bankable. My

career really at this juncture rests in your hands. You could

force me into bankruptcy and take me through the law courts which

I believe would be non-productive and completely destructive of any

chance that I have in trying one day to put aside some money for

my loved ones and myself.

Hopefully, you will allow me to continue in my profession

and make the best pictures that I possibly can. I sincerely hope

that we will work together again on other pictures. After all, if

the film does what United Artists' now predicts it will do, you will

have received well over $2,000,000 for four (4) weeks work. I, on

the other hand, will have received a producer's fee that has long

since been spent plus a sick stomach caused by my pride and yes,

-3-

let's say it, ego. Thus, the ball is in your court Jack. My

lawyer has made certain proposals which would allow me to con-

tinue making films and hopefully satisfy the mistake which I

made, vis-a-vis you.

I hope you will see your way clear to go along with me.

With best regards, I remain,

Yours sincerely,

Elliott Kastner

152 Wadsworth
Santa Monica, CA   90405

July 26, 1976

Dear Fred:

I have been thinking a lot since we spoke last and I have come
to feel that I must see Lillian if only for part of a day. I
am playing her, not just a character based on her (even though
many licenses must be taken), and I need to feel her presence,
get a flesh and blood sense of her. I am immersing myself in
her books and plays, and it has proved immensely helpful--a
whole complex subtext with all the contradictions that exist
in life is there for me to draw from.

But the woman is alive with her memories to help me fill in
the gaps and to not tap this resource, to play Lillian Hellman
without even having talked to her, is a very disturbing situation for me. Then there is another point--I am a grown person,
not particularly fragile or unduly flappable. I can certainly
take Lillian's criticism of the script in stride.

I don't know the specifics of her criticism, only the general
outlines. I do not agree with her basic criticism that Lillian
shouldn't be in the center of the story as much as she is since
she is a "passive" character. I don't think she is central; I
think the relationship with Julia is what is central, but perhaps she is right. God knows she's got enough expertise on the
subject of structure. But in any case, we have committed ourselves to Alvin's structure and it's too late to go back.

There are other criticisms. Maybe I'll agree with some of them
and maybe not. Perhaps her views will help me in areas (like
her fear) where I am having trouble understanding her. I hope
so.

Mr. Fred Zinneman
Page Two
July 26, 1976

Finally, I feel that I at least owe the woman the respect to
talk with her and to try to come to a principled relationship;
not to exclude her because of disagreements. That will be
bad for our morale, our sense of decency, and if worse comes
to worst, it could look bad in the press. Avoidance, as a
tactic, smacks too much of the worst traits of Hollywood.

I don't like the idea of our beginning the film with differences
between us. I don't function well in conflict and I am sure you
don't either. But I feel strongly about this and hope you will
understand me. Please call.

                          With warmest regards,

                          Jane

JF:re

Jane Fonda to Fred Zinnemann

JULY 26, 1976

Jane Fonda's brave and uncompromising work as the playwright and screenwriter Lillian Hellman in *Julia*, based on a chapter in Hellman's memoir *Pentimento*, was just one of the roles that made Fonda one of the most important actresses of the 1970s. The acerbic Hellman had clashed with screenwriter Alvin Sargent and director Fred Zinnemann about the best way to adapt her work, and clearly Zinnemann was worried that an encounter between Fonda and the famously difficult writer might have a negative effect on Fonda's performance. Although Fonda does not mention the meeting in her autobiography, the two apparently did come together to discuss the film. Their encounter is described in the Fonda biography by Patricia Bosworth, who wrote that the actress spent a day and a half with Hellman at the writer's home in Martha's Vineyard, giving Fonda the chance not only to discuss Sargent's script, which Hellman still claimed to dislike, but also to observe the formidable Hellman in an informal setting. Fonda was nominated for an Academy Award for her performance in the film. Her costars Vanessa Redgrave, who played Julia, and Jason Robards, who played Dashiell Hammett, took home the supporting-actress and -actor Oscars, and Sargent also won for his screenplay adaptation.

Permissions & Sources

12 Letter from Harry Houdini. From the Adolph Zukor correspondence, Margaret Herrick Library, Academy of Motion Picture Arts and Sciences (AMPAS). | **16** Letter from Roscoe Arbuckle. From the Adolph Zukor correspondence, Margaret Herrick Library, AMPAS. | **20** Letter from Mabel Normand. From the Adolph Zukor correspondence, Margaret Herrick Library, AMPAS. | **23** Letter from Irving Thalberg. From the Erich von Stroheim papers, Margaret Herrick Library, AMPAS. | **25** Telegram from Cecil B. DeMille. From the Cecil B. DeMille Collection, MSS 1400. L. Tom Perry Special Collections Library, Harold B. Lee Library, Brigham Young University, Provo, Utah. Courtesy of the DeMille Estate. | **27** Letter from Lou Marangella. From the MGM Collection, Cinematic Arts Library, University of Southern California. | **30** Letter from William Wyler. From the William Wyler papers, Margaret Herrick Library, AMPAS. Courtesy of the Family of William Wyler. | **33** Letter from Will Rogers. From the Cecil B. DeMille Collection, MSS 1400. L. Tom Perry Special Collections Library, Harold B. Lee Library, Brigham Young University, Provo, Utah. | **34** Letter from Will Hays. From the Hal Roach Collection, Cinematic Arts Library, University of Southern California. | **37** Letter from Sol Wurtzel. From the Madge Bellamy papers, Margaret Herrick Library, AMPAS. Courtesy of Sol Wurtzel's great-granddaughter Sharon Rosen-Lieb. | **38** Letter from Ronald Colman. From the Samuel Goldwyn papers, Margaret Herrick Library, AMPAS. | **40** Letter from Jack L. Warner. From the Hunt Stromberg papers, MHL. Courtesy of the Jack Warner Family. | **41** Letter from Bela Lugosi. Courtesy of the Bela Lugosi Family. | **43** Letter from Mrs. Alonzo Richardson. From the Red-Headed Woman file, Motion Picture Association of America. Production Code Administration records, Margaret Herrick Library, AMPAS. | **45** Letter from John Barrymore. From the Edward G. Robinson Collection, Cinematic Arts Library, University of Southern California. | **48** Letter from Bert Glennon. From the Katharine Hepburn papers, Margaret Herrick Library, AMPAS. Courtesy of the Glennon Family. | **51** Letter from Jean Bello. From the Jean Harlow letters to Arthur Landau, Margaret Herrick Library, AMPAS. Courtesy of the heirs of Jean Harlow. | **52** Partial letter from Don Eddy. From the Ronald Haver collection, Margaret Herrick Library, AMPAS. | **55** Letter from Gregg Toland. From the Fred Zinnemann papers, Margaret Herrick Library, AMPAS. | **56** Letter from Boris Karloff. Private collection. Reprinted by permission of Sara Karloff. | **58** Letter from Humphrey Cobb. Correspondence from the Fritz Lang Papers, courtesy of the American Film Institute. | **60** Letter from Tallulah Bankhead. From the David O. Selznick collection, Harry Ransom Center, The University of Texas at Austin. | **63** Letter from Dashiell Hammett. From the Lillian Hellman papers, Harry Ransom Center, The University of Texas at Austin. Courtesy of the Dashiell Hammett Estate. | **66** Letter from Mary Pickford. From the Gloria Swanson papers, Harry Ransom Center, The University of Texas at Austin. Courtesy of The Mary Pickford Foundation. | **68** Telegram from Henry Fonda. From the William Wyler papers, Margaret Herrick Library, AMPAS. Courtesy of Jane Fonda. | **69** Telegram from William Wyler. From the William Wyler papers, Margaret Herrick Library, AMPAS. Courtesy of the Family of William Wyler. | **70** Telegram from Greta Garbo. From the Marion Davies papers, Margaret Herrick Library, AMPAS. The Name and Likeness of Greta Garbo are the property of Harriet Brown and Co., Inc. | **72** Letter from Pandro Berman. From the Mark Sandrich papers, Margaret Herrick Library, AMPAS. Courtesy of The Pandro S. Berman Estate. | **74** Memo from Miriam Howell. From the Samuel Goldwyn papers, Margaret Herrick Library, AMPAS. | **77** Letter from Carl Laemmle. From the William Wyler papers, Margaret Herrick Library, AMPAS. Courtesy of the Laemmle Family. | **81** Letter from Alfred Hitchcock. From the Myron Selznick papers. Selznick Agency Files, Harry Ransom Center, The University of Texas at Austin. Courtesy of Mary O'C. Stone. | **85** Letter from Lewis Meltzer. From the Daniel Taradash papers, Margaret Herrick Library, AMPAS. Courtesy of Joshua Meltzer. | **86** Letter from Jennings Lang. From the H.N. Swanson Agency records, Margaret Herrick Library, AMPAS. Courtesy of The Family of Jennings Lang. | **89** Letter from Bette Davis. From the Warner Bros. Archives, School of Cinematic Arts, University of Southern California. Courtesy the Estate of Bette Davis. | **95** Letter from David Niven. From the Samuel Goldwyn papers, Margaret Herrick Library, AMPAS. Courtesy of the David Niven Family Estate. | **98** Letter from Fred Astaire. From the David O. Selznick collection, Harry Ransom Center, The University of Texas at Austin. License courtesy of and Copyright © Mrs. Fred Astaire, Beverly Hills, California.

All rights reserved. | **101** Letter from Constance Collier. From the Hedda Hopper papers, Margaret Herrick Library, AMPAS. | **105** Letter from Hedda Hopper. From the Hedda Hopper papers, Margaret Herrick Library, AMPAS. Courtesy Joan Hopper Peat-James. | **106** Letter from Victor Potel. From the Preston Sturges papers, UCLA Library Special Collections, Charles E. Young Research Library. | **108** Letter from Peter Ballbusch. From the Charles Laughton papers, UCLA Library Special Collections, Charles E. Young Research Library. Courtesy of Peter Fischer. | **110** Letter from Irving Berlin. From the Mark Sandrich papers, Margaret Herrick Library, AMPAS. Reprinted by special permission of The Rodgers & Hammerstein Organization on behalf of the Estate of Irving Berlin. All Rights Reserved. | **112** Telegram from David O. Selznick. From the Warner Bros. Archives, School of Cinematic Arts, University of Southern California. Courtesy of Daniel Selznick. | **115** Telegram from Joseph M. Schenck. Correspondence from the Charles K. Feldman Papers, courtesy of the American Film Institute. | **116** Letter from Virginia Mayo. From the Virginia Mayo Collection, Cinematic Arts Library, University of Southern California. Courtesy of the Johnston Family. | **121** Letter from Joseph Breen. From the Double Indemnity file, Motion Picture Association of America, Production Code Administration records, Margaret Herrick Library, AMPAS. | **124** Letters from Sam Fuller. From the Universal Pictures Collection. Cinematic Arts Library, University of Southern California. Courtesy of Christa and Samantha Fuller, Chrisam Films, Inc. | **127** Letter from Dorothy Arzner. From the Preston Sturges papers, UCLA Library Special Collections, Charles E. Young Research Library. | **129** Letter from Mary C. McCall, Jr. From the Screen Writers Guild records, Writers Guild Foundation Library and Archive, Writers Guild of America West. Courtesy of Sheila Benson and Mary-David Sheiner. | **130** Letter from Tyrone Power. From the Darryl F. Zanuck papers, Margaret Herrick Library, AMPAS. Courtesy of the Tyrone Power Estate. | **132** Letter from Raymond Chandler. From the Billy Wilder papers, Margaret Herrick Library, AMPAS. Copyright © Raymond Chandler. Reproduced by permission of the estate of the author c/o Rogers, Coleridge and White, 20 Powis Mews, London W11 JN. | **134** Letter from Robert E. Sherwood. From the Samuel Goldwyn papers, Margaret Herrick Library, AMPAS. Courtesy the Estate of Robert E. Sherwood. | **137** Letter from Frank Sinatra. From the Albert Maltz papers (U.S. Mss 17AN), Wisconsin Center for Film and Theater Research. Courtesy of Frank Sinatra Enterprises. | **139** Letter from Oscar Hammerstein II. From the Alfred Newman Collection, Cinematic Arts Library, University of Southern California. Courtesy The Hammerstein Family Collection. | **140** Letter from Darryl F. Zanuck. From the My Darling Clementine file, Motion Picture Association of America, Production Code Administration records, Margaret Herrick Library, AMPAS. Courtesy of the Darryl F. Zanuck Estate and DARRYL F. ZANUCK LETTER DATED MARCH 5, 1946 Courtesy of Twentieth Century Fox. All rights reserved. | **142** Letter from Jean Negulesco. From the Oscar Levant Collection, Cinematic Arts Library, University of Southern California. | **144** Letter from Hattie McDaniel. From the Hedda Hopper papers, Margaret Herrick Library, AMPAS. | **146** Letter from Dalton Trumbo. From the Dalton Trumbo papers (U.S. Mss 24AN), Wisconsin Center for Film and Theater Research. Courtesy of the Trumbo Family. | **147** Letter from Ginger Rogers. From the Hedda Hopper papers, Margaret Herrick Library, AMPAS. Ginger Rogers Is used with permission from The First Church of Christ, Scientist. | **149** Letter from Ezra Goodman. From the Ernest Lehman papers, Harry Ransom Center, The University of Texas at Austin. | **150** Letter from James Bridie. From the Hume Cronyn and Jessica Tandy papers, Manuscript Division, Library of Congress, MSS17301. Reproduced by permission of The Agency (London) Ltd. 1948 © James Bridie. | **152** Letter from Robert Lord. From the In a Lonely Place file, Motion Picture Association of America, Production Code Administration records, Margaret Herrick Library, AMPAS. Courtesy of the family of Robert Lord. | **155** Letter from Gloria Swanson. From the Gloria Swanson papers, Harry Ransom Center, The University of Texas at Austin. Courtesy of Gloria Swanson Inc. | **156** Letter from Jerry Lewis. From the Hal Wallis papers, Margaret Herrick Library, AMPAS. Courtesy of the Jerry Lewis Family. | **158** Letter from Louis Calhern. From the Louis Calhern correspondence with Leonard Lyons, Margaret Herrick Library, AMPAS. | **161** Letter from Gilbert Roland. From the Clara Bow papers, Margaret Herrick Library, AMPAS. Courtesy of Gyl Roland. | **163** Letter from Errol Flynn. From the Lewis Milestone papers,

Margaret Herrick Library, AMPAS. Courtesy of the Family of Errol Flynn. | **165** Letter from Marlon Brando. From the Fred Zinnemann papers, Margaret Herrick Library, AMPAS. Courtesy of The Marlon Brando Estate, | **168** Memo from Joseph L. Mankiewicz. From the Joseph L. Mankiewicz papers, Margaret Herrick Library, AMPAS. Courtesy of the Joseph L. Mankiewicz Estate. | **171** Letter from Preston Sturges. From the Preston Sturges papers, UCLA Library Special Collections, Charles E. Young Research Library. Courtesy of the Preston Sturges Collection at UCLA. | **175** Letter from Kirk Douglas. From the private collection of Kirk Douglas. Courtesy The Bryna Company. | **177** Letter from John Huston. From the Katharine Hepburn papers, Margaret Herrick Library, AMPAS. Courtesy of Anjelica Huston. | **178** Letter from Charles Brackett. From the Gloria Swanson papers, Harry Ransom Center, The University of Texas at Austin. Courtesy of the Charles W. Brackett Estate. | **180** Letter from George Cukor. From the Ruth Gordon and Garson Kanin papers, Manuscript Division, Library of Congress, MSS85114. Courtesy George Cukor Estate. | **181** Letter from Alan Ladd. From the George Stevens papers, Margaret Herrick Library, AMPAS. Courtesy David Ladd. | **183** Letter from Carl Foreman. From the Fred Zinnemann papers, Margaret Herrick Library, AMPAS. Courtesy of the Family of Carl Foreman. | **186** Letter from Philip Dunne. From the Alexander Knox papers, Margaret Herrick Library, AMPAS. Courtesy of the Family of Philip Dunne. | **188** Letter from Daniel Taradash. From the Daniel Taradash papers, Margaret Herrick Library, AMPAS. Courtesy of the Taradash Family. | **191** Letter from Humphrey Bogart. From the John Huston papers, Margaret Herrick Library, AMPAS. Courtesy of Stephen Bogart. | **195** Letter from Paul Kohner. From the John Huston papers, Margaret Herrick Library, AMPAS. Courtesy The Kohner Family Collection. | **198** Letter from John Wayne. From the Jack L. Warner Collection, Cinematic Arts Library, University of Southern California. John Wayne Letter © John Wayne. Used with permission of John Wayne Enterprises, LLC. All Rights Reserved. wwwljohnwayne.com. | **201** Letter from Geraldine Page. Correspondence from the Charles K. Feldman Papers, courtesy of the American Film Institute. Courtesy of the Estate of Geraldine Page. | **207** Letter from Elia Kazan. From the East of Eden file. Motion Picture Association of America, Production Code Administration records, Margaret Herrick Library, AMPAS. Courtesy of the estate of Elia Kazan. | **208** Letter from Bert Allenberg. From the Joseph L. Mankiewicz papers, Margaret Herrick Library, AMPAS. Courtesy of John Allenberg. | **211** Letter from Ray Bradbury. From the John Huston papers, Margaret Herrick Library, AMPAS. Reprinted by permission of Don Congdon and Associates, Inc. and Ray Bradbury Literary Works, LLC. | **212** Memo from Dorothy Jeakins. From the Paramount Pictures production records, Margaret Herrick Library, AMPAS. Courtesy of the Jeakins Family. | **214** Letter from Katherine Albert. From the George Cukor papers, Margaret Herrick Library, AMPAS. Courtesy of Joan Katherine Weatherly. | **217** Letter from Sal Mineo. From the Claudia Franck papers, Margaret Herrick Library, AMPAS. Courtesy of the Mineo Family. | **220** Letter from Marlene Dietrich. From the Ernest Hemingway papers, John F. Kennedy Presidential Library. Courtesy Die Marlene Dietrich Collection GmbH. | **223** Letter from Charles Chaplin. From the John Howard Lawson papers, Special Collections Research Center, Morris Library, Southern Illinois University Carbondale. Reproduced from Association Chaplin. | **224** Letter from Yul Brynner. From the Charles Brackett papers, Margaret Herrick Library, AMPAS. Courtesy of The Estate of Yul Brynner. | **227** Letter from Deborah Kerr. From the John Huston papers, Margaret Herrick Library, AMPAS. Courtesy of Francesca Shrapnel. | **229** Letter from Joan Crawford. From the Jane Ardmore papers, Margaret Herrick Library, AMPAS. | **231** Letter from Ingrid Bergman. From the Cary Grant papers, Margaret Herrick Library, AMPAS. Courtesy of Pia Lindstrom, Ingrid Rossellini, Isabella Rossellini and Roberto Rossellini. | **233** Letter from Clifford Odets. From the Hedda Hopper papers, Margaret Herrick Library, AMPAS. Courtesy of Walt Odets. | **234** Letter from Shelley Winters. From the George Stevens papers, Margaret Herrick Library, AMPAS. Permission granted by Victoria Gassman. | **236** Letter from Charles Laughton. Private collection. | **238** Letter from Tom Parker. From the Hal Wallis papers, Margaret Herrick Library, AMPAS. Courtesy Tom Parker Estate. | **240** Memo from Eddie Lewis. From the Kirk Douglas papers (U.S. Mss 102AN), Wisconsin Center for Film and Theater Research. Courtesy of the Bryna Company. | **243** Letter from Claudia McNeil. From the Daniel Mann papers, Margaret Herrick Library, AMPAS. | **247** Letter from Joseph Stefano. From the Janet Leigh papers, Margaret Herrick Library, AMPAS. Courtesy of Marilyn and Dominic Stefano. | **248** Letter from Cary Grant. From the Eva Marie Saint papers, Margaret Herrick Library, AMPAS. Courtesy of the Cary Grant Family. |

250 Letter from Charles K. Feldman. Correspondence from the Charles K. Feldman Papers, courtesy of the American Film Institute. | **252** Telex from Albert "Cubby" Broccoli. From the Eon Productions Archives. © 1961 Metro-Goldwyn-Mayer Studios Inc. and Danjaq, LLC. Courtesy of Barbara Broccoli and Michael Wilson. | **253** Letter from Henry Bumstead. From the Henry Bumstead papers, Margaret Herrick Library, AMPAS. Courtesy of The Bumstead Family. | **257** Letter from Jerry Wald. From the Fred Zinnemann papers, Margaret Herrick Library, AMPAS. Courtesy of Andrew Wald. | **260** Letter from Groucho Marx. From the Groucho Marx papers, Manuscript Division, Library of Congress, MSS47845. Courtesy of Groucho Marx Productions Inc. | **262** Letter from Stuart Heisler. From the Boris Leven correspondence, Margaret Herrick Library, AMPAS. Courtesy of Stuart Barker. | **265** Letter from Joel McCrea. From the Sam Peckinpah papers, Margaret Herrick Library, AMPAS. Courtesy Frances Dee McCrea Trust/Estate of Joel McCrea—Wyatt McCrea, Trustee. | **267** Letter from James Wong Howe. From the Sanora Babb papers, Harry Ransom Center, The University of Texas at Austin. Courtesy of the estate of Sanora Babb Howe. | **270** Letter from Alex North. From the Joseph L. Mankiewicz papers, Margaret Herrick Library, AMPAS. Courtesy of the North Family. | **273** Letter from Rex Harrison. From the Arthur P. Jacobs Collection, Loyola Marymount University, Department of Archives and Special Collections, William H. Hannon Library. Courtesy of the estate of Rex Harrison. | **280** Letter from Robert Mulligan. From the Gregory Peck papers, Margaret Herrick Library, AMPAS. Courtesy of Sandy Mulligan. | **283** Letter from Audrey Hepburn. From the George Cukor papers, Margaret Herrick Library, AMPAS. Courtesy of Sean Hepburn Ferrer & Luca Dotti. | **290** Letter from Sidney Lumet. From the Katharine Hepburn papers, Margaret Herrick Library, AMPAS. Courtesy of The Lumet Family. | **292** Letter from Budd Schulberg. From the Samuel Goldwyn papers, Margaret Herrick Library, AMPAS. Reprinted by permission of Betsy Schulberg. | **295** Letter from Jay Presson Allen. From the Alfred Hitchcock papers, Margaret Herrick Library, AMPAS. Courtesy of the Family of Jay Presson Allen. | **296** Letter from Saul Chaplin. From the Ernest Lehman papers, Harry Ransom Center, The University of Texas at Austin. Courtesy The Estate of Saul Chaplin. | **298** Memo from Ernest Lehman. From the Ernest Lehman papers, Harry Ransom Center, The University of Texas at Austin. Courtesy of the Ernest Lehman Family. | **300** Letter from Hedda Hopper. From the Katharine Hepburn papers, Margaret Herrick Library, AMPAS. Courtesy Joan Hopper Peat-James. | **301** Letter from Katharine Hepburn. From the Katharine Hepburn papers, Margaret Herrick Library, AMPAS. Courtesy The Estate of Katharine Hepburn. | **302** Letter from Walter Matthau. From the Billy Wilder papers, Margaret Herrick Library, AMPAS. Courtesy of Charles Matthau. | **304** Letter from Francis Ford Coppola. From the Samuel Goldwyn papers, Margaret Herrick Library, AMPAS. Courtesy of Francis Coppola. | **307** Letter from Michael Wilson. From the Arthur P. Jacobs Collection, Loyola Marymount University, Department of Archives and Special Collections, William H. Hannon Library. Courtesy of Rosanna Wilson-Farrow and Becca Wilson, daughters of Michael Wilson. | **309** Letter from Paul Newman. From the William Wyler papers, Margaret Herrick Library, AMPAS. Courtesy of Newman's Own Foundation. | **311** Letter from Milton Pickman. From the George Seaton papers (U.S. Mss 75AN), Wisconsin Center for Film and Theater Research. Courtesy of the Estate of Milton Pickman. | **313** Letter from Paul Jarrico. From the Waldo Salt papers, UCLA Library Special Collections, Charles E. Young Research Library. Courtesy of Lia Benedetti. | **315** Letter from Hal Ashby. From the Hal Ashby papers, Margaret Herrick Library, AMPAS. Hal Ashby to Norman Jewison re: "The Landlord", courtesy of the Hal Ashby Trust, Copyright, 2018. All Rights Reserved. | **320** Letter from Norman Jewison. From the Hal Ashby papers, Margaret Herrick Library, AMPAS. Courtesy of Norman Jewison. | **323** Letter from Sydney Pollack. From the Sydney Pollack papers, Margaret Herrick Library, AMPAS. Copyright 2019 Pollack 1988 Trust. | **327** Letter from Charlton Heston. From the William Wyler papers, Margaret Herrick Library, AMPAS. Courtesy of the Heston Family Estate Archives. | **328** Letter from Ross Martin. From the Martin Ritt papers, Margaret Herrick Library, AMPAS. Courtesy of Phyllis Rosenblatt. | **331** Letter from Tom Hanks. From the George Roy Hill papers, Margaret Herrick Library, AMPAS. Courtesy of Tom Hanks. | **333** Letter from George Roy Hill. From the George Roy Hill papers, Margaret Herrick Library, AMPAS. Courtesy of the Family of George Roy Hill. | **335** Letter from Ellen Burstyn. From the private collection of Paul Clemens. Courtesy of Ellen Burstyn. | **339** Letter from Elliott Kastner. Courtesy of the Estate of Elliott Kastner. | **342** Letter from Jane Fonda. From the Fred Zinnemann papers, Margaret Herrick Library, AMPAS. Courtesy of Jane Fonda.

Acknowledgments by Rocky Lang

When writing a book like this, we had to rely on so many people. Some were old friends, some new. On this project, there was a good deal of chasing down leads and uncovering stones along the way. Once we found a letter we hoped to include in the book, we needed to find the author or the estate of the letter writer to grant us permission to use it in this collection. It's often not easy to find people. Families die out. People change their names, or really don't want to be found. Some just go off the grid. To each and every family member and estate holder who was kind enough to give us permission to use a letter: thank you.

I would also like to thank David Stenn and David Frankel, both great friends and colleagues. Thank you for always being there and offering your thoughts, ideas, and support. And, to David Cashion, our editor at Abrams Books, thank you for your belief in this three-year project.

Thanks to the entire Abrams team of Connor Leonard, Liam Flanagan, Gabby Fisher, and everyone else who helped make our book a reality. We send a super special thanks to Ashley Albert, who came in and pinch hit in the ninth inning. We deeply appreciate your contribution.

Thanks to my longtime and ultracool agent, Uwe Stender, whose honesty and sense of humor keeps me moving along. (Sigh.) Across the pond, Dillon Kastner was a huge help along the way and never said a word about how much I was bugging him. Alan Nevins, thanks for believing and pushing. To my old William Morris agents and dear friends, John Ptak, Liz Robinson, and Jim Crabbe, you know how helpful you have been. Pete Saphier, the guy who discovered *Jaws*, thanks for the vine.

There are no words to express my gratitude to Fred Specktor at CAA, my old friend who broke down some doors and was incredibly helpful. Joel Drucker, the southpaw from the north, thanks for our early emails and your continued support. Marlo Carruth, your sage advice is as good as your backhand. Bobby Schwartz, thanks for never saying no to a question . . . ever. Michael Lynton, you have the key to every door, thank you. Ron Meyer and Jeff Shell, you guys listened and helped when others didn't. Nat Rosenberg, thanks with Mother Jean. That was a big one. Michael Donaldson and Katy Alimohammadi, your knowledge of copyright law and your enthusiasm for our project will never be forgotten. A special thanks to "Charlie," my Deep Throat contact, who in the dark of the night supplied me with tips.

Thanks to the kid in New Jersey, Phillip Portera, "The Spokeo Kid," who was our intern and turned up some great finds. Many thanks to David Gurvitz, our own private eye, for finding the tough ones. Hey, Fred Fuchs! You tossed me a very good vine, and the *Titanic* rises again. And, thanks to Chris Lemmon, Jeff Sanderson, Bonnie Garvin, Courtney Garcia, Matthew Younge, Peter Gethers, Alan Eichler, Sean O'Neil, Charles Drazin, Barry McPherson, Mick Garris, Peter Gethers, Mike Medavoy, Paul Clemens, Jeff Pirtle, Alfie Coates, Michael Berman, David Cohen, Wendy Prober-Cohen, Vincent Jefferds, Joel Gotler, Stephanie Wenborn, Caren Roberts, Big Brother Mike Lang, Nick Meyer, David Craig, Linda Berman, Steve Fisher, Nancy Josephson, Ben Dey, Barbara Broccoli, Tony Broccoli, Steve Ransohoff, Lee Wilcox, Mark Teitelbaum, Paul Legrand, Meg Simmonds, Kate Kelly, Mark Williams, Andy Moreton, Bruce Ferber, Lynne Lugosi, Tom Doherty, Joan Harrison, Robert Finkelstein, Peter Gladysz, Rex Sikes, Peter Crabbe, Jon Segar, Jay Jorgenson, and Janet Pattiselanno. Dean Lamana, your awesome eye and editorial suggestions are amazing. Hey, Joan Golub! You know how incredible you have been and how supportive you are.

I would like to give a huge shout-out to Howard Prouty at the Margaret Herrick Library for his patience, help, enthusiasm, and everything else he has done for this project, including introducing me to the great and multi-talented Barbara Hall. Louise Hilton, thank you so much for everything. Thank you, Val Almendarez, who worked in the shadows and hit home runs for us. Thanks to Nora, Chris, and Debi for your continued enthusiasm for this project, and the laughs and great dinners. Carla Morris—the light that has led me for so many years, thanks. There are many others who had a lead or an idea or met me on a street corner to give me a tip or pass me a letter. There were agents and assistants, archivists and research assistants who were invaluable. Thanks to all of you.

I want to thank my Dea, who has shown me what life and love are really about. Thank you to my daughters, Nikki and Erica, for tolerating a lifetime of me making you watch old movies and becoming the young women I had hoped for. And, to my stepdaughter, Annie, whose curiosity inspires me and who is game to watch black-and-white films. Eddie, Tommy, Bobby . . . well, FIFA lives, but you guys are the best. Michael, thanks for letting me grab you in the kitchen and for your patience in letting me tell you about this project . . . over and over. Finally, to my writing partner, Barbara Hall, I would need an entire book to thank you for everything.

Acknowledgments by Barbara Hall

First and foremost, I need to thank all of my friends and former colleagues at the Margaret Herrick Library of the Academy of Motion Picture Arts and Sciences, especially archivist Sam Gill and library director Linda Harris Mehr who gave me my first opportunity at the library and sent me down the path that would become my career. Much of the research for this project was done at the library, which is practically my home away from home, and it's hard to express how much it means to me to be able to share a selection of items from the library's holdings in our book. I especially want to thank my longtime Academy colleagues Jenny Romero, Kristine Krueger, and Lucia Schultz for their years of friendship, support, and encouragement. My good friend Howard Prouty, who as the library's acquisitions archivist has worked so tirelessly to build up its unparalleled collections, deserves special thanks not only for his guidance and generosity, but also for introducing me to my coauthor, Rocky Lang, and suggesting that we collaborate on this book together. For their tremendous assistance on our project, I am also very grateful to Louise Hilton, Marisa Duron, Clare Denk, Stacey Behlmer, and the outstanding Special Collections desk staff: Andrea Battiste, Devon Bloore, Cindy Desir, Mona Huntzing, Jeff Miller, Amber Sykes, Kevin Wilkerson, and Galen Wilkes. I also want to acknowledge the invaluable support of the library's photograph curator, Matt Severson, and his dedicated and patient team, especially Christina Ha, Allison Francis, John Damer, Faye Thompson, and Jeanie Braun, and, in the digital studio, Michael Tyler, Barbara Bunting, Alan Duignan, and Sean Khao.

My work on *Letters from Hollywood* is dedicated to my husband, film historian Val Almendarez, who is also the collections archivist at the Margaret Herrick Library. We met at the library in 1983 and have been partners ever since, building a life centered around movies, books, friends, family, theater, music, travel, and pets. His support, feedback, and encouragement, as well as his invaluable suggestions for letters that we should consider including in the collection, helped make this book a reality. Of course, Rocky and I are not the only authors to benefit from Val's knowledge and expertise. In his more than thirty years as an archivist at the Academy, Val has shaped generations of film history research by creating hundreds of detailed and thoughtful inventories that make the contents of the Academy's vast collections searchable by historians, students, and scholars. Val's work is rarely in the spotlight, but

it is invaluable to the process of doing archival research, and he and his team at the library, and indeed all archivists and curators, deserve a great deal of appreciation for the painstaking work that they do on behalf of film history.

In addition to the staff at the Margaret Herrick Library, I am also indebted to archivists and librarians at many other fine institutions. I was ably assisted by, at the USC Cinematic Arts Library, the irreplaceable Ned Comstock, as well as Sandra Garcia-Myers and Steve Hanson, and at the Warner Bros. Archive, Brett Service, who all offered valuable suggestions and unbridled enthusiasm for our project. I was very lucky to have the opportunity to make a research visit to the Harry Ransom Center at the University of Texas, where Steve Wilson was generous with both his knowledge and his time and Cristina Meisner facilitated our reproduction request. At the American Film Institute's Louis B. Mayer Library, librarian Robert Vaughn, archivist Emily Wittenberg, and licensing manager Mike Pepin were very kind and welcoming, as were Cynthia Becht, Head of Archives and Special Collections at Loyola Marymount University, and the staff at UCLA Library Special Collections, especially Molly Haigh. Thanks also to Cindy Brightenburg and Ben Harry of Tom L. Perry Special Collections at Brigham Young University, who assisted me from afar with the Cecil B. DeMille archive, and film historian Phil Wagner, who generously pointed me toward the DeMille telegram that we selected for the book. We also received valuable assistance and advice from Sean D. Noel and Jane Parr at the Howard Gotlieb Archival Research Center at Boston University, Hilary Justice at the John F. Kennedy Presidential Library, Rebecca Baumann at the Lilly Library, Meg Simmonds and Stephanie Wenborn at Eon Productions, Jeff Pirtle at NBCUniversal, and Charles Drazen at Film Finances. I also wish to thank Rorri Feinstein at the Samuel Goldwyn Company for granting me access to the Goldwyn collection, which is housed at the Margaret Herrick Library. Thanks also to Cari Beauchamp, Matthew Bernstein, Anne Coco, Joanne Dearcopp, Tom Doherty, Maria Cooper Janis, Nathalie Morris, and Harlow Robinson for their suggestions and advice.

Special thanks must also go to my friend, film historian Christopher Husted, who offered to mine the treasures at the Wisconsin Center for Film and Theater Research on our behalf, and to the staff there who assisted us on the project, especially Mary Huelsbeck. I also want to thank Hilary Swett, Javier Barrios, and Lauren O'Connor at the Writers Guild Foundation Library and Archive, both for their support for my project and for being great colleagues and friends during my fellowship at the Foundation in 2017–2018.

Working with Rocky on this undertaking has been a wonderful experience, and I will always be grateful to him for asking me to be his collaborator and for encouraging me to stay the course even as the project grew into something bigger than either of us could have imagined. His passion and determination were the engines that kept the book moving forward and got us past the finish line. I also want to sincerely thank all of the family members and other heirs who have made our book possible by allowing us to publish the exceptional letters found on these pages. I personally want to offer special thanks to Katharine Houghton, Don Lee, Laurie Lehman, Joshua Meltzer, Julie Rivett, Mary Stone, Tom Sturges, and Bill Taradash for their generous assistance and support. Thanks also to our editor, David Cashion, and our agent, Uwe Stender.

Much appreciation as well to Gerald Ayres, Abele Doremus, Jed Feuer, Elizabeth Frank, the Ava Gardner Trust, Babbie Green, Harold Hecht, Monika Henreid, the Kohn family, Joanna Lancaster, Peter Larsen and Pamela Fridie, Steven Panama, Mark Penn, Thomas Prior, Terry

Taylor, John Valenti, Beverly Walker, and William Wellman Jr. Your stories, and the stories of your family members, inspired us.

Over the years, I have been very lucky to have found so many kind and brilliant friends, who have enriched my life in so many ways. Thanks from the bottom of my heart to all of you, especially Mary Desjardins and Mark Williams, who have been such an important part of our lives for more than thirty years and who have taught me so much about watching and loving movies. I also owe a debt of gratitude to professor and film historian Richard B. Jewell. When I was a student at USC, it was Rick's remarkable classes that inspired me to become a cinema major, and his belief in me that helped me land the job at the Academy that would change my life. That friendship continues to this day, and it means the world to me. Finally, I would like to thank my late parents, Margaret and Charles Hall, who instilled in me and my sisters a love of learning, reading, and history. I would not be the person I am without them, and without my sisters, Nancy Hall Gingsjö, Suzy Hall Jurgensen, and especially Mary Kathleen Hall, who was one of the first people to foster my interest in old movies.

Photo Credits

8 Courtesy of Rocky Lang | 10 Author's collection | 13 Library of Congress | 14 From the collections of the Margaret Herrick Library, Academy of Motion Picture Arts and Sciences (AMPAS) | 22 Courtesy of NBC-Universal | 26 From the collections of the Margaret Herrick Library, AMPAS | 32 From the collections of the Margaret Herrick Library, AMPAS | 36 Media History Digital Library | 39 Author's collection | 41 Courtesy of Lynne Lugosi | 42 Special Collections and Archives. Georgia State University Library | 44 Author's collection | 50 From the collection of Darrell Rooney | 57 Bison Archives and HollywoodHistoricPhotos.com | 59 From the collections of the Margaret Herrick Library, AMPAS | 67 From the collections of the Margaret Herrick Library, AMPAS | 71 Photofest | 76 Photograph from the Wyler family collection | 80 Photofest | 87 From the collections of the Margaret Herrick Library, AMPAS | 100 Wisconsin Center for Film and Theater Research | 104 Photofest | 114 From the Los Angeles Times Photographic Archive, Library Special Collections, Charles E. Young Research Library, UCLA, and the collections of the Margaret Herrick Library, AMPAS | 120 From the collections of the Margaret Herrick Library, AMPAS | 128 Photofest | 136 Photofest | 138 Author's collection | 153 From the collections of the Margaret Herrick Library, AMPAS | 154 From the collections of the Margaret Herrick Library, AMPAS | 160 Author's collection | 174 Photofest | 176 From the collections of the Margaret Herrick Library, AMPAS | 179 From the collections of the Margaret Herrick Library, AMPAS | 194 Bison Archives and HollywoodHistoricPhotos.com | 209 Getty Images | 210 From the collections of the Margaret Herrick Library, AMPAS | 213 From the collections of the Margaret Herrick Library, AMPAS | 216 From the collections of the Margaret Herrick Library, AMPAS | 232 From the collections of the Margaret Herrick Library, AMPAS | 237 Getty Images | 242 From the collections of the Margaret Herrick Library, AMPAS | 246 Courtesy of Dominick Stefano | 255 From the collections of the Margaret Herrick Library, AMPAS | 263 From the collections of the Margaret Herrick Library, AMPAS | 264 From the collection of Wyatt McCrea | 266 Courtesy of Don Lee and Joanne Dearcopp | 305 Moviestills | 306 From the collections of the Margaret Herrick Library, AMPAS | 310 From the collections of the Margaret Herrick Library, AMPAS | 314 From the collections of the Margaret Herrick Library, AMPAS | 319 AGE Fotostock America Inc. | 322 Photograph by Terry O'Neill. Courtesy of Iconic Images | 326 Photograph from the Wyler family collection | 338 Courtesy of Dillon Kastner

Index

Editor: David Cashion
Designer: Liam Flanagan
Production Manager: Rebecca Westall

Library of Congress Control Number: 2018958272

ISBN: 978-1-4197-3809-8
eISBN: 978-1-68335-666-0

Printed and bound in China
10 9 8 7 6 5 4 3 2 1

Abrams books are available at special discounts when
purchased in quantity for premiums and promotions as well
as fundraising or educational use. Special editions can also
be created to specification. For details, contact specialsales@
abramsbooks.com or the address below.

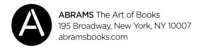
ABRAMS The Art of Books
195 Broadway, New York, NY 10007
abramsbooks.com

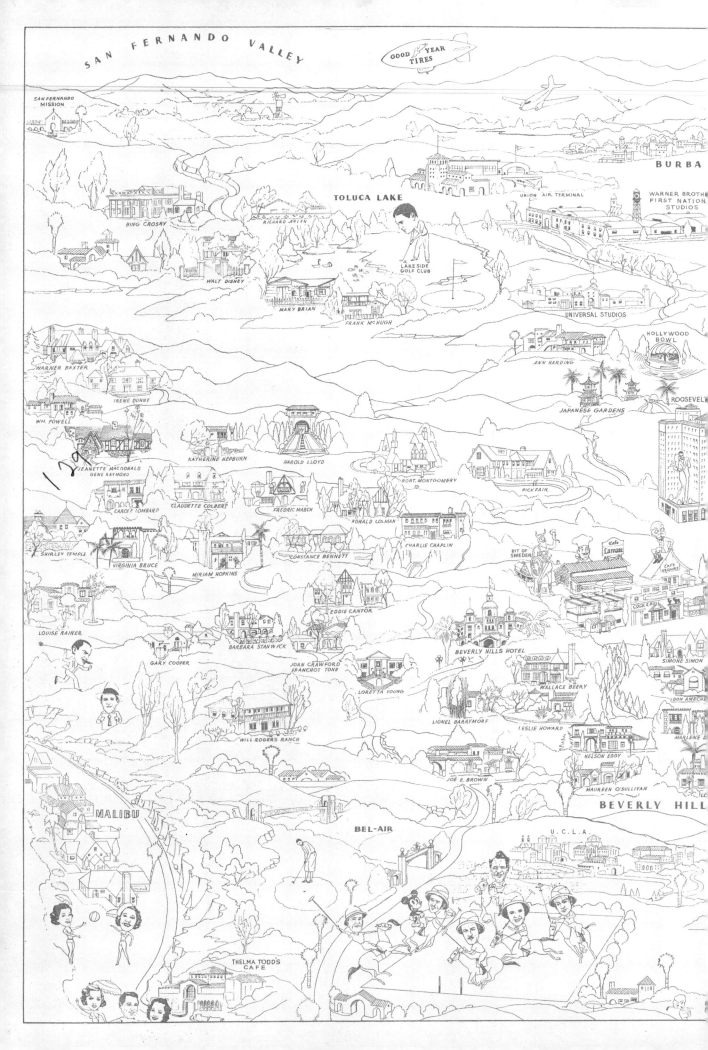